THE CANADIAN FEDERALIST EXPERIMENT

The Canadian Federalist Experiment

From Defiant Monarchy to Reluctant Republic

FREDERICK VAUGHAN

McGill-Queen's University Press

Montreal & Kingston · London · Ithaca

Legal deposit second quarter 2003
Bibliothèque nationale du Québec

Printed in Canada on acid-free paper that is 100% ancient forest
free (100% post-consumer recycled), processed chlorine free.

This book has been published with the help of a grant from the
Humanities and Social Sciences Federation of Canada, using funds
provided by the Social Sciences and Humanities Research Council
of Canada.

McGill-Queen's University Press acknowledges the support of the
Canada Council for the Arts for our publishing program. We also
acknowledge the financial support of the Government of Canada
through the Book Publishing Industry Development Program
(BPIDP) for our publishing activities.

National Library of Canada Cataloguing in Publication

Vaughan, Frederick
 The Canadian federalist experiment: from defiant monarchy
to reluctant republic/Frederick Vaughan.

 Includes bibliographical references and index.
 ISBN 0-7735-2533-5

 1. Canada – History – Confederation, 1867. 2. Canada – Polities and
government – 1867. I. Title.

JL15.V38 2003   320.971   C2002-905620-9

Typeset in Palatino 10/12
by Caractéra inc., Quebec City

For Carol

Contents

Preface

This book retells the story of how a group of men – whom we call the "Fathers of Confederation" – forged a new nation, Canada, out of the splintered remains of a failed British North American empire. But this retelling differs from other accounts inasmuch as it tells the story as one of moral as well as political defiance. For our constitutional beginnings took place in the nineteenth century, well after the time when nations of the Western world had repudiated kings and monarchies and had begun to champion the cause of "the people" and republican government.

During the period when the Fathers of Confederation were preparing their constitution, the new commercial successes of the Industrial Age were spawning the most abysmal working conditions in fetid shops and factories throughout Britain, as the great nineteenth-century English novelist Charles Dickens chronicled so powerfully for the world to see. The dreadful conditions prompted the revolutionary writings of Karl Marx in London, where – on the eve of Canada's Confederation – he wrote the first part of *Das Kapital*, calling for hostile revolt against the new commercial aristocrats.

In a time when the crowns of European monarchies had either been overthrown or become tarnished by incompetence and corruption, England elevated to the throne a "fairy-tale Queen," the young Victoria. No-one expected very much of her. She had inherited a monarchy widely held in disrepute, the butt of vulgar working-men in their ale houses and the embarrassment of unkempt old aristocrats. As one historian of the period has observed: "Her wicked uncles, particularly the wickedest and cleverest of them, George the Fourth, had made such heavy drafts upon the people's loyalty that there were, so to speak, but a few farthings left in the till for the child to set up her housekeeping. The great boors of the House of Hanover, the

Dukes with their thick German accents, their dismal mistresses, and their visible distaste for the ways of the English, had exhausted the affections of the people for the Royal family."[1] Despite these inauspicious beginnings, Victoria's reign proved a glorious one, so glorious that the age has borrowed her very name. The new nation, Canada, was to be one of its most enduring achievements.

The century immediately preceding Victoria and the founding of Canada as a nation was a violent and revolutionary one both on this continent and in Europe: first in the United States, where the thirteen British colonies had resorted to arms against the mother country and boldly shucked off monarchy and declared to the world that the future liberty and happiness of humankind lay with the republican form of government; then in France, where the revolutionary fires of republican government set Europe ablaze in long years of terror and bloody war. It was the age when "royal sovereigns" were forcibly dethroned and beheaded, the age when "the people" proclaimed their "sovereign" right to govern[2]: a pivotal time in the annals of modern history.

Yet the Fathers of Confederation stubbornly sought to lay the foundations of a *monarchical* regime in the teeth of those violent republican times; they were defiantly determined to stem the tide of republicanism with a "piece of solid British masonry."[3] And however much some would insist that our nation was not truly "founded," as Machiavelli would have had it, Confederation was a nation-making achievement worthy of our admiration and gratitude. Canada was consciously constructed in such a way as to give to future generations a "constitution similar in principle to that of the United Kingdom," complete with the Crown, the Christian religion, and a semblance of aristocracy (however modified by the emerging commercial aristocracy). Our constitution was, accordingly, meant to place Canadians permanently in the posture of defiant opposition to the "vulgar" or popular American commercial republic. Thus, in addition to the geographic border designated by formal treaty, the framers of that constitution erected a psychological barrier, one meant to shield Canada from the democratic passions that were embroiling Americans in civil war – the worst of all possible kinds of war, as Thomas Hobbes, one of the greatest English political philosophers, had reminded Englishmen a century before. Canadians have long boasted that our nation was not founded in the ashes of revolution and war but evolved peacefully out of an ordered constitutional process.

But who were these men who claimed that they had fashioned the best of the British and American constitutions into a unique blend of monarchy and federalism, at the same time charging it with the benefits of the new English commercial spirit? The principal constitutional framers (as we shall call them) – John A. Macdonald, George Etienne Cartier, George Brown, Alexander Galt, Thomas D'Arcy McGee, Charles Tupper, Leonard Tilley, Christopher Dunkin, and others – walk through the pages of current histories as men with characters as weak as cardboard; men pushed from behind by the winds of the lowest political and personal motives; men never motivated by high virtue or noble ambitions. Very rarely are we permitted to see them as men genuinely committed to the highest personal and political virtues. Very seldom, if ever, are we permitted to look upon them as genuine historic heroes. As a result, Canada has become a nation without heroes. Our historians almost brag that we do not have a Washington or Jefferson or Hamilton. Indeed, to seek for historic heroes is so we are told – "unCanadian."

We shall see, however, that the leading constitutional framers – those men throughout the North American provinces in the nineteenth century who laboured hard to fashion a genuine nation "from the fragmentary portions of the provinces of Britain on this continent"[4] – understood the task of nation-building better than we have been told. Above all, they viewed republican or popular government as morally inferior to monarchical government and were determined to leave their nation a form of government that would serve higher ends – public and private virtues – not simply lower ambitions. They were resolved on bequeathing to their countrymen a regime where the community would take precedence over the individual, where "peace, order and good government" would redound to the benefit of the entire community, not to the selfish benefit of commercial individualists. For them, monarchical parliamentary government guaranteed to future generations of Canadians moderate and prudential government, where governments would be responsive to the needs of a people deferential to duly constituted authority. They were convinced that republican government pandered to popular excess and public intemperance and disrespect for authority, with self-serving individuals claiming priority over the community. Above all, these men knew they were attempting to stem a veritable flood in resisting the spread of democratic or republican government into Canada. They understood these things and were prepared to defend their vision with passion and conviction. This book is a retelling of their story and of the legacy they bequeathed to us. It is also an account of the decline of that legacy, of the succumbing of monarchic virtue to republican enticements.

I have resisted throughout this study the current academic fashion of filtering thoughts and deeds through the clouded prisms of ideological categories; indeed, I have resisted, even such soft categories as "toryism" and "liberalism" and the like. Filtering the thoughts of great men and women in this manner leads to distortions within which the historic participants are destined to remain trapped for generations. I have permitted the Fathers of Confederation to speak their own language, and have attempted to understand them as I believe they would want us to understand them.

I would like to thank a number of people who have assisted me with this book. First and foremost I want to thank my wife, Carol, who for many years has listened with patience to my musings on its subject matter. Her unflagging enthusiasm and insistence to get on with it have led to its completion, albeit not as soon as she would have wished. It is for this and many other reasons that I am dedicating this book to her. I also wish to thank our sons, Geoffrey and Kevin, who have read most of the manuscript and were generous with their advice and criticism. I would like to thank Olga Domján as well, for her keen editorial assistance. I am deeply indebted to the Earhart Foundation, Ann Arbor, Michigan, for generously providing me with funding at a critical juncture when Canadian sources were not forthcoming. Finally, I am especially indebted to the late Herbert J. Storing of the University of Chicago, who first prompted me to explore the themes treated in this book. I hope he would be pleased with the finished product. Naturally, I alone am responsible for any shortcomings.

THE CANADIAN FEDERALIST EXPERIMENT

An Improbable Ambition

The principal intention of this book is to direct the attention of Canadian readers and students of federalism back to the constitutional history of Canada by reflecting on the *spirit* – the internal driving force – of our constitution in light of the powerful influences of British and American constitutional developments and history. Canada was conceived in the minds of men and born of the efforts of men who were subjected to internal and external pressures, both personal and political. By returning to the historic records of Confederation – to the many public and private speeches and addresses and archival sources – and by "conversing" with the men who struggled with the turbulent forces of our colonial past, it is hoped that all Canadians will appreciate more fully the true character of their ambitions. Above all, it is my hope that revisiting the constitutional conditions and events that led to the confederation of Canada will lead to a better understanding of the intellectual and political forces that eventually undermined the original constitutional vision for Canada and reduced it to an "improbable ambition." Finally, my hope is that all Canadians will begin to admire the men who wrestled with the events and complexities of the nation throughout the formative years of its history. Contrary to what we may have been taught, the formative period in our history – roughly the years between 1840 and 1867 – was an exciting time containing the story of the stubborn defiance of the men who drafted the terms of the constitutional union of the provinces. They set out not simply to resist the spread of democracy, which they viewed as "mob rule," but to lay the solid foundations for a qualitatively new kind of nation, one blending the best of the American regime's commercial spirit with the British monarchical regime's spirit of ordered deference to ancestral authority. For they also believed strongly that monarchical constitutions gave rise to qualitatively different kinds of citizens from those produced by republican or democratic constitutions. As Thomas D'Arcy McGee, one of the more thoughtful of the constitutional framers, said in 1864, the democratic spirit "is very like pride – it is the 'good-as-you' feeling carried into politics. It asserts an unreal equality between youth and age, subject and magistrate, the weak and the strong, the vicious and the virtuous. But the same virtues which feed and nourish filial affection, and conjugal peace in private life, are essential to uphold civil authority; and these are the virtues on which the monarchical form of government alone can be maintained."[1] McGee went on to suggest that it was time that a "negative to the prevailing democratic theories" be asserted in British North America. The basic principle of the monarchic or aristocratic form of government – that is, "the divine origin of society," as maintained by "Burke, Washington [sic], Bossuet, and Shakespeare" – challenges "the theory of its human origin, upheld by Jefferson, Paine, Rousseau, and John Locke."[2] McGee stood squarely with Edmund Burke, his acknowledged mentor, against the powerful modern republican doctrine of the "rights of man," which Burke had called "that grand magazine of offensive weapons."[3] Thus we shall see that the discerning among the constitutional framers were motivated by a moral vision or virtue – one which it is our task to recover. It can be said provisionally at this point that the moral vision of Canada's founders can be seen in the focal point to which we used to turn for continued inspiration and confirmation: the British constitutional Crown.[4] It will be shown that theirs was not an unreflective vision, as McGee made clear in a public lecture on Shakespeare's "philosophy of State affairs" when he outlined how the framers appropriated the playwright's "high concerns [for] peace and war, rule and misrule,"[5] and asserted that they understood the extent to which private passions can convert one into a tyrant. Their moral vision was, accordingly, comprehensive and rooted in the English constitutional tradition.

As Thomas Pangle has shown in *The Spirit of Modern Republicanism*,[6] the character or spirit of the American regime can best be understood by comprehending John Locke's powerful influence on the moral and political principles that shaped American republican government at the founding. Likewise, I say, the character of the Canadian regime can be understood more clearly by identifying the powerful influence that Thomas Hobbes had on the principles that informed Canada's constitution at Confederation. As well, recognizing the Hobbesean character of the constitution will enable us to understand more clearly the roots of our recurring constitutional crises.

Above all, the Canadian efforts to found a regime in British North America must be seen in the stormy vortex of the Enlightenment and the two great modern revolutions. We must therefore understand the new dynamics at the heart of both British and American institutions and view Canadian constitutional origins in light of the transformations in British and American constitutional law and practice taking place at the time. In a certain sense, Canada's constitutional regime attempted to do the impossible: to bind the northern half of the American continent to a monarchical form that was itself undergoing dramatic changes. Moreover, the constitutional framers deliberately and defiantly attempted to resist the inroads of certain of the intellectual forces unleashed by the Enlightenment's faith in republican government. They also resisted the Enlightenment's repudiation of revealed religion. Canada was firmly rooted in Christian principles, especially those of the Protestant Church of England. This commitment too Protestantism became one of the grounds for recurring animosity between the large French Catholic population and other segments of the populace from the very beginning.

Has Canada experienced, as Robert Vipond has suggested,[7] a breakdown in the federal institutional character of the constitution, or was the failure more deeply rooted in the moral and political vision of the framers? Did the Fathers of Confederation fail by not providing the country with an indigenous point of national coalescence – a national centre of gravity – without which no state can long survive? Did they, with the best of intentions, err by not comprehending sufficiently that the attachment to the British Crown meant that the point of national coalescence resided externally to the nation's borders, across thousands of miles of ocean? In brief, did they fail from the very beginning to provide a cementing force for national unity? Why did they not see that the affectionate attachment to the British monarchy would become increasingly tenuous with time and hence was destined to disintegrate under the unrelenting hammer of American commercial republicanism? Can the constitutional framers be faulted for the failure to appreciate the irresistible pull of the powerful democratic forces emanating from the United States? The great critical observer of democracy Alexis de Tocqueville, writing two decades before Confederation, believed that "the democratic revolution occurring before our eyes is an irresistible fact and ... it would be neither desirable nor wise to try to combat it."[8] Indeed, de Tocqueville regarded the spread of democracy as being much like a political virus, observing its diffusion from Revolutionary France and worrying about the willingness of democratic peoples to sacrifice their liberty for equality. Few forces in human history have been more influential in shaping the lives and fortunes of people than the spirit of the American democratic republic. But that magnetic force of America, which continues to draw millions of people to its shores, radiates from the moral vision of liberty and the political promise of abundance at the heart of republican government.

This book explores Canada's efforts to establish its constitutional foundations as a nation midway through the nineteenth century, when the American half of the continent was embroiled in a bloody civil war and continental Europe was in political and intellectual disarray in the wake of the French Revolution. It was not the most auspicious of times for statecraft. Yet a group of our forebears was determined to succeed. Could their constitution, which imported "a constitution similar in principle to that of the United Kingdom" and which promised "Peace, Order and Good Government," provide durable conditions for a prosperous and virtuous citizenry better than, or even as well as, "Life, Liberty and the Pursuit of Happiness" or "Liberty, Equality, Fraternity"? John A. Macdonald, George Etienne Cartier, Alexander Galt, George Brown, D'Arcy McGee, Charles Tupper, and the rest believed that their constitution, with its strong central Parliament, was better than either the American or the French republican constitutions. Many at the time, of both French and English ancestry, supported them in their determination to establish it and have it succeed. We shall now see how well they navigated the shoals and reefs on the way to those ambitions.

1

The Enlightenment and the Foundations of Modern Government in England and America

Politically, democracy is majority rule; but its spirit is classlessness
or the absence of any distinction between ruler and ruled.

Seth Benardete, *Socrates' Second Sailing*[1]

The Western liberal democratic state, as we have come to know it, was forged in the fires of civil war in monarchical England one hundred years before the French Revolution in 1789 and two hundred years before the political union of the British North American colonies in 1867. Freedom from the arbitrary rule of kings was wrested from them by men determined to become free to pursue commercial gain; to throw off the yoke of a tradition they viewed as oppressive. They did so with pikes, longbows, and gunpowder. They were encouraged to these revolutionary ends by the moral and political teachings of the new natural philosophers; the fires of revolutionary war were preceded by a war of liberation in ideas. After several centuries of covert but persistent effort, the philosophies of the seventeenth and eighteenth centuries burst through the thin veneer of European order dominated by kings and popes, and the political landscape of the West was changed forever. Following the clarion call of Machiavelli, Thomas Hobbes and John Locke in England and, later, the like-minded philosophers on the continent (such as Jean-Jacques Rousseau) unleashed a flurry of writings challenging the long dominance of monarchs and the political theology of the divine right of kings. "In the development of political thought, " Ernst Cassirer has written, "the eighteenth century, the period of the Enlightenment, proved to be one of the most fertile ages. Never before had the philosophy of politics played such an important and decisive role. It was no longer regarded as a special branch but was the very focus of all intellectual activities."[2] The ambition of the great Enlightenment philosophers was to make a political difference in the way men were governed;

they rejected the theological foundation of political legitimacy and replaced it with a new basis founded not in God but in the consent of men themselves. Above all, following the lead of Descartes and Bacon, the new order was to be scientific. As Richard Kennington has observed, Francis Bacon was the first to propose a "project," one that "promised maximum benevolence to society by a universal method, and hence inaugurated the politics of Enlightenment."[3]

A new age of popular "enlightened" citizenry was trumpeted under the banner of the new science, which promised (in Bacon's words) "to relieve man's estate" in this world – in explicit opposition to the religious promise of glory in the next. The political revolution was therefore most assuredly to be founded on a thorough re-examination of the foundations of political legitimacy. Hence the emergence in England of such powerful works as Hobbes's *Leviathan, or the Matter, Forme and Power of a Commonwealth Ecclesiasticall and Civil* and Locke's *An Essay Concerning the True Original, Extent and End of Civil Government.* These and other seminal writings introduced novel teachings on the "natural rights" of men, on the "state of nature" and the "social compact." Such novel *moral* teachings were intended to have a formal impact on the structure of modern governments. And they did. The new Canadian regime, formed in 1864–67 out of the entrenched French colonial fragment and the northern English colonies left behind by the American rebellion, was forged on the anvil provided by the Enlightenment – or at least in reaction to the Enlightenment. The Enlightenment was, first and foremost, a *moral* achievement with monumental importance for politics. However one viewed the it – whether as a threat or as a promise – no-one could ignore it. For the Enlightenment reshaped permanently the moral core of modern public and private life.

The intellectual, theoretical importance of the Enlightenment was made concrete in the two major revolutions (that were its direct off-springs: the one in America in 1776 and the other in France in 1789. They shook the foundations of Europe and America and permanently altered the world, guided as they were in different ways by the philosophers of the Enlightenment. The Americans rebelled on the authority of "unalienable Rights" and the promise of "Life, Liberty and the Pursuit of Happiness." The French, little more than a decade later, proclaimed in the blood of their king and their aristocracy the "rights of Man" and promised France a new order based on "Liberty, Equality and Fraternity." In so doing, they set continental Europe afire with revolution for the next fifty years, and all in England, and not a few in America, watched in horror as Europe burned.

The Enlightenment philosophers became teachers. At first condemned and persecuted by the royal and religious authorities, they taught that the old order dominated by Christian morality was a form of repression. Indeed, the civil wars that exploded upon English history were preceded by an intellectual civil war, a war of minds encouraged in their boldness by the Reformation in religion, for it was the Protestant Reformation that first challenged the authority of tradition and proclaimed the private right to interpret the Bible, which led in due course to the philosophic private interpretation of nature. Under the direction of the new natural philosophers, reason emerged liberated from the constraints of faith. Bacon's *Advancement of Learning* and *The Great Instauration* presented this project with an unprecedented sweep and boldness. Indeed, reason now defiantly expropriated the throne once occupied by faith. The modern natural philosophers moved, in short order, to throw off the shackles of a decayed Aristotelianism of the Schools with a promise of greater material comforts. In the words of Bacon: "That wisdom which we have derived principally from the Greeks is but like the boyhood of knowledge, and has the characteristic property of boys: it can talk, but it cannot generate, for it is fruitful of controversies but barren of works."[4] As noted, the revolution of ideas led by philosophers paved the way for the political revolutions that erupted first in England, then on the continent. Indeed, the political revolutions of the eighteenth and nineteenth centuries cannot be understood apart from the intellectual revolution that paved the way for the new political order.

It is well known that the English Enlightenment philosophers Hobbes and Locke played an important role in those great historic battles, at least on the theoretical, philosophical level. Their writings had a profound impact on the entire Western world, including, of course, British North America. Under the inspiration of Machiavelli they undermined the political foundations that had prevailed for more than a millennium throughout Christian Europe. Hobbes and Locke were true subversives who sought to overthrow the traditional claim of kings to rule by a rational appeal to more solid grounds of legitimacy in the new understanding of human beings as fundamentally hostile to one another. They laboured to repudiate in principle the foundations of monarchy, striking at the heart of the doctrine of the divine right of kings: no God gave kings the right to rule over others. Human beings themselves possessed the right to rule over one another, and the power to rule could only be given to another – to a person or an assembly – by consent or contract. Thus, the modern political philosophers sought nothing less than to replace the old monarchical foundations with the new republican principle of the consent of the governed. Their enterprise was subversive on two planes: the political and the religious. In politics, republican principles repudiate the flow of virtue from the top down, substituting a bottom-up spirit of legitimacy, an egalitarian spirit. Every member of a republic has, at least in principle, the claim to rule. The principle of divine equality taught by Christianity was taken over by Hobbes and his followers and transformed into a civil principle. Christianity taught a vertical equality: all men are equal in the eyes of God. While it provided a major impulse towards political equality, Christianity always did so with a firm acknowledgement that this vertical equality was the touchstone of political equality. Hobbes rejected the idea of vertical equality and replaced it with horizontal equality: all men are equal to one another in the critical respect that each possesses the power to kill the other. Hence the chief concern of the civil authority must be containing the fierceness of men by strict laws and procedures. The proponents of republican government saw the regime as resting on a more secure foundation than monarchy, with its legitimacy founded on God. But the perpetual challenge for a republic was to produce an aristocracy based on merit that would not present itself as being what it truly was: superior to those upon whose consent its political power rested. The leaders in a republic must never appear to the people to be "to the manor born." On the religious plane, the church and its claims were thus subordinated to the claims of the civil sovereign. Under the direction of Hobbes, Church and State would be fused in such a way as to ensure that the Church would serve the ends established by the civil sovereign.[5]

Hobbes and Locke, as proponents of the new political philosophy and as Englishmen, were at the epicentre of the movement to refashion the English monarchical regime into a republican one. More than anyone else, they liberated the "individual." As C.B. MacPherson has written: "Individualism, as a basic theoretical position, starts at least as far back as Hobbes. Although his conclusions can scarcely be called liberal, his postulates were highly individualistic. Discarding traditional concepts of society, practice, and natural law, he deduced political rights and obligations from the interest and will of dissociated individuals ... And individualism has a large, if ambiguous, place in Locke's political theory. All these theories were closely related to the struggle for a more liberal state."[6] In the final analysis – and after a great deal of bloodshed – the efforts of Hobbes and Locke bore some fruit. But unlike in America, the new regime emerged in England as a republic encased in the trappings of monarchical form. The king or queen remained, but his or her rule was tempered by the legitimacy of the people. The new English monarchy emerged as "constitutional" monarchy, with the kings and queens reigning but no longer ruling arbitrarily. But both Hobbes and Locke stated clearly that the new English rulers had to be able to rule effectively without fear of being overthrown by the people. The foundations of hereditary king's authority to rule was too uncertain and hence too insecure, in their view. The new "sovereign" of Hobbes or the new "prince" of Locke would be securely founded in the "brutish" nature of men and would be fully armed with all power necessary to ruling decisively. The philosophers were clearly aware of the potential for instability that republican government, based in the consent of the individual, contained within itself, and they were fully determined that the new English "republican" political institutions would be formally and effectively insulated from the democratic spirit lying at the roots of all republican governments. Not for nothing did Hobbes entitle his principal political work *Leviathan*, the new state was a monster, and the monster would be bridled by inherited aristocratic institutions complete with the Crown, as well as by men prepared to rule aggressively. Hobbes recognized that the tenuous hold of republican government on public order required a strong "monarch" – whether one or many fully armed.

Hobbes's and Locke's new constitution framed a form of government that permitted the rulers – that is, the "executive" – to rule with the support of public force.[7] There was to be no separation of powers or checks and balances beyond the apparent in the new English constitution. On its face, it would appear from a statement Locke made in *Two Treatises of Government* that he advocated a strict separation of powers: in "well-ordered commonwealths," the chief powers were separated "because it may be too great a temptation to human frailty, apt to grasp at power, for the same persons who have the power of making laws to have also in their hands the power to execute them."[8] However, this separation applied only to the legislative and executive functions of government; Locke spoke of the judicial power as part of the legislative and did not countenance their separation. Moreover, the initial appearance of formal separation of the legislative from the executive functions became radically diluted in later discussion of the prerogative power of the executive. "The power to act according to discretion for the public good, without the prescription of law [i.e., without legislative endorsement] and sometimes even against it, is what is called *prerogative*."[9] Geoffrey Marshall has succinctly summarized Locke's teaching on the separation of powers: "Locke certainly did not believe in the separation of powers in the sense of 'independence and equality' of executive and legislature; for he held: 'There can be but one supreme power, which is the legislative, to which all the rest are and must be subordinate.'"[10] Neither Hobbes nor Locke would have recognized the prince or the executive of the American constitution. Gridlock between the "branches" of government was virtually impossible under the English system of government, where Parliament was so strong. The virtual fusion of powers in the English constitution permitted the sovereign Parliament to rule energetically and effectively. The body politic could not possess two souls, Hobbes taught; it could not contain two sources or motive principles any more than the human body could.[11]

The English monarchy, reformed and reshaped under the influence of the Enlightenment philosophers, thus combined elements of the old monarchical order and the new republican order. The people were encouraged to continue to pay homage to the Crown while the politically ambitious were free to rule in Parliament on behalf of the people and in their best interests – the best interests of the people, of course, being understood as synonymous with the best interests of the new ruling elites, primarily and increasingly the new commercial aristocracy. Further, the church's the influence of the Church was brought to heel; the Church was permitted to retain its ceremonial role but lost its formal political authority over the people, especially over the new commercial elites motivated solely by Locke's "acquisitive spirit."

By the time the Fathers of Confederation sat down to design a new constitution in the 1860s, the British constitution had undergone a series of radical transformations from absolute monarchy to constitutional monarchy. From the Glorious Revolution of 1688 to well into the nineteenth century, it continued to undergo serious modification prompted by the Enlightenment. As Gordon Wood has observed: "[T]he Age of Enlightenment was also the classic age of the English constitution. Perhaps never before and surely never since has any single nation's constitution so dominated Western man's theorizing about politics ... By the beginning of the eighteenth century the English government was obviously 'the most free and best constituted in all the world.'"[12] The British constitution also responded earlier than others to the democratic pressures that began to erupt late in the seventeenth century. It made a successful transition from absolute monarchy to responsible parliamentary government, but only after a flirtation with Leveller demands for universal suffrage and a bloody civil war culminating in Cromwell's republican experiment.[13]

THE ENGLISH CONSTITUTION AND COMMERCE

The seventeenth and eighteenth centuries were the most turbulent in Western constitutional history, in both the old world and the new. From the beheading of Charles I until the late nineteenth century, the efforts of English reformers were directed to wedding the best of the past with demands for more democratic or republican institutions. The middle decades of the 1800s in England – known as the Age of Reform – were especially energetic years. They witnessed a long process of constitutional reform culminating in the Reform Acts of 1832 and 1867. Throughout this period the British constitution underwent serious changes, ones that were to be reflected in the new constitution of Canada. It was the peculiar genius of the English constitution, as de Tocqueville noted with admiration, that it accommodated the democratic spirit in stages and without completely abandoning monarchical character and institutions.[14]

By the nineteenth century the British constitution had produced, as Baron de Montesquieu observed," a nation that may be justly called a republic, disguised under the form of monarchy."[15] The Reform Acts were the results. In addition, the commercial spirit had gripped Britain. The constitution was made to accommodate that spirit as the new commercial classes began to displace the old landed gentry in the House of Commons, the dominant legislative body. I. Deane Jones has summarized its actions thus: "Between 1689 and 1714 the functions of Crown and the House of Lords were defined and limited; but the body that prescribed the limits for others set none for itself. The all-embracing and encroaching activities of the Commons defy classification; there was little they could not do and dared not do."[16] If there is one dominant Hobbesean characteristic of the British constitution that stands out more than any other, it is that the government has full power to govern. The British constitution learned from Hobbes that those who exercise the sovereign authority must not be "content with less power, than to the peace, and defence of the commonwealth is necessarily required."[17] From John Locke it learned that the one who "has the executive power" must be fully conscious of and fully prepared to use all those prerogative powers.[18] As Harvey Mansfield has observed," Locke's constitution attempts to contain a power that admittedly cannot be contained."[19]

It is a tribute to the genius of the British constitution that it was able to accommodate the ambitions of the new commercial age under an executive government that could act with dispatch and authority. Above all, the constitutional processes embodied in Parliament conspired to channel the conflicting passions of the two great traditions of modern British politics that emerged out of the Glorious Revolution of 1688: the one Whig, with its "tradition of independence, opposition to the Crown, alliance with the dissenting religious sects, and often also sincere liberalism" the other; Tory, embracing "the great mass of small village squires and gentlemen farmers [who remained] Tory, conservative, loyal to the King and the established Church."[20]

It was this genius that saved Britain alone among European nations from the upheavals of the revolutions that swept Europe in 1848 and 1849. The seeds of stability of the English constitutional reforms of the franchise of 1832, later consolidated by the reforms of 1867, had been sown deeply in the nation's constitution over several centuries; thus, they were there when they were needed to channel the emerging popular pressures and provide stability. The English constitution, under the inspiration of Hobbes and Locke, had institutionally absorbed the democratic spirit almost two centuries before the rest of Europe. By the time France erupted into civil war, England had pacified the democratic spirit within a constitution that retained its monarchic and aristocratic form, established on an electoral foundation giving it a limited democratic legitimacy.

Moreover, the class structure was reshaped around the twin commercial forces of labour and management, worker and entrepreneur. The constitution remained structurally the same but its complexion was altered with the extension of the franchise and the rise of the commercial aristocracy. Montesquieu paid no small compliment to English political genius when he wrote in *The Spirit of the Laws* that the English "know better than any other people upon earth how to value, at the same time, these three great advantages – religion, commerce, and liberty."[21] The effect of the new commercial spirit on the laws and institutions of Britain cannot be exaggerated, for while the constitution accommodated the spirit of commerce, in due course the spirit of commerce shaped the course of the laws and the lives of the people. England became, in Marx's contemptuous phrase, "a nation of shopkeepers." No-one made the point more succinctly than Voltaire, when he observed as early as 1726 that "[c]ommerce, which has enriched English citizens, has helped to make them free, and this freedom in its turn has extended commerce, and that has made the greatness of the nation."[22] The nation had listened to Locke, who had proclaimed that "[t]he great and chief end of men united into commonwealths, and putting themselves under government, is the preservation of their property."[23] The leading public men were landowners and merchants armed with the support of bankers determined to mobilize the powers of government behind their commercial ventures. As I. Deane Jones has explained it, "[t]he Commons, therefore, representing economic power, took from the Crown its Prerogative of economic regulation. Men like Montagu, Godolphin and Walpole became political leaders on the sole ground of financial genius; economic issues decided the fate of nations and governments ... No Dutch alliance or King could remove the economic barriers of the Navigation Acts; no Crown Prerogative could stop the Commons

from regulating Crown grants of land, from interfering in the government of colonies and Chartered Companies."[24] Thus, Britain was the
first modern state to constitutionally entrench the commercial spirit,
the first to provide the politically stable order for the pursuit of
wealth. "For this reason," Jones continues, "England from 1689 drew
farther and farther ahead of her European rivals, who lacked the
blessings of a capitalised Constitution."[25] In so doing Britain became
the foremost nation of the new age of commercial expansion and colonialism. It left the rest of Europe behind to squabble over the parochial
ambitions of petty princes.

MODERATION GUIDES REFORM

The Glorious Revolution of 1688 ended absolute monarchy. In its
wake, reformers struggled to retain the initiative and maintain the
monarchical and aristocratic character of the regime while at the
same time conceding a sufficient measure of democracy to satisfy
radical reformers. It was no easy matter. On the one hand, radical
reformers such as David Williams, were shouting that the English
constitution "was one of the most awkward and unmanageable fab-
rics which has ever been produced by human folly."[26] On the other,
no less a parliamentary force than Charles James Fox praised the
French Revolution as "the greatest event ... that ever happened in
the world, and ... the best."[27] Fox went so far as to call the draft of
the new French constitution "the most stupendous and glorious edi-
fice of liberty which had been erected on the foundations of human
integrity in any time or country."[28] He was dead wrong, as Edmund
Burke was quick to remind him.

In rejecting the French republican revolution Burke was not
implying he preferred the absolute monarchy that the French had
overthrown. Far from it. As he noted in Parliament: "None of us love
absolute and uncontrolled monarchy."[29] Indeed, he favoured constitutional monarchy. But he saw clearly that the task for all reformers
of the English constitution was to replace absolute monarchy with a
form of government that would ensure the preservation of English
liberty and good government, the legacy of a prescriptive tradition,
not the fruit of some abstract theory. English liberty was understood
to be a commercial liberty wherein individual Englishmen were free
to pursue their commercial interests; it was never understood to be a
"rights-based" liberty, as in France. The focal point of the struggle
involved the institutions of Parliament and the reform of the franchise.

Both Montesquieu and Burke saw the Church of England as central
to the English constitution. The sovereign was and remains the head

of the Church of England as well as the head of state, exactly as Hobbes had suggested. However, where Montesquieu saw religious freedom in England as posing a problem when fused with the commercial spirit,[30] Burke extolled it as "the first of our prejudices, not a prejudice destitute of wisdom. I speak of it first. It is first, and last, and midst in our minds."[31] So it was that the Church played no insignificant role in keeping in check the potential danger of the newly enfranchised working class after 1832, for it urged the people to do their duty, the chief of which was to obey the law.

Despite the changes wrought by the Reform Acts, the central aristocratic institutions of the British constitution remained fundamentally intact. The lower house, the House of Commons, contained the elected representatives of the people (narrowly understood until well into the nineteenth century) and jealously preserved the right to introduce money bills and thus control the power to tax and to spend. The House of Lords contained the remnants of the old aristocratic orders and exercised "a second sober thought" over the Commons. The highest judicial office, for example, was that of Lord Chancellor, and the highest court of appeal continued to be the House of Lords. The prime minister and all other ministers of the Crown were required to be members of either house, thereby preserving the responsibility of the executive to the legislative body. Under the British constitution there was no possibility of gridlock; the executive – especially under a majority government – could always govern. The constitution was not based on the fear of executive power or excessive government. However, this fragile equilibrium between the legislature and the executive could only be maintained, as Blackstone explained,[32] by a continuous reverence for the royal dignity. Monarchy as it emerged in England is a political regime consisting of a genuine monarch and subjects who give willing obeisance to the king or queen because of their kingly or queenly virtue. The regime is characterized by the clear manifestation of the subjects' love for the monarch and by the monarch's genuine concern for the subjects of the realm. It is this *spirit*, intangible but real, that cements monarchies to their citizens and distinguishes them from other kinds of regimes. Few English monarchs in history won and maintained the affection of the people more than Queen Victoria in the nineteenth century. Her reign was, in all important respects, the high point of modern English monarchy. As Walter Bagehot remarked in 1865, "the mass of the English people ... say it is their duty to obey 'the Queen', and they have but hazy notions as to obeying laws without the Queen."[33] Canadians at Confederation incorporated into their own constitution that affection for her person and for the institutions supporting her.

In Edmund Burke's view, the British reformers had an easier task than the American constitutional framers in accommodating republican (or democratic) reforms because it was easier to fuse republican principles with monarchical government than to fuse monarchical (or aristocratic) principles with democratic institutions, as Alexander Hamilton attempted to do at Philadelphia in 1787.[34]

MONARCHS BRIDLED

The British monarchy, now constitutionally checked by the requirement of formal ministerial advice, was consolidated, especially under the long and popular reign of Queen Victoria. It is no accident that Walter Bagehot discussed the cabinet before he treated the monarchy in his celebrated book on the English constitution. For the sovereign reigns but does not govern. "The efficient secret of the English Constitution," wrote Bagehot, "may be described as the close union, the nearly complete fusion, of the executive and legislative powers."[35] That fusion takes place in the cabinet. But as Bagehot went on to explain, "[t]he English system ... is not an absorption of the executive power by the legislative power: it is a fusion of the two. Either the Cabinet legislates and acts, or else it can dissolve. It is a creature, but it has the power of destroying its creators. It is an executive which can annihilate the legislature, as well as an executive which is the nominee of the legislature. It *was* made, but it *can* unmake; it was derivative in its origin, but it is destructive in its action."[36] The English constitution is not simply the product of a theory of government and therefore vulnerable to other competing theories; it is, rather, the result of long and painful practice and is supported by a certain kind of deeply felt and widely shared reverence that has the force of a religion. It is, as Bagehot noted, supported by the "mystic reverence, the religious allegiances, which are essential to a true monarchy; imaginative sentiments that no legislature can manufacture in any people."[37]

Under the English constitution Parliament remained supreme, with the executive as part of the legislative branch and the judicial power subordinate to the legislative function. It is for this reason that Harvey Mansfield could write that "[e]xecutive power in [Locke's] *Second Treatise* is a thinly veiled description of English constitutional monarchy."[38] In Locke's account the government can act with dispatch, unfettered by countervailing power. Indeed, it is permitted to function under its prerogative powers in such a way as to make up for the deficiencies of the law. In some modern republics, such as the United States, this function has been usurped by the judicial power.[39]

As the history of the movement towards constitutional monarchy in England reveals, the intention was to restrict the arbitrary executive power of the king. Bagehot wrote: "One of the most curious peculiarities of the English people is its dislike of the executive government."[40] But there was no intention to extinguish the effective exercise of executive power to command through the force of laws. The popular or republican principle was, accordingly, absorbed in the House of Commons, but reined in by an executive that commanded the confidence of the elected representatives. So long as it could command that confidence it could govern effectively. It is no accident that under this constitutional form – operative in Britain and Canada – governments have become "executive dominant." But the end result can be said to be stable, durable, and effective government. It is not unfair to observe that, to the extent to which it is executive dominant, it is *not* democratic government. The constitution of Britain in the nineteenth century thus emerges as a cautious constitutional monarchy, where the shell or outward appearance is monarchical while the inner substance pays discreet but firm obeisance to republicanism. Clearly, under the influence of Hobbes and Locke, the constitution of England became at its core republican. It was designed to have what Alexander Hamilton called "energy in the executive." Or, as Bagehot put it: "The English Constitution, in a word, is framed on the principle of choosing a single sovereign authority and making it good."[41]

THE GREAT AMERICAN
REPUBLICAN EXPERIMENT

A first look at the constitution of the United States prompts the observation that it has little in common with the English constitution. Such a first impression is predictable, given that the former is a written document, defining the legislative jurisdictions of the national and state governments, and specifying the separation of the three operations of government into three distinct branches. But that impression is mistaken.

The one thing that both constitutions strove to incorporate was the moderation or restraint of the unruly democratic spirit by institutions that would distance the people from the selection of the highest officers of government. It is important to recall that the United States was founded to be a republic, not a democracy, as the authors of *The Federalist Papers* emphasized;[42] that its structure was designed to accommodate the direct influence of the people at the lowest level – in the biannual election of members to the House of Representatives – but to dilute their influence at the highest level. It is for this reason that the president was to be chosen indirectly by the electoral college, not directly by the people, and senators were to be chosen for six-year terms by the state legislators. As Alexander Hamilton explained in *The Federalist Papers* 9: "The regular distribution of power into distinct departments – the introduction of legislative balances and checks – the institution of courts composed of judges, holding their offices during good behaviour – the representation of the people in the legislature by deputies of their own election – these are either wholly new discoveries or have made their progress towards perfection in modern times."[43]

More importantly, the American constitution is a conscious construct born out of revolution against abusive monarchic power. The American founders thought deeply and read the ancient sources studiously in their efforts to design a form of government suited to their needs. They fully understood that they stood on the edge of anarchy once they had severed ties with Great Britain. Indeed, the years between 1776 and 1789 were characterized more by anarchy than by ordered government. The driving passion of Americans was for liberty – but a liberty they knew had to be restrained by law. For this reason the place to begin a study of the American constitution is the Declaration of Independence. It is clear from that document that, while the American colonists appealed to universal principles, they were rebelling as Englishmen; they rebelled on the principles and practices of the English constitution. This is why Edmund Burke spoke in favour of the American cause. But the American founders were confronted with a major practical problem: how to form a diverse people scattered over a vast territory into one people. They had to meet the objections of Montesquieu that republics could only be secure and survive as small states. The American founders responded with the federal form of government, defining the powers of the national government clearly and leaving the residual power to the state legislatures.

The distinctiveness of the American constitutional form was inspired by a judicious blend of Locke's and Montesquieu's writings on government. Morton J. Frisch has concluded that "Locke took the first step in the direction of the American Constitution by separating and equalizing legislative and executive power in order to maintain limited government and at the same time by providing for the independence of the executive power through prerogative. Montesquieu completed the transformation of thought which Locke had initiated through the incorporation of executive power into republicanism by the substitution of constitutional power for prerogative power, and through assimilating the judiciary into his account of separation of powers in order to make the regime of liberty more moderate."[44]

Unlike the British constitution, the American constitution was to provide for limited government constrained by institutional checks and balances. The former followed more closely the thought of Hobbes, who was more concerned than any of the earlier political philosophers with the power of governments to govern and the duty of the citizens to obey. "Hobbes argued that the liberty of the citizen was not inconsistent with the unlimited power of the sovereign and that separation of powers tended to undermine or destabilize government."[45] Montesquieu was more clearly interested in the liberty of individual subjects. "Hobbes' remarks therefore were directed to the support of authority whereas Montesquieu's were meant to give freedom a greater latitude."[46] Frisch observed further: "The American Constitution is a new kind of constitution in the sense that it provides the citizens with a sphere of private liberty derivative from the modern doctrine of natural right."[47]

The American constitutional framers learned from Hobbes that the ancient republics of Greece and Rome were faulty models inasmuch as they did not espouse or provide for the liberty of the individual. The absence of individual rights in the ancient regimes was a crucial defect, even for Hobbes.[48] The concept of individual rights was perhaps the most powerful political force unleashed by the Enlightenment, an achievement of enormous proportions. The American framers were the first to enshrine it in constitutional form. They thereby went well beyond the English Bill of Rights of 1689, which does not contain the concept of individual rights.

What emerged from the Philadelphia constitutional convention in 1787 was a constitution that provided for the institutional guarantees of individual freedom based on modern natural right, the social contract, government by consent, and limited government – all within the framework of a commercial republic. It set down the terms of the first truly modern liberal republican government in history.[49] Since that time the American constitution has become the model for modern free governments. Small wonder that Gladstone could call it "the greatest instrument of government ever struck off by the mind of man."

CONCLUSION

By the time the Canadian framers were contemplating the form of their own constitution, the great revised constitutions of Britain and the United States were firmly in place. They understood clearly the virtue of their English constitutional heritage and the serious challenge posed by the close proximity of the radical alternative: American

republican government. They also understood that American republicanism gave freer rein to the people; under republican government
most public offices – especially those closest to the people – were elective. Moreover, they understood that throughout the several states the
judicial offices were also elective. They saw all these things and they
were not impressed, because they also saw civil war and social instability and they remembered Hobbes and his dire warnings about civil
war. The Fathers of Confederation lived under the British form of
government where the public offices, especially the judicial, were
appointed at "the royal pleasure." The choices confronting them were
serious and troubling, especially in the face of sympathetic pressures
throughout the colonies to absorb at least some of the commercial
features of the great republic that was beginning to show signs of
economic success despite the tensions between north and south. President Abraham Lincoln's determination to expunge slavery from the
life of the republic by civil war did much to encourage British North
Americans to take refuge in their Hobbesean proclivities. They closely
followed the events of the civil war, which was almost always referred
to in the press as the "American revolution."[50] Joseph-Edouard
Cauchon, a member of the Parliament of the United Canadas, related
in 1865: "We have seen military rule extending over the entire face of
the great neighbouring republic, lately so proud of its popular institutions. And we have seen also that people, so proud of their liberty,
humbly bend their necks to the sword of the soldier, allow their press
to be muzzled, after having condemned the system of censorship
legalized in France, and suffer their writers to be imprisoned without
a protest. M. de Tocqueville has lived too long; his admirable work
on democracy in America produces upon our minds, at the present
day, only the effect of an heroic poem; it is the Isle of Calypso, so
admirably sung by Fenelon, but which fades away when you have
closed *Telemachus*."[51] This same Quebec member of the legislature
sang the praises of the British monarchical system of government: "We
wish in America, as elsewhere, for a monarchy tempered by the parliamentary system and ministerial responsibility, because, without
interfering with liberty, it renders institutions more solid and secure."[52]
That is precisely what the Canadian constitutional framers set out
to achieve.

2

From Royal Prerogative
to Responsible Government

The idea of republicanism, of independence, of severance from the mother
country never crossed my mind ... but as there is now no occasion, so
have I no wish for republican institutions, no desire to desert the mighty
mother for the great daughter who has sprung from her loins.

Joseph Howe, 1837

War lurks somewhere in the past history of almost every country.
Canada's history is no exception. Although Canada has never been
the central playing field of a major war, save perhaps for the War of
1812, the results of a major European war brought the nation into
existence. The Seven Years War between France, Spain, and Britain
ended with the Treaty of Paris on 7 February 1763. The terms of that
treaty ceded to Great Britain, among other things, all the French
possessions in North America (with the exception of two small
islands in the Gulf of St. Lawrence, St Pierre and Miquelon). In
negotiating the treaty Britain chose Canada over Guadeloupe (which
it returned to France) because the large French population north of
the thirteen American colonies posed a serious security threat to
British possessions in North America. But while it made strategic
sense to claim the vast French territories, the sudden acquisition of
120,000 French-speaking people accustomed for over a century to
living under French civil law and the seigneurial system posed new
challenges to British colonial ingenuity. Never before had the Crown
acquired half a continent of white settlers speaking the language and
enjoying the laws and customs of another major European power
with which it had been at war several times over the past century.
In addition, the population was almost universally Catholic, a religion formally proscribed under the terms of the British constitution.

From every vantage point – civil, military, political – the task of
melding the newly conquered populace with the laws and traditions
of England appeared almost impossible. It would take the skills of
Solon and the judgment of Solomon to recast these traditionally

hostile people into loyal and willing subjects of the British Crown. General James Murray was chosen as the first governor, with the mandate to begin the process.

Murray was chosen to serve at pleasure by George III as "Captain General, and Governor-in-Chief" of the province of Quebec on 21 November 1763. It was a wise choice, for he was a good man fully qualified to undertake the task. Armed with the Royal Proclamation of the same year and a commission bearing formal instructions, Murray set out to negotiate the shoals and whirlpools of nationality and religion that awaited him. He would prove to be one of the most enlightened – however short-lived – of British governors in North America. Under the terms of his royal mandate, Murray was to enjoy full executive authority, aided by a council appointed by the Crown. He was instructed to convoke an assembly similar to those already in existence in the Thirteen Colonies "as soon as the state and circumstances of the said colony will admit thereof." However, Murray quickly realized that prospects of an assembly were remote because of the paucity of English settlers and the formal constitutional exclusion of Catholics – and hence the new French subjects – from public office. He was fully aware that the central thrust of his mandate was to secure "the Commercial Advantages" of the recent acquisition, not merely the military security of His Majesty's North American colonies. This commercial focus was emphasized by the fact that the Treaty of Paris was formally submitted by the king to the Lords of Trade and Plantations for their explicit recommendations in order that "the most extensive Commercial Advantages may be derived from those Cessions."[1] The Lords of Trade were also requested to draft the terms of Murray's instructions and commission and to advise the king on all administrative and military matters. Thus the Lords of Trade, in writing the terms of the Royal Proclamation and of Murray's instructions and commission,[2] can in truth be called the real authors of Murray's mandate. The powerful influence of the Board of Trade would, alas, prove too strong for Murray's great virtues.

The Earl of Egremont had formally requested on behalf of the king that the Lords of Trade advise "how far it is expedient to retain, or depart from the Forms of Government which His Most Christian Majesty [the King of France] had established in those Colonies."[3] The Lords of Trade replied one month later in a lengthy memorandum in which they outlined the most obvious commercial advantages to be derived from the new acquisitions – principally relating to the fishery, fur, and timber trades. They also recommended that the long-established tripartite division of the province of Quebec be retained but that the French governors be replaced by British military commanders. Murray was, accordingly, appointed governor general of the entire province, with his residence in Quebec City, while lieutenant governors were appointed to the two districts centred in Montreal and Trois Rivieres.

Almost from the moment he began his tenure, Murray was faced with a host of problems, which were soon to prove intractable. To begin with, the British military commanders at Montreal and Trois Rivieres refused to accord him command over their forces. A handful of British merchants in Quebec City and Montreal quickly accused him of ignoring his instructions by manifesting an undue generosity towards the French inhabitants. The merchants wanted to anglicize the new colony at once and wanted no concessions made to the Canandians, whom they were determined to exploit and subjugate. Their solution to the problem of a French subject population was to absorb them into English customs and laws as quickly as possible. Murray thought this policy contrary to the king's intentions and thoroughly unjust.

Murray showed an intelligent sensitivity to the French, and especially to the difficulty of imposing on them an alien criminal and civil law. As a group of French leaders complained in a letter to the king two years after his arrival, "we have seen with grief our fellow citizens imprisoned without being heard, and this at considerable expense ruinous alike to debtor and creditor; we have seen all the family affairs, which before were settled at slight expense, obstructed by individuals wishing to make them profitable to themselves, who know neither our language nor our customs and to whom it is only possible to speak, with guineas in one's hand."[4] They had no complaints against Murray, who they said "has up to the present time, at the head of a Military Council administered to us all the justice that we could have expected from the most enlightened jurists." It was the "four or five jurists" who spoke only English and were ignorant of the established French laws and customs that caused the problems. In a letter to the Lords of Trade one year after his appointment to Quebec, Murray claimed that "[L]ittle, very little, will content the New Subjects but nothing will satisfy the Licentious Fanaticks Trading here, but the expulsion of the Canadians who are perhaps the bravest and the best race upon the Globe, a Race, who cou'd they be indulged with a few privileges which the Laws of England deny to Roman Catholics at home, wou'd soon get the better of every National antipathy to their Conquerors and become the most faithful and most useful set of Men in this American Empire." However, his advice was consistently overruled by the commercial interests at the Board of Trade.

The Lords of Trade had insisted from the beginning that the instructions governing Quebec contain the "power of calling Assemblies." They recommended that "so soon as the Circumstances of the Colonies will admit thereof, to summon and call General Assemblies of Freeholders in their respective Governments in such manner as is practiced in Your Majesty's other Colonies."[5] Murray's commission, accordingly, contained explicit instructions that "the persons thereupon duly Elected by the Major Part of the Freeholders of the respective parishes, or precincts, and so returned, shall before their sitting take the oath mentioned in the said act." Governor General Murray was, – with the advice and consent of his council and assembly – granted "full power and authority, to make, Constitute or Ordain, Laws and Statutes and Ordinances for the publick peace, Welfare and good Government" of the new province. But his task was rendered impossible by the rider that "said Laws and Statutes and Ordinances are not to be repugnant, but as near as may be agreeable, to the laws and Statutes of this our Kingdom of Great Britain." Murray understood perfectly that the oath required of members of the assembly and the "laws and Statutes of this our Kingdom of Great Britain"[6] formally excluded Catholics; under the circumstances, he judged it inopportune to call an election for the assembly. The delay stuck in the craw of the merchants, who knew they would control any assembly so defined. Their animosity towards Murray increased, as did their determination to have him recalled. Accordingly, Murray was not given an opportunity to pursue his generous impulses towards the new Canadian subjects for long. The Lords of Trade were more in sympathy with the "Licentious Fanaticks" than with him, and in April 1766 he was ordered home. This man of foresight and virtue lost out to lesser men and baser motives.

He was replaced by Sir Guy Carleton, whose tenure in office was likewise marked by generosity towards the French inhabitants and who also ran afoul of the British merchants at Montreal and Quebec. Carleton saw the necessity of securing the allegiance of the French in the event of a war with the increasingly rebellious American colonies. He was therefore prepared to concede to them the continued use of their laws and their land system, as well as the practice of their religion. The merchants protested that they had been promised the benefits and protection of the British constitution, which included an assembly. Pointing at the commercial terms of Murray's instructions, they demanded that his successor comply.[7] But the times became dominated by the furious outcry throughout the American provinces against the imposition of the Stamp Acts. The most pressing need became military security. Carleton grew even more determined to defer to the French in order to obtain their support in case of an invasion from the south. Commercial interests would have to take a back seat, he insisted, until the military position of the new colony was more secure.

A NEW CONSTITUTION:
THE QUEBEC ACT OF 1774

From that time until the introduction of the Quebec Bill in Parliament in 1774, relations between the French and their English political masters did not improve. Widespread dissatisfaction with the constitutional arrangements in Britain's new acquisition, coupled with the merchants' persistent agitation for reforms that would permit them to dominate the French population, made it clear to the British government that a new constitution had to be devised for Quebec. On 2 May 1774, Attorney General Edward Thurlow introduced a "Bill for Making More Effectual Provision for the Government of the Province of Quebec" in the house of Lords. In so doing, Thurlow showed a remarkably enlightened sense of fairness. He said: "[Y]ou ought to change those lawsonly which relate to the French sovereignty, and in their place substitute laws which should relate to the new sovereign; but with respect to all other laws, all other customs and institutions whatever, which are indifferent to the state of subject and sovereign, humanity, justice, and wisdom equally conspire to advise you to leave them to the people just as they were."[8] He drew attention to the fact that, as far back as the Royal Proclamation of 1763, the government had instructed the governor of Quebec in terms almost identical to those addressed earlier to the governor of New York. The population of New York at the time had been 1,700 English-speaking people, whereas that of Quebec was approximately 120,000, virtually all exclusively francophone. The official colonial tradition had been to respect, as far as possible, the local customs and laws of newly acquired peoples. In the case of Quebec this largely meant respecting a system of law that was at variance with long-established English common and statute law. Nevertheless, Thurlow continued – almost certainly with the commercial factions in mind: "If the English laws would be a prejudice to them, it would be absurd tyranny and barbarity to carry over all the laws of this country, by which they would lose the comfort of their property, and in some cases the possession of it. As far as that goes, I consider it merely a gift of the conqueror to the conquered people, whom he does not mean to treat cruelly."[9]

Opposition members in Parliament were quick to pounce on Thurlow's explanations. Colonel Isaac Barre, who had served with General James Wolfe at the Battle of the Plains of Abraham, took special issue with the provisions permitting the practice of the Catholic religion. "By this bill the Roman Catholic religion has its establishment," he thundered. He was joined in this view by several other members of the house.

The main objective of the opponents of the Quebec Bill – including of course the English merchants – was assimilation. Many members of the house, including John Cavendish, recommended that the French be assimilated "as much as possible, that they might become fitter subjects of Great Britain."[10] Cavendish worried about the long-term prospects for making willing citizens out of "a people acquired by conquest, and differing in laguage and religion from the conquerors." But it was Serjeant Glynn who hit a sensitive constitutional chord when he observed that failing to import the laws of England into Quebec denied British emigrants their entitlement to those laws. People who had already gone there to settle, he argued, had done so on the understanding that they would be governed by English laws; it "inflicts the cruelest injury the hand of power ever inflicted, in taking from them the laws of their country."[11] The opposition asserted that the English population in Quebec had a right to the English constitution; the clear implication was that the anglophone populace would increase substantially over time with emigration from the British Isles.

Thurlow and the government formally rejected assimilation as cruel and unworkable. He rebuffed even the argument for the right of the English population to the English constitution: "When the Crown of Great Britain makes a conquest of any foreign established country," he informed the House of Commons, "if it be true that it is an article of humanity and justice to leave the country in possession of their laws, then, I say, if any English resort to the country, they do not carry the several ideas of laws that are to prevail the moment they go there." He went on, "It would be just as wise to say, if an Englishman goes to Guernsey the laws of the City of London were carried over with him."[12]

The government was determined to pass the Quebec Bill. Solicitor General Alexander Wedderburn explained in his defence of it that passing it was a matter of the right: "The principles of humanity, the principles of natural justice, demand this at our hands, as a recompense for the evils, by a total subversion of all those particular forms and habits, to wich the conquered party have been for ages attached."[13] In short, the government was determined to pursue this course because it was right.

But the new legislation was a far cry from what the vociferous British merchants in Quebec wanted. It conceded little to the commercial factions, for it reaffirmed in detail the essential elements of the Royal Proclamation of 1763. The Anglican forces, ever active behind the merchants, were especially inflamed, for French Canadians were given formal assurance of the right to practise their religion and to use their language and civil law. Up to this point these privileges had been accorded by the king's prerogative; now they had the support of Parliament. In this respect if in no other, Parliament acceded to the recommendations of Baron Maseres, who had urged such a move: "The authority of Parliament seems to be a much safer foundation to establish this measure upon, in a manner which neither the new English inhabitants of the province can Contest, nor the French Catholics suspect to be inadequate."[14]

It was reserved for the devious Charles James Fox to subject the Quebec Bill to the closest scrutiny. He began by claiming that permitting Catholic clergy to continue to enjoy the privilege of receiving tithes amounted to permitting the Catholic Church to tax the people of Quebec, now British subjects. Fox was not impressed with the Thurlow's response, which reminded him that the fourth article of the Treaty of Paris, 1763 implied the preservation of the right of tithes. Fox was, of course, right, since the Royal Proclamation itself neither stated nor implied anything about the right to tithes or even of the right of the French in Quebec to practise their religion. He shifted his efforts at scuttling the Quebec Bill, showing that the provision preserving the right to tithes made it a money bill; money bills could not be lawfully introduced in the House of Lords, as this bill had been. It was a clever parliamentary ploy, but even it was ineffectual; the government successfully defeated it.

Fox moved to a higher plane. It was not right, he claimed, "for this country to originate and establish a constitution, in which there is not a spark or semblance of liberty." He pleaded for the introduction of the laws of England, calling the Quebec Bill "a perfectly despotic government," one "contrary to the genius and spirit of the British Constitution," and declaring it a design "to enslave the people of America." "My idea is, that America is not to be governed by force, but by affection and interest," he pleaded.[15]

On this occasion, Fox had the full support of Edmund Burke, whose first tactic was to call for a delay of the bill. "There can be no mischief in postponing it; but there may be much mischief, if you give the French people despotic government, and Canadian law, by act of parliament." Burke joined Fox in characterizing the terms of the Quebec Bill as despotic. "If you were prepared to give them a free constitution, I should be in haste to go on; but necessity – 'necessity, the tyrant's plea' – is urged for proceeding immediately." One quickly sees in Burke's case against the bill the depth of his distrust of the French constitution, even before the revolution of 1789. "I, for one," he exclaimed with reference to Quebec, "will never give my vote for establishing the French law in that country."[16] Burke saw the preservation of the French civil law as the perpetuation of the old French regime, which in effect was the perpetuation of an order of government unworthy of Englishmen. To preserve the French civil law was, for Burke, to divide the regime between two incompatible forms: one free, the other slave. To propose that present and future British emigrants should be forced to live under French laws was to subject them to giving up their freedom and beccoming slaves. Burke's comments on the despotic character of the Quebec Bill bear citing in full:

I should be sorry to see his Majesty a despotic governor. And am I sure that this despotism is not meant to lead to universal despotism? When that country cannot be governed as a free country, I question whether this can. No free country can keep another country in slavery. The price they pay is one which men never will, and never ought to bear. When we are sowing the seeds of despotism in Canada, let us bear in mind, that it is a growth which may afterwards extend to other countries. By being made perpetual, it is evident that this constitution is meant to be both an instrument of tyranny to the Canadians, and an example to others of what they have to expect; at some time or other it will come home to England.[17]

Some of Burke's strongest feelings about the virtues of the English versus the French form of government emerged in the course of the debates over the boundary to be drawn for the southern and western borders of New York and Quebec. Lord North wished to leave the matter to Canadians to determine "on the spot." Burke, however, wanted the boundary clearly marked and proposed a set of coordinates to do just that. He saw the issue in broader terms: not simply as one of geography, but as one of preserving the rights of Englishmen, a subject on which he was stubborn to a fault. For him it was not merely a matter of drawing a line on a map; the line was one "that best becomes the regulation of right"; one "which is to separate a man from the right of an Englishman." He elaborated: "It provides for individuals, that they may hold their property; but they must hold it subject to the French laws, subject to French judges, without benefit of trial by jury." These were the important questions: "Whether what they [French Canadians] ask is a favour which can be granted them, without doing a material injury to the most substantial rights of others? – whether the effect of the power given by this clause may not be to reduce British free subjects to French slaves?"[18] On the question of English versus French government, there could be no compromise. Said Burke: "The government of France is good – all government is good – but, compared with the English government, that of France is slavery. We have shed oceans of blood for that government, and are ready, I hope, to shed oceans of blood again for it … Let us consider, then, whether it is worth while to give a clear boundary, and to let the man know whether he is or is not an Englishman."[19]

Above all, Burke regarded the efforts to perpetuate French law in Canada as an impediment to the eventual firm establishment of the English constitution. "Where there is a basis of French judicature, of French law, the legislature will never think of grafting upon it an English constitution," he protested in the closing days of the debate on the Quebec Bill. [20] In a final plea, he proclaimed: "In order to make Canada a secure possession of British government, you have to bind the people to you, by giving them your laws. Give them English liberty – give them an English constitution – and they, whether they speak French of English, whether they go to mass of attend our own communion, you will reder them valuable and useful subjects of Great Britain. If you refuse to do this, the consequences will be most injurious: Canada will become a dangerous instrument in the hands of those who wish to destroy English liberty in every part of our possessions."[21]

Thus, two years before the American colonies proclaimed the Declaration of Independence and fifteen years before the French Revolution, Burke was warning about the prospects of despotic and tyrannical government and extolling the virtues of the English constitution. By extending the boundaries of Quebec, regulated in large part by the old French law, Parliament was extending that law over the lives and property of people in a territory that ought to be governed by English law. Burke saw Englishmen as enjoying liberty while Frenchmen lived as slaves. The lines could hardly have been more severely drawn.

But Burke's dark forebodings went unheeded. The bill became law, and, despite the fact that the Quebec Act of 1774 was later hailed by historians as "one of the most enlightened pieces of colonial admin-istration in the history of European colonial expansion,"[22] it was greeted with anger throughout English-speaking North America, even the loyal colonies of Nova Scotia and New Brunswick. But their rage was tame by comparison with the violent reaction that swept the Thirteen Colonies. American Puritan and Presbyterian divines, as well as public figures, stormed from their pulpits and podiums that, by granting the French the right to practise their religion, the Quebec Act presaged nothing short of the end of stable government and religious freedom in America.[23] Such a chorus of pulpit oratory was rarely heard before or since; scarcely a Protestant divine from Massachusetts to Virginia could resist the temptation to rage against this act of British perfidy. To grant French Catholics a right under the British flag to practise the religion of the "Whore of Rome" was far worse than taxation without representation. No less a personage than the venerable Sam Adams had warned against the evils of Catholicism a full six years before the Quebec Act in the Boston *Gazette*: "I did verily believe and I still do, that much more is to be dreaded from the growth of Popery in America, than from Stamp Acts or any other Acts destructive of civil Rights; Nay, I could not help fancying that the Stamp Act itself was contrived with a design only to inure the people to the habit of contemplating themselves as the slaves of men; and the transition thence to a subjection to Satan is mighty easy."[24] The redoubtable Dr Johnson expounded on the same theme in *Hypocrisy Unmasked*: "The disaffected colonies have for some time played off their spiritual artillery ... by representing the grant of the Popish religion, have suddenly started up as the champions of the orthodox faith, and hence the whole army of patriots have pronounced the Quebec Bill a more dangerous innovation, if possible, than even the imposition of a revenue upon the Americans."[25] Clearly, the Quebec Act did much to enflame the hearts and minds of the colonial Americans a short two years before the revolutionary war began in 1776. It undoubtedly played a large role in their determination to shrug off the imperial yoke.

The English minority in Quebec was outraged over the British government's failure to extinguish the remnants of French colonial laws and customs, which they saw as conflicting with their rights as British subjects. Granted, the English criminal law was to be applied to all, replacing the harsh French version, but even this proved difficult to administer where the defendants were unable to understand the language or procedures of the criminal courts. A far greater perceived insult to the conquerors was that the English in Quebec were now required to live under French civil laws and listen to a language they had been taught from childhood to despise.

The English merchants took small comfort in the fact that the Quebec Act established an Executive Council that they would dominate; they wanted a broader, more complete sway over their new home providing them with the full range of English law and privilege. How could they enjoy these prerogatives when the predominant laguage was foreign to them and the Church of England was virtually swallowed up by the overwhelming and noisy presence of the Church of Rome? They protested that it was inconsistent with the laws of

England to tolerate the free exercise of the Catholic religion, and scorned the claim that such toleration was grounded in the 1759 Articles of the Capitulation of Quebec, which virtually dictated the terms of surrender to the conquerors. The terms, presented by de Ramezay, included the stipulation that "the exercise of the Catholic, Apostolic and Roman religion shall be maintained."[26] From that point on, every royal instruction and constitutional document has included this or an equivalent provision. Thus, from the very beginning of the British rule in Canada, the French population has been accorded the privilege of practising the Catholic religion and the right to use the French language at home, at school, and in public. Almost to a man, the English settlers resented these consessions and wanted Parliament to repudiate them.

Thus the seeds were sown which have flowered like stubborn weeds into a permanent cause of discord in Canada ever since. The current debate over the nature of Quebec as a "distinct society" within Confederation and hence in need of special legislative powers and the right to a veto over the alteration of federal institutions can be traced to the issues raised by Burke more than two hundred and thirty year ago.

THE CONSTITUTION ACT, 1791

It came as no surprise to British North Americans that less than two decades after it was passed, in 1791, the Quebec Act was back before the British Parliament. Constant tension and public dissatisfaction, especially among English-speaking Canadians, led to repeated calls for amendments to which Parliament finally consented. Those amendments were incorporated in the Constitution Act, 1791. Thus, while the Quebec Act of 1774 was drafted and debated two years before the American Revolution, the Constitution Act, 1791 was drafted and debated two years after the French Revolution of 1789. The principal achievement of the latter was to divide the colony, by subsequent Order in Council, into two separate provinces: Lower Canada (Quebec) and Upper Canada (Ontario). This development was greeted with much satisfaction among the French population of Lower Canada; they were to enjoy a degree of self-government with their own legislative assembly. The English merchants of Montreal and Quebec City, on the contrary, were not at all pleased; they were reduced to a minority under the new constitution, at the mercy of a French majority. At least, that is how they perceived it. From the beginning, the Constitution Act, 1791 was doomed to failure.

In introducing the bill on 4 March 1791, William Pitt claimed that the division into two separate colonies "would put an end to the competition between the Old French inhabitants and the new settlers from Britain or British colonies."[27] The constitutional reforms, said Pitt, purported to imitate "the mother-country, a Council and House of assembly for each." He proposed that members of the Legislative Council be appointed by the Crown for life and that the Assembly be chosen by election every seven years. James Charles Fox objected to the attempt to make the members of the Legislative Council hereditary; "it would only add to the power of the king and the governor," he protested.[28] Fox urged this time more forcefully than he had in 1774 that, rather than divide Canada into two parts, "the French and the English inhabitants of Canada should unite and coalesce, as it were, into one body; and that the different distinctions of the people might be extinguished for ever ... He wished the people of that country to adopt the English laws from choice, and not from force; and he did not think the division of the provinces the most likely means to bring about this desirable end."[29] Fox repeatedly argued that the French Canadians ought to be encouraged to adopt the laws of England by choice; "it could not possibly be kept by any other means," he reasoned.

The government forces, led by Pitt, rejected any suggestions that would introduce an elective Legislative Council "in the manner which had been lately established in America." He argued forcefully against republican principles, wary of any suggestions that they might be grafted onto the British form of government. "An aristocratical principle being one part of our mixed government, he thought it proper there should be such a council in Canada as was provided for by the bill."[30] The full extent of Pitt's naivete became apparent when he suggested that the French inhabitants of Quebec would eventually come to prefer the English constitution: "Dividing the province is considered to be the most likely means to effect this purpose [of having French adopt the English constitution], since by doing so, the French subjects would be sensible that the British government had no intention of forcing English laws upon them, and therefore they would, with more facility, look at the operation and effect of those laws, compare them with the operation and effect of their own, and probably in time adopt them with conviction ... Experience would teach them that the English laws were best."[31]

Edmund Burke entered the debate with the assertion that "to appoint a legislature for a distant people, and to affirm a legal authority in itself to exercise this high power" was a high and important act. He accordingly began by looking to the constitutional authority for governing other people. He pointedly rejected the "new code imported from a neighbouring country" commonly called "the rights of man." According to this "new code," all men were by nature free, as well as equal in respect of rights, and continued so in society. "If this code were admitted then this House could extend no further than to call together all the inhabitants of Canada, and recommend to them the free choice of a constitution for themselves. On what then was this House to found its competence: there was another code, on which men of all ages had acted, viz., the law of the nations; and on this code he thought the competence of the House must rest. This country had acquired the power of legislating for Canada, by right of conquest; and in virtue of that right, all rights and duties of the old government had devolved on us."[32]

Burke could not resist the opportunity to denounce the French Revolution once again, in the course of his remarks on the 1791 Quebec Bill. His obsession struck many in Parliament as an unnecessary and unwelcome diversion in the debate on Canadian affairs. Burke, however, saw the proposed new constitution for Canada as no-one else appears to have seen it: as an inadvertent way of introducing the principles of revolution into French Canada. Accordingly, he defended his remarks on the evils of the French Revolution before the house. The corrosive principles of that revolution must not be permitted to work their way into the fabric of the constitution of Canada by default or by negligence, he protested. He was mindful of the powerful presence of the American republics and demanded of his parliamentary colleagues "that the people of Canada should have nothing to envy in the constitution of a country so near to them." The people of the British North American colonies, he insisted, were favourably disposed towards the English form of government. As for the French population, he expounded at length: "The ancient Canadians were next to be considered, and being the most numerous, they were entitled to the greatest attention. Were we to give them the French constitution – a constitution founded on principles diametrically opposite to our's, that could not assimilate with it in a single point, as different from it as wisdom from folly, as vice from virtue, as the most opposite extremes in nature – a constitution founded on what was called the rights of man?[33]

Burke then proceeded to recount in grim detail the recent history of the French West Indies where, he said, the *practical* effects of the cursed "rights of man" doctrine were all too visible. "As soon as this system arrived among them, Pandora's box, replete with every moral evil, seemed to fly open, hell itself to yawn, and every demon mischief to overspread the face of the earth."[34] Had the French revolutionists not encouraged the export of this pernicious form of government, Burke said in defence of his comments on France in this debate on Canadian affairs, he would not have raised the matter. He called them "one of the most desperate and most malignant factions that ever existed in any age or country."[35] The constitution of France was nothing less than "[a] shapeless monster, born of hell and chaos." In conclusion, he urged that Canadians "be governed upon the nature of men, the only wise foundation of all governments; and let there not be adopted any wild theories, more unknown than the north west coast of America."[36] Burke preferred governments based on the "rights of nature" to the chimerical "rights of man."

When the final terms of the Constitution Act, 1791 are reviewed in retrospect, it is difficult not to concur in the misgivings of those like Burke and Fox. In the matter of finances, the governor exercised control over certain Crown revenues in addition to the military chest, which was replenished by the British government. The assembly controlled only those revenues raised by provincial legislation, which were few in number. Hence, the governor and his government were not dependent on the general revenues; he could, and frequently did, proceed in opposition to the wishes of the elected assembly. As well, there was no clear indication of where the provincial power of legislating resided. The British Parliament appeared to retain full legislative jurisdiction over the colonies, despite the existence of a legislative assembly. Nor was the Legislative Council, appointed by the governor and removable by him, responsible to the assembly. Thus, the executive was constitutionally and financially independent of the assembly. Small wonder that clashes arose almost as soon as the ink on the Constitution Act, 1791 was dry. As a result, the period between 1791 and 1840 was one long series of petitions for redress. Clashes between French and English within the government of Quebec and general discord persisted. Is it any wonder that from this time on the pressure arose for "responsible government"; for government where an elected assembly controlled the policies and revenues and where the executive offices of government were *responsible* to the elected assembly? Such was the minimum set of conditions put forth by the British North American colonists from the very beginning.

CONTINUING DISCONTENTS

Petitions for greater popular control or self-government began to be heard not many decades after the peace with the American colonies in 1783. Patrick Morris's plea for self-government for Newfoundland, written in 1828, is a good place to begin to understand the nature and the depth of the discontent. Morris wrote the British authorities begging for "the same constitutional privileges which have been bestowed upon the neighbouring colonies."[37] He went on to express a sentiment deeply ingrained throughout the population of British North America outside Quebec: "I am one, that at the same time that I am enthusiastically attached to the people's rights, am of opinion that the constitutional prerogatives of the Crown is one of their greatest bulwarks. I am as strongly opposed to the democratic tyrant as to any other ... If I shall unfortunately be driven to a choice of tyrants, I shall prefer the tyranny of the one to the tyranny of the many; humanity may possibly influence the former, but it never moves the bowels of the later."[38] Drawing on Burke, Morris asserted that "it is not taxes, but the injudicious appropriation of them that is an injury to a country."

No-one figured more prominently in this crusade for responsible government than the fiery Halifax publisher, legislator, and orator Joseph Howe. On a trip to Southampton in 1851 to drum up support for the cause of self-government, Howe made the following plea:

From the moment of their independence when [America] was recognized [they] ... enjoyed the absolute control over their internal affairs. Fancy what this did for them, for more than half a century while the northern provinces were governed by politicians in and out of office by the fluctuations of opinion in England, or officers sent out, and by the permanent, irresponsible cliques that they almost invariably gathered round them. Down to the year 1839, when Lord John Russell's celebrated despatch was promulgated in the colonies – and the struggle was scarcely over till 1848, when the despatch was acted on and enforced by the present Government – the colonies were carrying on perpetual contests with Governors and Secretaries of State, to win that which Englishmen have enjoyed since the Revolution of 1688 – the privilege of managing their own affairs.[39]

Thus did Howe – appealing to the historic grounds of English liberty – lay his case before the people of England. In so doing he was arguing as Burke had done in his support of the American cause in 1775.

Howe led the movement for more representative institutions for the colonies with enthusiasm. He was no wild-eyed democrat, however, nor was he calling for the introduction of American republicanism into Nova Scotia. Loyal British North Americans, with the exception of those privileged few who enjoyed power and status, could not comprehend why they had to continue to live under a system of government that denied them their most fundamental rights as Englishmen. The governor was still appointed by the Crown and ruled along with his hand-picked council. The popular assembly had very little power over legislation, which could, in any event, be rejected by the governor – and indeed was routinely rejected.

Joseph Howe in Nova Scotia, unlike Louis Joseph Papineau and William Lyon Mackenzie in Lower and Upper Canada respectively, was in tune with the leading British public men of the time, who were decidedly anti-democratic. As Benjamin Evans Lippincott reminds us in *Victorian Critics of Democracy*, "Carlyle, Ruskin, Arnold, Stephen, Maine and Lecky were perhaps the most vigorous and distinguished critics of democracy in England in the nineteenth century. These men attacked, in varying degrees, the liberal tradition which was at its zenith in the Victorian age; above all, they attacked middle-class democracy."[40] Howe sought the support of these men, not of radical reformers.

British opinion was becoming informed through the daily press of the sorry state of affairs in the Canadian colonies. An editorial in the *Times* of London, 17 May, 1849, stated – in words not to be misunderstood and in a language that could have been borrowed from Howe himself: "In Canada we behold oligarchy, which has long reveled in the plunder of a province laboring to overawe a Senate, to bully a Governor, to paralyze a majority, and to degrade a people, merely that they may again monopolize office and divide official booty. The rebels of 1837 were patriots and honorable men compared with their present opponents. The former fought for free and equal institutions: the latter for the ascendancy of a faction and a race."[41]

The same forces of reform were gathering independently in Upper Canada under the direction of the moderate-minded Robert Baldwin and his cohorts. It is important to remember that these proponents of responsible government in British North America were not radical democrats attempting to overthrow monarchical government; rather, they were deeply loyal and for the most part deferential. It is perhaps for this reason that they were so singularly unsuccessful for so long. Reformers who keep insisting on their loyalty and their determination to pursue peaceful means are not likely to be taken seriously or, at least, are not likely to be perceived as posing a serious threat to the established government. Despite the fact, noted by J. Murray Beck in his study of Joseph Howe – that the system of government enjoyed throughout the British North American colonies was a pale reflection of the kind of government enjoyed by Englishmen, the colonial reformers were not firebrands.[42] No-one desired to weaken the ties with the mother country; if anything, they wanted to cement them more firmly. Reformers in the Maritime colonies as well as in the Canadas made it clear that they were seeking power to legislate over their own internal affairs, not to weaken the authority of the British Parliament. Robert Baldwin, for example, declared his willingness to acknowledge that Parliament had the right to determine the range of that internal control. Said he in 1841: "[T]he most important as well as the most undoubted of the political rights of the People of this Province is that of having a provincial Parliament for the protection of their liberties, for the exercise of a Constitutional influence over the Executive Departments of their Government, and for a Legislation upon all matters, which do not, on the ground of absolute necessity, constitutionally belong to the jurisdiction of the Imperial parliament, as the paramount authority of the Empire."[43] Baldwin was clearly prepared to accord full constitutional deference to Parliament, but the basic condition of self-government had to be met by right as Englishmen.

QUEBEC AND THE CAUSE OF SELF-GOVERNMENT

The French in Quebec were even more adamant in their pursuit of self-government than the English in Upper Canada. The course of events in Quebec took a slightly different course, however, as was to be expected in light of the French roots of the law and the influences from France working on the leading men there. One would think that the principles of the French Revolution would have become operative in Quebec soon after the normalization of relations between France and the American colonies following the peace with England in 1783. Given the fact that "the conquest" stuck uncomfortably in the throats of the French population of Canada, one would expect to find considerable sympathy with revolutionary France throughout the population. However, such was not the case. Jean-Pierre Wallot observed that radical revolutionary thinking did not penetrate the ruling elites until well into the 1830s.[44] The ruling elites of Quebec were of the *ancien régime* and wished to have nothing to do with the anti-monarchialism and paganism of post-revolutionary France. The French ambassador to the United States, Citizen Genet, was not a little frustrated to find his Canadian fellow francophones unreceptive to his overtures to free themselves from the British yoke and align themselves with the more free Americans. In the summer of 1793, Genet distributed 350 copies of a pamphlet entitled *"Les Français libres a leurs frères canadiens"* formally inviting French Canadians to open rebellion against the Crown. According to Wallot this *"cathechisme"* produced a profound impression on the people of Quebec throughout the autumn and winter of 1793-94. It became the subject of animated conversation "outside churches, in the public places and at the markets." But despite the further propaganda efforts of Henri de Mezière, *"un revolutionnaire"* who corresponded with Genet, the attempts to ignite fires of rebellion in Quebec were ineffectual.[45]

The reason for which the people of Quebec were so impervious to the revolutionary blandishments was that the powerful ruling elites, the haute bourgeoisie and the clergy, were hostile to everything the French Revolution stood for. Fernand Ouellet has written about the frequent railing by the Bishop of Quebec, Joseph-Octave Plessis, against the "monstrous principles" of the philosophers of the Enlightenment, such as Diderot, Voltaire, Rousseau, and d'Alembert.[46] In a sermon to his flock in 1798, Plessis summarized the advantages of living under the British administration in Lower Canada over that of living under the French regime. He contrasted the lot of the habitant and small tradesman of the 1750s with that of their descendants of the 1790s. Touching upon the free exercise of religion, popular participation in government, the absence of heavy taxation, the adoption of English criminal law, the retention of the *Coutume de Paris*, and finally, the British respect for Catholic institutions in Quebec and their sanction of episcopal succession.[47] In another sermon of 1 April, 1810, Plessis called the doctrine of popular sovereignty the "most evil, the most false and most absurd," destined to dispose nations to revolution. Taking *"une pièce de monnoie d'Angleterre"* in his hand, the bishop asked: "Whose image does it contain? The People's? No, it is the King's. It is that King who is sovereign, not the people." Therefore, he concluded, "following St. Paul," it is the king who deserves the respect, homage, and loyalty of all citizens. He urged his compatriots to remain – as he was – "loyal and sincerely attached to the Government of Great Britain."[48] It will come as no surprise to learn that Plessis was in due course, invited to become a member of the Legislative Council of Lower Canada.

Despite these powerful pro-monarchical sentiments among Quebec religious elites, the seeds of the French Revolution were planted deep in the soil of Quebec, though they did not flower in the eighteenth century. Groups of bourgeoisie formed organizations such as the Club des Patriotes and the Club constitutionnel. In 1806, *Le Canadien* appeared on the scene with the unambiguous motto: *Notre langue, nos institutions, et nos lois*. The *parti canadien*, which gradually absorbed this radical sentiment, became in due course the ground out of which the ever-recurring nationalist movement in Quebec has seemed to emerge.

Elzear Bedard introduced ninety-two resolutions in the Lower Canada Assembly in February 1834. They amounted to a collective "declaration of independence" of the Quebec reformers, who in this respect differed from their moderate English-speaking colleagues, led by John Neilson. The resolutions were at length forwarded to England, where they were debated in the House of Commons on the insistence of J. A. Roebuck, M.P. for Bath and agent in England for Lower Canada since 1833. Appearances to the contrary, the document does not read as the platform of a group of hotheads. It begins with a statement of loyalty to the Crown: "His Majesty's loyal subjects, the people of this province of Lower Canada, have shown the strongest attachment to the British Empire, of which they are a portion; that they have repeatedly defended it with courage in time of war; that at the period which preceded the Independence of the late British Colonies on this continent, they resisted the appeal made to them by those colonies to join their confederation."[49]

Bedard's resolutions proceded to emphasize that the French inhabitants of Quebec had continuously supported His Majesty's Government, even "when the government of the province has been administered by men who trampled under foot the rights and feelings dearest to British subjects; ... these sentiments of the people of this province remain unchanged." Yet despite repeated efforts to have the government authorities consider their legitimate complaints, these remained uncorrected. "In the year 1827," the document recalled, "the great majority of the people of this province complained, in petitions signed by 87,000 persons, of serious and numerous abuses which they prevailed, many of which had then existed for a great number of years, and of which the greater part still exist without correction or mitigation."[50] It went on to say that these earlier protests led the Parliament of the United Kingdom to appoint Edward Geoffrey Stanley to inquire into the complaints and make recommendations. Stanley ruled in favour of the complainants and recommended serious changes to the constitution and system of government of the province. But his efforts were to no avail, for "the recommendations of the Committee of the House of Commons have not been followed by effective measures of a nature to produce the desired effect."

The resolutions continued, in no uncertain terms:

The most serious defect in the Constitutional Act [1791], its radical fault, the most active principle of evil and discontent in the province; the most powerful and most frequent cause of abuses of power; of the infraction of the laws; of the waste of the public revenue and property, accompanied by impunity to the governing party, and the oppression and consequent resentment of the governed, is that injudicious enactment, the fatal results which were foretold by the Honourable Charles James Fox at the time of its adoption, which invests the Crown with that exorbitant power (incompatible with any government duly balanced, and founded on law and justice, and not on force or coercion) of selecting and composing without any rule or limitation, or any predetermined qualification, an entire branch of the legislature, supposed from the nature of its attributions to be independent, but inevitable the servile tool of the authority which creates, composes and decomposes it, and can on any day modify it to suit the interest or the passions of the moment.

Bedard's resolutions read like an updated version of the grievances of the American colonists more than half a century earlier. They allude to an "unlimited power" that has been "so exercised in the selection of the members of the Legislative Council of this province, as to favour the spirit of monopoly and despotism in the executive, judicial and administrative departments of government, and never in favour of the public interest." Moreover, Bedard insisted, things had gotten worse rather than better.

The picture painted of the abuse of political privilege and power by his resolutions almost defies belief. But it was an accurate one. The oligarchy ruled in virtual contempt of the wishes of the people of the province. In 1833, the Legislative Council rejected or radically altered twenty-eight of sixty-four bills passed by the Legislative Assembly. Is it any wonder that the colonial form of government throughout British North America was said to have been a mere caricature of the British parliamentary system of government? It is important to observe that the resolutions drew consistently upon the example of government enjoyed by Americans since 1789. When John Neilson went to England on behalf of the reformers of the United Canadas, he explained that the people, both French- and English-speaking, had become increasingly fond of popular government as they saw it being enjoyed in the United States. The major reform requested was representation by population, the fundamental democratic principle. The constitution of 1791, as administered, failed to protect the people "in their lives, their property and their honour."

Despite the fact that the resolutions were overwhelmingly the work of French reformers, their tone was one of deference and respect to the British government and Crown. They made consistent reference to "British subjects" and characterized Britain as "the mother country." The forty-ninth resolution, for example, stated: "That this House and the people whom it represents do not wish or intend to convey any threat"; that their requests were based on "the principles of law and justice." In accordance with those principles, the resolutions urged the government to make good the terms of the Constitution Act, 1791, and respect the French language, customs, and religion. The French majority in the United Canadas made it clear that they were "in nowise disposed to repudiate any one of the advantages they derived from their origin and from their descent for the French nation." The population at the time was estimated at approximately 600,000, of whom 525,000 were French and the remaining

75,000 were of British extraction. Yet there were, in 1832, 157 British or other nationals in the civil administration, and only 47 French Canadians – many of them dependent on higher-paid English-speaking functionaries. The matter was especially galling in the judicial department; "the judges for the three great districts having, with the exception of one only in each, been systematically chosen from that class of persons, who, being born out of the country, are at the least versed in its laws, and in the language and usages of the majority of its inhabitants." As a result, "the majority of the said judges have introduced great irregularity into the general system of our jurisprudence, by neglecting to ground their decisions on its recognized principles." Some judges even attempted to ban the use of French in their courts.

The repeal of the seigneurial system by the Tenure Act, which left tenants dispossessed of their property, was a special bone of contention. The legislation increased land speculation and made the inhabitants subject to the laws of England, to their permanent detriment. Small wonder they called for its repeal. Another source of the executive government's collection and spending of money without the consent of the legislature. A notable example was the routine sale of Crown land and timber titles. Indeed, "Governors, Legislative and Executive Councillors, Judges and subordinate officers have appropriated to themselves large tracts of the said lands; the monopoly of an extensive portion of the said lands in the hands of speculators residing in England."[51] Worst of all, the complete disregard for even a semblance of the separation of powers or functions of government reached the point of conflict of interest. It was common for members of the Court of Appeal to be at the same time members of the Executive Council. At times, "[T]he practice of illegally calling upon the judges, to give their opinions secretly on questions which may be afterwards publicly and contradictorily argued before them; and the opinions themselves so given by the said judge, as political partisans, in opposition to the laws, but in favour of the administration for the time being."[52] Even the military was known to interfere in the electoral process; on at least one occasion, the result was the killing of three citizens.

The Lower Canada Assembly, under the leadership of Louis Joseph Papineau, leader of the radical Reformers, adopted Bedard's ninety-two resolutions in 1834. They were considered to be too radical by the more moderate, mainly English-speaking Reformers, and thus caused a split in the Reform ranks. The British government saw the dissension but paid no heed. Three years later, in November and December 1837, armed skirmishes broke out. Papineau fled to the

United States following the failure of the Reformers to win the support of the Catholic hierarchy of Lower Canada, without which the required popular support could never be achieved. The Chateau Clique had won again – at least for a time, until events were to run a similar course in Upper Canada.

Led by William Lyon Mackenzie, who came from Scotland with the hot embers of the American Revolution in his belly, the radical reformers captured a majority of the Legislative Assembly of Upper Canada in the election of 1835.[53] A Special Committee of the Upper Canada Assembly drafted a "Seventh Report on Grievances," a milder version of the ninety-two resolutions adopted by their Reform counterparts in Lower Canada. The report was modelled after the American Declaration of Independence. A group of Toronto Reformers issued a declaration titled "The Declaration of the Reformers of the City of Toronto to their Fellow Reformers in Upper Canada." It constituted a lengthy plea for responsible government framed along these lines: "Government is founded on the authority, and is instituted for the benefit of a people; which, therefore, any government long and systematically ceases to answer the great ends of its foundation, the people have a natural right given them by their Creator to seek after and establish such institutions as will yield the greatest quantity of happiness to the greatest number."[54] The awkward amalgam of natural rights theory and utilitarian promise pleaded for no more than had been given to the Americans. But the call was for the same solution as presented by Lower Canada's Reformers: an elected Legislative Council and the end of oligarchy.

The British government responded by sending out Sir Francis Bond Head as the new governor of Upper Canada in 1836. Bond Head soon showed that he had "neither the head nor the heart" required by the office, for he was no more interested in conceding responsible government than his predecessors. It was clear to all in Canada that Britain was simply not getting the message, as evidenced by the appointment of Bond Head. When the assembly refused to pass the necessary supply shortly after his arrival, he dissolved the legislature. In the course of the ensuing election, he denounced the Reformers as republican sympathizers disloyal to the British Empire. And so, as in Lower Canada, the radical Reformers in Upper Canada took to the streets for the first time in the nation's history, and attempted to make their point with guns. They were easily subdued by the governor's troops. Mackenzie fled, like his Lower Canadian counterpart, to the United States, where he remained until he was pardoned by the government several years later. Once more, the hopes for Canadians of responsible government suffered a serious setback.

But the violence of 1837 had the effect of finally capturing the formal attention of the British government. In the words of Lower and Chafe, "The blood spilled in the rebellions … accomplished what years of verbal protest had failed to do: it brought decisive action from the government in England. When the news arrived, the authorities were surprised and perplexed. If the Rebellions were not directed against the mother country, what was it Canadians wanted?"[55] In an effort to find an answer to this question the imperial authorities sent out Lord Durham to investigate and make a report recommending a solution. He did just that in his now infamous *Report on the Affairs of British North America* of 1839. The principal recommendations were for a legislative union of the two Canadas and for a form of responsible government. But in the course of his report Durham outraged the population of Lower Canada with a litany of ill-advised observations on the cultural backwardness of the French people. The insults have never been forgotten by the people of Quebec and are to this day frequently trotted out as the historic reserve out of which the insensitive English view of things French is drawn. No-one has continued to occupy a presence in our history so out of all proportion to his merit and influence as the vain and feckless Lord Durham. In fact, he had very little influence on British policy, and his sentiments towards the French inhabitants of Canada were thoroughly out of touch with the official views expressed from the earliest days following the conquest. Janet Ajzenstat has attempted at considerable length to rescue Durham's place in Canadian history by explaining his mission and achievements in the context of liberal politics of the time.[56] As well, she has argued that Durham's recommendation in favour of the assimilation of the French can, in part at least, be ascribed to the influence of de Tocqueville's *Democracy in America*. But, as Stephane Dion has observed in his reply to Ajzenstat, there is nothing in the writings of de Tocqueville that supports such a recommendation.[57] Indeed, as noted earlier, the imperial policy governing the treatment of conquered or acquired peoples was one of respectful accommodation. W.L. Morton, for his part, has attributed the tone and content of Durham's report to the influence of the colonial advisors whom he met in the course of his travels throughout Upper and Lower Canada: Robert Baldwin, who persuaded him of the virtues of self-government, and Adam Thom, author of *Anti-Gallic Letters*, the "voice of the English party in Quebec," and a man who had "no intention of accepting the French as equal fellow-subjects." According to Morton, "Durham appointed Thom to his staff, and [he] was a member of the committee which prepared the material on municipal government for Durham's Report." Durham reflected Thom's hatred of the French and his perception of the need to make Lower Canada British by union with Upper Canada.[58]

Whatever credit is due to Durham for the eventual emergence of responsible government, his contribution pales in comparison with the determined efforts of the colonial advocates of responsible self-government, both English and French. Notable among them were Louis-Hippolyte Lafontaine, Mackenzie, Joseph Howe and Robert Baldwin, who over a long period had begged and badgered the authorities for the fundamental English right of self-government.

The Act of Union of 1840-41 was the chief and ill-fated achievement of Durham's report – "ill-fated," for it soon brought a host of new and intractable problems. In time, it proved to be one of the greatest constitutional disasters in Canada's history. Durham's design was to meld the two language groups into one, i.e., to assimilate the French. "I have little doubt," he wrote, "that the French, when once placed, by the legitimate course of events and the working of natural causes, in a minority, would abandon their vain hopes of nationality."[59] No-one has put the impossibility of the task set by the Act of Union more succinctly than Stephen Leacock:

It was easy for Lord Durham to recommend responsible government. It was another matter to know just how to put it into force, especially as between such ill-assorted partners as Upper and Lower Canada, one British, one French, one nearly all Protestant, one nearly all Roman Catholic, one with seigneurial land and one with individual ownership, one demanding municipal government, people's schools and secular control, the other opposing all of them. In such an environment how much was the royal governor to do and how much not? Can a majority of the elected assembly have anything they cared to ask or only what is good for them.[60]

A new governor, Poulett Thomson (Lord Sydenham), was sent out to Canada to superintend the new constitutional arrangement. One of his first acts was to select Kingston, in Upper Canada, as the capital of the United Canadas, removing the seat of government from Lower Canada and thereby robbing the French Canadians of the privilege of self-government within the confines of their own territory. As bad as the Constitution Act of 1791 was, it had at least given the French their own Legislative Assembly. Now they found themselves deprived of that privilege and living under an act of union whose sinister – and all too obvious – purpose was to assimilate them. Under the new constitution, Lower Canada and Upper Canada were each granted forty-two seats in the assembly, despite the greater population of the former. Could any beginning of good government have as many strikes against it as this one? To no-one's surprise, the arrangement did not provide the framework of peaceful responsible government.

With the arrival of responsible government in 1849, the ceaseless efforts of Howe in Nova Scotia and the reformers of Lower and Upper Canada, Lafontaine and Baldwin, finally bore fruit. But that milestone constitutional achievement was greeted almost immediately by one of the most violent public outbursts in Canadian history: a riot led by a Tory mob in Montreal over the passage of the Rebellion Losses Bill. In the words of W.L. Morton: "The outburst was the result of Tory opposition to a Rebellion Losses Bill, intended to compensate those who had suffered losses in the troubles of 1837-38. The truth was that French ministers were resolved to carry the bill, cost what it might, and their English colleagues were embarrassed but forced to remain silent. It was thus a first test of cabinet solidarity under responsible government."[61]

The central problem of the bill was that it did not distinguish between a legitimate claimant and a rebel. The Conservative administration of William Draper had determined in 1847 that a sum of £100,000 would be sufficient to meet all legitimate claims, but took no further action. When Lafontaine succeeded Draper, he took up the cause and introduced a bill providing for compensation in that amount. However, its terms failed to specify clearly what constituted a legitimate claim. Lafontaine knew that many of his francophone compatriots who took part in the rebellion of 1837-38 had never been convicted in court but had suffered property damage from the troops who put down the rebellion. Technically they were rebels, but since thet had not been convicted they sought compensation for their losses.

Naturally, the anglophone citizens of Montreal were outraged and took to the streets in protest. As Lord Elgin reported to Lord Grey, the English press of Montreal stirred the embers of outrage with language destined to incite riot. One newspaper shouted: "When French tyranny shall become insupportable, we shall find our Cromwell ... when we can stand tyranny no longer, it will be seen whether good bayonets in Saxon hands will not be more than a match for a mace and a majority."[62] The Tory mob not only pelted the carriage of Governor General Lord Elgin and insulted his person with hooting and shouting: it "proceeded to the House of Parliament ... and breaking the windows set fire to the building and burned it to the ground."[63]

The violence of the reaction to the bill was thoroughly disproportionate to its objectives. According to Morton, "The intent and substance of the bill were unexceptionable, being no more than an act of justice to the French sufferers in the rebellion, and an act intolerably delayed."[64] In Upper Canada, by contrast, those who has suffered losses during the rebellion had long since been compensated without incident.

The late 1840s and early 1850s were the period when the victory of responsible self-government, that uniquely cautious form of parliamentary government, began to take root in British North America. Throughout Europe, on the other hand, it was a period of explosive democratic unrest, as summed up by Ernest Barker:

The year 1848 was the *annus mirabilis* of the nineteenth century. A whole continent was in travail with new nationalities and new constitutions. If in England the days of that eventful year ran more quietly, they were nevertheless stirring ... The Chartist movement came to an abortive end; but the Christian Socialists attempted to found a cooperative movement ... A new school appeared in English art. While Thackeray was finishing *Vanity Fair* ... Macaulay was publishing the first two volumes of his *History of England* ... Ten years later, in 1858, the doctrine of natural selection was enunciated; and a new and powerful leaven was added to the fermentation of ideas already at work in the general mind. Men began to feel the need of a more scientific explanation of the facts, and a more scientific attempt to cure the defects of social life. Two revolutions had passed over the world in the last few decades – the political revolution which had started in France in 1789, and the industrial revolution which had begun in England in 1760.[65]

While the people of British North America were at a safe distance from the European centre of this momentous series of events, they were not entirely immune from its aftershocks. There can be no question that the educated elites of the colonies were aware of the new forces, that were unleashed, and took care to pronounce against them. Nowhere was this more true than in Quebec. The Catholic authorities knew full well that the leading intellectuals in France were intoxicated with the thoughts of re-invigorating the spirit of the French Revolution. Maurice Agielhon has commented: "In 1848 thinking about the Republic meant thinking about the French revolution."[66] The same authorities were also fully conscious of the words of Louis Saint-Just, who had proclaimed in 1789 that "a republic is the total destruction of that which is opposed to it."[67] The clerical elite wanted nothing to do with this destructive spirit. They did everything they could to keep Quebec's educational institutions free of the materialism and irreligion that emerged full blown from the ashes of the French Revolution.

HINDSIGHT

Looking back over Canadian history, as we have been doing, from the beginnings in 1763 to the Act of Union of 1840–41, we see one long train of constitutional crises. The constitutional solution of 1840–41 proved to be no solution at all, as events from that time until 1865 were to prove all too clearly. The political deadlock in the United Canadas became persistent and insoluble. No-one was happy with Durham's unenlightened legacy: neither French nor English, neither merchant nor farmer. The seeming hopelessness of attaining self-government led the exhausted politicians of the day, French and English alike, to explore the prospect of the union of all five British North American colonies. And so they swallowed their bitter partisan differences and embarked for Charlottetown, Prince Edward Island, in September 1864, to see if they could not themselves draw up a constitutional arrangement, one "made in Canada," which would provide the basis for sound and durable government. Each and every one of the delegates to the Charlottetown Conference was fully aware of the magnitude of the task before them. But they all came to Charlottetown prepared and determined to succeed.

3

The Foundations of Eddystone[1]

Of all men that distinguish themselves by memorable achievements the first place of honour seems due to legislators and founders of states who transmit a system of laws and institutions to secure the peace, happiness, and liberty of future generations.

David Hume

The physically weary and politically exhausted delegates from the United Canadas, led by John A. Macdonald, sailed from Quebec City on the *Queen Victoria* on Monday, 29 August 1864. After a brief stop at Gaspé, the delegates arrived in Charlottetown on 1 September. The Canadian delegates, unlike their Maritime counterparts, came prepared to discuss a union of all the British North American provinces into one large federation. The leading politicians of the Maritime provinces, for their part, had called The Charlottetown conference for the express purpose of discussing the prospects of uniting the three provinces of Nova Scotia, New Brunswick, and Prince Edward Island into one centrally administered colony. When the Americans repealed the Reciprocity Treaty of 1854, the three Maritime provinces had felt the need to consolidate their economic efforts in order to cope with the post-reciprocity order; up to then they had enjoyed successful open commerce with their cousins in the New England states.

On learning of the meeting planned for Charlottetown, the Canadian politicians requested to be permitted to attend, with a view to exploring the possibility of union of all the provinces. The Maritime leaders consented to listen to their proposals, though they were openly cool to the idea of such a union. The Canadas had a large debt, and the Maritime provinces were unwilling to embrace an impoverished partner.[2]

This was not the first time the idea of a union of all the provinces had been raised. As early as 1858 public leaders in Upper and Lower Canada formally requested permission to begin discussions of the subject. On 9 September, 1858, the governor-in-chief of Canada, Sir

Edmund Head, submitted to the colonial secretary a Canadian Minute of Council on the question of union. It suggested that the lieutenant governors of the other British North American colonies immediately request from the colonial secretary the authority to convoke a meeting of delegates from the several colonies "for the purpose of considering the subject of a Federative Union, and reporting on the principles on which the same could properly be based."[3] The prime mover behind the suggestion was Alexander Galt who entered the Canadian government in 1858 on the condition that union be made a government policy. The colonial politicians understood that they required formal authorization from the Britain before they could even begin discussions of such a matter. They knew they lacked the authority to initiate constitutional proceedings; there never was any doubt that constitutional affairs remained firmly with the Crown.

The colonial secretary, Sir Edward Bulwer Lytton, was cool to the proposal and refused to authorize the meeting requested in the Canadian Minute of Council. He replied to Governor Head that until he received similar requests from the other colonies he was reluctant to grant the necessary authority.[4] But Lytton's deeper reasons for refusing the request stemmed from his belief that the very initiative for such discussions properly belonged to "the executive Authority of the Empire, and not to that of any separate province."[5] And there the matter rested until John Manners-Sutton, lieutenant governor of New Brunswick, a firm champion of the political union of the Maritime provinces, wrote to the Duke of Newcastle, Lytton's successor as colonial secretary. Newcastle, more receptive than Lytton, indicated that he thought their union should precede a larger union of all the provinces.

Newcastle seized the initiative and sent a circular to all the British North American governors in which he expressed the belief that the subject of federal union of all the provinces might be introduced into the next session of the several legislatures. He warned, however, that in the event of a proposal for such a union no delegates would be authorized "without previous communication with the Secretary of State in order that the Mission of the delegates and the instructions to be given them may be known before hand to Her Majesty's Government."[6] He declined, moreover to take an active role in the process at that time. "I would avow readiness to entertain favourably any proposals which had the concurrence of all three [Maritime] Provinces, but I would caution the Governor and Lieutenant Governors not to come to too hasty conclusions."[7]

Newcastle's qualified approval for the talks contained the important element of permission for the colonial administrations to begin

discussions of political union, hitherto denied. Nevertheless, sufficient doubt remained as to the British government's enthusiasm for
union to prompt requests for clarification. Joseph Howe, for example,
introduced a resolution in the legislature of Nova Scotia on 15 April,
1861, asking that Her Majesty's Government make known its policy
regarding proposals for a union, either legislative or federal.[8]

The reply to Nova Scotia's request for clarification was encouraging inasmuch as it outlined the general procedure to be followed.
Newcastle suggested that proposals for union – whether of the
Maritime provinces or of all the colonies – were of a nature making
it "especially fit that if either of them should be proposed for adoption it should emanate in the first instance from the provinces and
should be concurred in by all of them which it would affect."[9] The
significant difference between Newcastle's reply in 1862 and Lytton's
in 1858 was that the Colonial Office, while still reluctant to initiate
proceedings, was now (in 1862) abandoning any attempt to discour-
age or control colonial initiation of discussions of union.

Union of the Maritime provinces received the formal consideration
of all three of them in 1864. Once more, the leadership came from Nova
Scotia. On 29 February, 1864, Major General Hastings Doyle, the
administrator of Nova Scotia, forwarded to the lieutenant governors
of New Brunswick and Prince Edward Island a copy of a resolution
that the Nova Scotia government planned to introduce into the Legislative Assembly. Doyle requested that resolutions "as nearly identical
as possible" be introduced by the other two governments.[10] The Nova
Scotia resolution requested the governors "to appoint delegates [not
to exceed five] to confer with delegates, who may be appointed by the
Governments of New Brunswick and Prince Edward Island, for the
union of the three Provinces under *one government and legislature*,[11]
such a union to take effect when confirmed by the legislative enact-
ments of the various Provinces interested and by the Queen."[12] In light
of subsequent events, it is instructive to note that a *federal* union of the
maritime provinces was not contemplated at this stage.

The resolution was approved by the legislatures of Nova Scotia
and New Brunswick but not by that of Prince Edward Island. The
reluctance of the people of Prince Edward Island to lose their legislature was too strong for them to enter into union discussions. They
did, however, at length agree to discuss the "expediency" of union.[13]
The province's politicians had been unreceptive to all suggestions
made between 1858 and 1862 for closer political and economic ties
with Canada, and were now no more responsive to political union
with the other Maritime provinces if it meant giving up their own
Legislative Assembly.

Preparations for a conference nevertheless proceeded. Where to hold it became the first serious problem. Prince Edward Island insisted on making it clear that union was out of the question and that it had agreed to attend solely out of courtesy. Now, however, the island's politicians demanded that the conference take place in Charlottetown. But this location was unacceptable to both Nova Scotia and New Brunswick. Hence, by June 1864, prospects for a conference on Maritime union appeared remote.

THE CHARLOTTETOWN CONFERENCE

Meanwhile, political events in the United Canadas were running a steady downward course. The Act of Union of 1840–1, which united Upper and Lower Canada under one legislature, was turning out to be no better than the previous constitutions. The government stumbled from one crisis to another; ministries fell like ninepins. No matter what combination was tried, it resulted in defeat. In short, Canadian politicians showed beyond dispute that under the prevailing constitutional arrangement they could not govern the province.

The only ray of hope emerged from George Brown's committee on constitutional problems. Brown, the leader of the Upper Canada Reform Party, suggested on 23 June 1864 that the legislature give serious consideration to a federal union of the two Canadas or of all the British North American provinces.[14] But this glimmer was darkened by the fall – the very some day – of the Tache-Macdonald ministry. It was, as one observer noted,"the fourth ministry to fall in four years, years in which even the turmoil of two general elections had failed to avert deadlock."[15] Something had to be done. The leading figures of both dominant political factions, led by Brown and Macdonald, temporarily stifled their deep personal and partisan differences and agreed to explore seriously the possibilities of federal union.

One week later, Governor General Lord Monck wrote to the lieutenant governors of the Maritime provinces at the request of the Canadian cabinet asking for information on the proposed conference on their union. Monck also asked whether their governments would permit delegates from the United Canadas to attend "to ascertain whether the proposed Union may not be made to embrace the whole of the British North American Provinces."[16] The request received a favourable but restrained response. Nevertheless, the interest shown by Canada had the effect of reviving the dormant conference preparations. A time and place were quickly decided by giving in to Prince Edward Island's demand that it be held in Charlottetown and setting a date of 1 September. The explicit purpose was discussing the union of the Maritime colonies; if the delegates were inclined, the Canadian suggestion of union of all the provinces would also be considered.

Both official and unofficial accounts of the meeting reveal that the Canadian delegation virtually hi-jacked the agenda, subsuming the proposal for legislative union of the three Maritime colonies within their vision for a larger federal union. The newspaper accounts of the conference confirm that the Canadian delegates presented a detailed plan for such a union. While those present did not formally, consider the plan, they did review it in general terms. They also decided to meet the following month in Quebec City to discuss it officially and in detail.

The official Canadian account of the Charlottetown Conference stressed the informal and exploratory character of the discussions. In a document entitled *Confederation of British North America*, the government of the United Canadas announced that "thus far all the proceedings of the Canadian Government have been entirely unofficial and informal ... Thus far nothing definite as to the details of the scheme has been agreed upon; notwithstanding the discussions of the last three weeks, every point will be open to unfettered inquiry by the Quebec conference."[17] The second meeting, held in October 1864, was therefore the more important of the constitutional conferences; accordingly, it deserves fuller attention because it placed all future discussions of the union of the provinces in the context of a *federal* union.

THE QUEBEC CONFERENCE

The Quebec Conference was the first and only time the confederation of Canada as a whole received formal consideration by all parties. Delegates from the United Canadas (modern-day Quebec and Ontario), Nova Scotia, New Brunswick, Prince Edward Island, and Newfoundland all converged on Quebec City on 10 October 1864. The conference lasted eighteen days, at the end of which the delegates had approved seventy-two resolutions that were to become the basis of the Constitution Act, 1867. They contained the only plan of federal union that was submitted to the various provincial governments for their legislative approval.

Federation and Representation

The first point on which the politicians assembled in Quebec agreed was to hold their meetings in secret. The press complained bitterly over the decision and submitted a formal request for access to the deliberations to the chairman of the conference, Sir Etienne P. Tache.[18] He replied on behalf of the delegates that members of the press would receive copies of whatever resolutions emerged at the end of the conference, but would not be permitted to attend the daily sessions.

Although the formal minutes of the Quebec Conference are fragmentary and incomplete, they do shed considerable light on the proceedings and provide a reliable guide to the daily debates.[19] In addition to official minutes there exist two sets of private notes taken during the Charlottetown and Quebec conferences that provide a valuable supplementary source of information.[20]

In his address of welcome, Sir Etienne P. Tache announced that "the object of the conference was to do away with some of the internal hindrances to trade, and to unite the Provinces for mutual defence."[21] Several other speakers, such as George Etienne Cartier from Lower Canada and Ambrose Shea from Newfoundland, picked up these themes and commended any effort to enhance relations between the provinces in the wake of the repeal of reciprocity with the United States. Alexander Galt, the principal force behind the suggestion for federal union, spoke in the same vein urging successfully that the conference adopt a resolution favouring the construction of a railway in the interest of binding the commercial lines of communication between the provinces.

When Charles Tupper of Nova Scotia called for a "fuller exposition" of the Canadians' intentions, John A. Macdonald stated that the conference was being held "for the purpose of discussing the general principles of a Federal Constitution."[22] Macdonald at length introduced the first resolution of the conference, which stated: "The best interests and present and future prosperity of British North America will be promoted by a Federal Union under the Crown of Great Britain, provided such union can be effected on principles just to the several Provinces." It apparently caused little debate; it was approved unanimously the same day. Everyone had had time to at least think about the idea it embodied before coming to Quebec. According to George Brown, the delegates from the Maritime provinces at Charlottetown the previous month "were unanimous in regarding Federation of all the Provinces to be highly desirable, if the terms of union could be made satisfactory."[23] His statement is made credible only by emphasizing the clause "if the terms of union could be made satisfactory," since Prince Edward Island was in no wise disposed to enter a union that would impair its legislative authority. Nor was Newfoundland. As events turned out, these two colonies refused to enter Confederation in 1867 because they viewed the terms of union as encroaching upon their hard-won right to self-government. They

THE FOUNDATIONS OF EDDYSTONE

were, however, prepared to entertain and discuss back in their respective legislative assemblies the Canadian plan of federal union of all the provinces.

Even though the Quebec Conference unanimously approved Macdonald's first resolution, the delegates did not assent without serious misgivings. There was a widely held preference among them for the British legislative union or unitary form of government. But as Cartier explained to the conference, "We thought that a Federation scheme was the best because these provinces are peopled by different nations and by peoples of different religions."[24] French Canadians were adamant in their desire to control their own institutions, free of Protestant and English interference; hence, they insisted on some federal form of government. The Maritime provinces, notably Prince Edward Island, were reluctant to give up their provincial legislatures and so supported the French in their request for a federal union, whatever that might mean in its details. For their part, English-speaking Canadians demanded assurances from their French colleagues that Confederation would not weaken the tie to the monarchy. Cartier smoothly provided these by reminding them that French Canadians, while truly French, were of the *ancien regime* and therefore monarchists at heart.[25] In Charlottetown Cartier had said: "We are French by origin, but French of the old regime."[26]

It is clear from the conference records that from the very beginning only one plan of union was considered by the delegates to both Charlottetown and Quebec City. It was the brainchild of George Brown's constitutional committee, formed two and a half months before the Charlottetown Conference. Unfortunately, very little is known about the early stage of its development.[27] And since no official transcript of the Charlottetown Conference was kept, we must look elsewhere for information about the content of the Canadian plan of federal union submitted at the Quebec Conference.

One of the most reliable accounts of what transpired at Charlottetown is contained in two official despatches from Lieutenant Governor Arthur Gordon to Colonial Secretary Edward Cardwell. Gordon, an observer at the conference, wrote that he had a "good deal of conversation with the Canadian Ministers especially with Mr. Galt ... who developed to me at considerable length the details of the scheme of federation which had been agreed upon by the Canadian Cabinet."[28] As well, *Le Courrier du Canada* published an account of the Charlottetown Conference in September 1864.[29] Included in it was an outline of the plan of union proposed by the Canadian delegates. The accuracy of Gordon's despatch and of the other reports on the Charlottetown Conference, such as that in *Le Courrier du Canada*, is confirmed upon comparison with the seventy-two resolutions adopted and later published at Quebec. No one attempted to disguise the Canadian origins of the Confederation scheme; in fact, several of the Maritime provinces' delegates at Quebec repeatedly referred to it as the "Canadian plan."[30]

Quebec delegates to the conference agreed to a federal union only after Macdonald, McGee, and others promised that it would be done within the framework of the British monarchical form. The major proponents of the Confederation plan therefore adopted the strategy of minimizing its federal character by stressing its monarchical character. In the resolution referring to the composition of the new central government, for example, the constitutional framers carefully avoided use of the term "federal"; the emphasis was on how closely it would approach the British model. The third resolution accordingly stated: "In framing a constitution, for the general Government, the Conference, with a view to the perpetuation of our connection with the mother country, and to the promotion of the best interests of the people of these provinces, desire to follow the model of the British constitution so far as our circumstances will permit." The previous resolution made it clear that existing circumstances best designed to promote the diversified interests of the several provinces "would be a general Government charged with the matters of common interest to the whole country; and Local Governments ... for each of the Canadas, and for the Provinces of Nova Scotia, New Brunswick and Prince Edward Island, charged with the control of local matters in their respective sections." A discussion of the federal character of the new constitution in a later chapter will disclose how the draftsmen understood the expressions "matters of common interest to the whole country" and "local matters."

The delegates proceeded to adopt without dissent the sixth resolution, which called for the establishment of a "General Legislature or Parliament ... composed of a Legislative Council and a House of Commons." All readily assented to the proposition that population should be the basis of representation in the House of Commons, and that the number of members would increase proportionately when population increased. Neither these resolutions nor those relating to the composition of the House of Commons generated much discussion or controversy. The same was not true, however, of the resolutions on the Senate,[31] which prompted much heated exchange evidencing a great division of opinion.

When John A. Macdonald introduced a resolution on October 13 suggesting the composition of the Senate, he initiated the most fiery debate of the meetings. It lasted a full six days, one-third of the entire conference. Macdonald moved, "That for the purpose of forming the Legislative Council, the Federated Provinces shall be considered as consisting of three divisions. 1st Upper Canada; 2nd Lower Canada; and 3rd, the four Maritime Provinces, and each division shall be represented in the Legislative Council by an equal number of members."[32]

Most delegates from four colonies in Macdonald's third division expressed dissatisfaction with this motion, fearing that they would be at the mercy of the larger provinces under such a plan. Newfoundland delegates, in particular, resented being lumped in among the "Maritime Provinces"; they had never been party to discussions of union with the three Maritime colonies and were fiercely protective of their ancestral position. The delegates reacted to Macdonald's proposal with an amendment calling for equal representation from each province, but their motion was quickly defeated by Quebec and Ontario, who would not countenance the idea of equality of the provinces. Indeed, the smaller provinces received little support because several of their own influential delegates, notably Charles Tupper of Nova Scotia and Leonard Tilley of New Brunswick, opposed the motion. Their ambition was one day to see a union of the three Maritime colonies into one large province that would enjoy equal representation with Quebec and Ontario in the Senate. Believing that Macdonald's resolution would give impetus to their long-cherished vision, they threw their weight behind it. After much acrimonious debate, the conference adopted the resolution. But bitterness lingered beyond the conference and resurfaced in the Maritimes and Newfoundland in legislative debates on Confederation when the delegates returned home.

As would be expected, the manner of selecting senators was also a major cause of controversy at the Quebec Conference. Some wanted to provide for popular election; others, led by Macdonald, favoured royal appointment for life. Two delegates from Prince Edward Island introduced a motion calling for the election of senators by both houses of the provincial legislatures, but it was never seriously entertained.[33] Once again, the insistence of the combined force of Quebec and Ontario eventually led the conference to approve Macdonald's resolution: "That the members of the Legislative Council shall be appointed by the Crown under the great seal of the General Government and hold office for life." It is clear that the Senate of the proposed confederation was designed to have more in common with the British House of Lords than the United States Senate, to which each state, regardless of size, sends two senators.

In introducing the resolutions on the Senate, John A. Macdonald disclosed his understanding of what the Senate should be: the place where the interests of property-holders would be foremost, since they had a greater stake in the stability of the regime. Accordingly, another of the resolutions adopted at Quebec stipulated that senators "shall possess a real property qualification of four thousand dollars over and above all encumbrances and shall be and continue to be worth that sum over and above their debts and liabilities." In defence of this motion Macdonald explained that, since men of wealth are always in the minority, they ought to have the means by which they could protect their property.[34] In a conscious effort to dilute the democratic principle, the most influential delegates at Quebec argued that men of property had a larger stake in the community and therefore ought to have a weighted voice in its affairs. The constitution should prevent those who had no property from "imposing the burden on those who had the property."[35] Macdonald confidentially expressed the belief that British North America should preserve "some gradation of classes" in imitation of British society and as a counterweight to American democratic influences.[36] The purpose of the Senate was thus to maintain this gradation and simultaneously provide men of property the means of protecting it. In the absence of such, Macdonald claimed, these men would be forced "to seek refuge in despotism, as in France."[37]

Who Will Make the Laws?

Once the delegates had determined the composition of the two houses for the new central government, they set about to define their respective legislative powers. The majority agreed with Macdonald when he insisted that the error of the American founding had to be avoided: "The primary error at the formation of their constitution was that each state reserved to itself all sovereign rights, save the small portion delegated." "We must reverse that process," he continued, "by strengthening the General Government."[38] One of the first steps taken, therefore, was to agree with Charles Tupper that "all the powers not given to the Local Legislatures should be reserved to the Federal Government."[39] Determined to eliminate from the very beginning a weakness of the American constitution that placed the residual powers in the several states, the delegates agreed that the central government would be the repository of those powers.

It is significant to note at this point that the politicians at Quebec clearly had before them the constitution of the United States and were determined to avoid its major features. There can be no question that they were familiar with its terms; how well they understood it emerged in the debates of 1865 when the Confederation plan was discussed in the provincial legislatures.[40]

One of the most striking features of the twenty-ninth resolution, which enumerated the thirty-six areas where the federal government was empowered to make laws, is the depth to which the delegates were willing to allow Parliament to penetrate into the legislative life of the provinces of the new nation. This matter bears special emphasis in light of recent attempts to claim that the resolutions adopted at the Quebec conference were consistent with the later emergence of provincial rights in Canada.[41]

According to the resolution, the federal government was to be granted, among other things, the "regulation of trade and commerce, ... banking – the incorporation of banks, and the issue of paper money, ... immigration, ... agriculture" and even marriage and divorce. The delegates at Quebec granted eighteen areas of jurisdiction to the provincial legislatures. However, even a few of these, such as agriculture and immigration, were to be shared with the central government, with federal dominance in the two cases named. Further, the forty-third resolution, outlining the powers of the local legislatures, stated that they "shall have power to make laws respecting the following subjects," then listed the eighteen areas. What is instructive is the ambiguity pervading this resolution as to the limits of provincial or local jurisdiction. At times it appears that the delegates circumscribed the provincial governments within the limits of the eighteen subjects listed, yet the resolution continues: "And generally all matters of a private or local nature." There would be little controversy if the sentence stopped there, but it does not. The entire sentence reads: "And generally all matters of a private or local nature, not assigned to the general Parliament." The clear implication seems to be that there are matters which – though properly local or provincial – come under federal jurisdiction wherever "assigned to the general Parliament." Subsection 37 of 29 resolution contains the important clause establishing that "all matters of a general character not specially and exclusively reserved for the local Governments and legislatures" belong to the central government. The question is, then, what matters are "specially and exclusively" assigned to the local legislatures?

Not even the power of taxation can be claimed as an exclusive provincial right. According to subsections 3,4, and 5 of resolution 29, Parliament was to be given the authority to raise money by customs duties on imports and exports (except on timber), excise duties, and "[T]he raising of money by all or any other modes or systems of Taxation." The provincial legislatures, on the other hand, were restricted in subsection 1 of resolution 43 to "Direct Taxation and the imposition of Duties on the Export of Timber; Logs, Masts, Spars, Deals and Sawn Lumber, and of Coals and other Minerals."

Nor were matters relating to property and civil rights designated as exclusively provincial areas of jurisdiction in light of subsection 15 of the same resolution, which covered "Property and civil rights, excepting those portions thereof assigned to the general Parliament." Subsection 33 of resolution 29, however, also refered to property and civil rights, stating that the federal government had power to render "uniform all or any of the laws relative to property and civil rights in Upper Canada, Nova Scotia, New Brunswick, Newfoundland and Prince Edward Island ... But any statute for this purpose shall have no force or authority in any Province until sanctioned by the Legislature thereof." Quebec was not included in this provision because it operated under the civil law imported from France.

The provinces were accorded wide authority over the sale and management of public lands, "excepting lands of the general Parliament." But according to the fifty-ninth resolution, "The several Provinces were permitted to retain all other public property [other than already subsumed under general jurisdiction] therein, subject to the right of the general Government to assume any lands or public property required for fortification of the defence of the country."

Even provincial jurisdiction over education was restricted. The provinces were not permitted to violate "the rights and privileges which the Protestant or Catholic minority in both Canadas may possess as to their denominational schools at the time when the union goes into operation." However, they were granted complete and exclusive jurisdiction over curricula and schools.

The only areas of the eighteen listed under provincial jurisdiction that are unequivocally local are these:[42]

- "Borrowing money on the credit of the Provinces." (2)
- "The establishment and tenure of local officers, and appointment and payment of local officers." (3)
- "The establishment, maintenance and management of penitentiaries, and of public and reformatory prisons." (9)
- "The establishment, maintenance and management of hospitals, asylums, charities, and eleemosynary institutions." (10)
- "Municipal institutions." (11)
- "Shop, saloon, tavern, auctioneer and other licences." (12)
- "Local works." (13)
- "Inflicting punishment by fine, penalties, imprisonment or otherwise, for the breach of laws passed in relation to any subject within their jurisdiction." (16)

However, despite subsection 13 of resolution 43, even some local works were to fall under the jurisdiction of Parliament. Subsection 11 of resolution 29, for example, stated that the central government had power over "[a]ll such works as shall, although lying wholly within any Province, be specifically declared by the Acts authorizing them to be for the general advantage." Since this stipulation was included under the head of powers of Parliament, it seems to have intended that the central government could enter any province and declare a purely provincial project as being for the public advantage and so, presumably, preempt the local jurisdiction. The proceedings of the Quebec Conference shed some light on this interesting point.

During discussion of the powers to be given to the provinces, George Brown stated, "As to local Governments, we desire in Upper Canada that they should not be expensive, and should not take up political matters."[43] This was George Brown, the leader of the Upper Canada Reform Party, speaking in defence of restricting the powers of provincial legislatures. Whatever his motives, he was joined in this view by Charles Tupper of Nova Scotia, who urged the delegates to strengthen the central legislature and reduce the power of the provincial governments. It comes as no surprise, therefore to find that the powers that are exclusively provincial are scarcely major ones. Under the resolutions adopted at the Quebec Conference, the federal government controls all the main areas of legislation.

No decision of the conference indicated more plainly the intention of the delegates to form a strong central government than the section of resolution 29 providing for federal regulation of trade and commerce. Alexander Galt explained to the delegates that since trade and commerce "were subjects in reference to which no local interest could exist, it was desirable that they should be dealt with throughout the Confederation on the same principles."[44] Galt went on, "It was most important to see that no local legislature should by its separate action be able to put any … restrictions on the free interchange of commodities as to prevent the manufactures of the rest from finding a market in any one province, and thus from sharing in the advantages of the extended Union." Clearly and emphatically, there were to be no barriers to trade between the provinces.

As already noted, the plan of Confederation provided for several areas of concurrent jurisdiction, including agriculture, immigration, and sea-coast and inland fisheries, which appeared identically and without qualification in both resolutions 29 and 43. However, in order to avoid uncertainty in the event of a clash over matters of concurrent jurisdiction, the Quebec delegates provided clear instructions in resolution 48: "In regard to all subjects over which jurisdiction belongs to both the general and local legislatures, the laws of the general Parliament shall control and supercede those made by the local legislature, and the latter shall be void so far as they are repugnant to, or inconsistent with, the former." This resolution, perhaps more than any other, provides an insight into the peculiar "federal" character of the plan. When taken together with other provisions, in which federal powers are clearly dominant, it demonstrates that the delegates at the Quebec Conference consciously set out to devise a unique form of federal government, one that was not simply an imitation of the American model with minor modifications. Resolution 48 clearly implies that Parliament could conceivably pass legislation on a matter of concurrent jurisdiction even after a provincial legislature had done so, and that the federal law would replace the provincial version. More to the point, which level of government would decide whether a given provincial law was "repugnant to" or "inconsistent with" an Act of Parliament? Certainly not the provinces.

To what extent, then, did the Quebec Conference delegates desire Parliament to control the provincial legislatures? They were in agreement that the federal government should appoint and pay the lieutenant governors of the provinces. The formal resolutions said no more than that lieutenant governors should be appointed "during pleasure" and paid by Parliament.[45] But the minutes of the conference testify that they were intended to serve as representatives of the federal government. George Brown stated emphatically that the principal duty of the lieutenant governor of a province was to bring the provincial governments "into harmony with the General Government."[46] To achieve this end, the delegates adopted a resolution stipulating that "any bill of the Local Legislatures may ... be reserved for the consideration of the Governor General." The conference proceedings and the resolutions adopted unmistakeably imply that the lieutenant governor of a province was to be an agent of the federal government, *not* the representative of the Crown.[47]

Bound Together by a Strong Central Government

The delegates to the Quebec Conference believed that their most important achievement was the establishment of a strong central Parliament and government (following Hobbes). They accomplished it by rendering the provincial governments subordinate to and dependent on the federal government. Ontario and Quebec, supported by important delegates from the Maritimes, espoused a strong central Parliament as a means of binding the country together around the Crown-in-Parliament. This powerful legislature would be the forum where *national* objectives would be enunciated and local or regional aspirations subsumed into the great *national* vision. Even the principal French Canadian delegates supported this ambition under the conviction that it would provide attachment to the Crown and at the same time give Quebec sufficient legislative jurisdiction over its own linguistic and religious affairs. John A. Macdonald viewed this feature of the new constitution as an essential protection against the centripetal forces of the federal form of government. The politicians at the conference were deliberating over these matters as the United States engaged in a bloody civil war, which many of them believed was the result of a federal government. The Canadians were determined not to sow the seeds of civil war in devising their unique federal system, and believed that a strong central government would avert such an outcome. Central to their ambition was the idea of a single national economy; there were to be no barriers to interprovincial trade. (This was made clear by the blanket endorsement of full jurisdiction of the Parliament over trade and commerce.) The Canadian constitutional framers had learned a critical lesson from the Americans' abortive Articles of Confederation, by which individual states jealously attempted to protect their own economies from competition from other states. Some even went so far as to coin their own currencies and build an economic wall around themselves. The chaos that resulted prompted the constitutional conference at Philadelphia in 1787, where the delegates quickly jettisoned the unworkable Articles of Confederation and set about redesigning the "more perfect union." The Canadians were inflexibly dedicated to a national economy and took measures to prevent the fragmentation of the economic life of the new nation by not only granting the central legislature the lion's share of legislative power over trade and commerce but also subordinating the provincial legislatures to Parliament. To the latter end, they further provided for federal disallowance of provincial legislation. Resolution 51 stipulated that "any bill passed by a local legislature shall be subject to disallowance by the Governor General within one year after the passing thereof." The governor general would, of course, exercise this authority only upon instructions from the federal government.

Resolution 60 promised that the federal government would "assume all the debts and liabilities of each Province" and also stipulated that it would provide an annual grant in aid to each of the provinces "in consideration of the transfer to the general Parliament of the powers of taxation." It is here that the seeds of "equalization payments," which have characterized Canadian fiscal federalism ever since, were sown. George Brown later gave at least a partial explanation for this decision in the Canadian debates on the Quebec plan of union. "Two courses were open to us, either to surrender to the local governments some source of indirect revenue, some tax which the General Government proposed to retain – or collect the money by federal machinery, and distribute it to the local Governments for local purposes. And we decided in favour of the latter."[48] But he did not explain why the general government proposed to retain such comprehensive control over provincial revenues in the first place. Alexander Galt, the financial expert among the delegates to Quebec, revealed other motives behind the course taken at the conference. It was decided, he affirmed later, to take away from the provinces "every source of revenue they possessed except minor local revenues, and then to give them from the public chest a sufficient subsidy to enable the machinery [of local government] to work."[49] He continued:

The estimate was that eighty cents a head of population of Nova Scotia would be sufficient to enable her to work her local system ... Therefore the subsidy proposed to be given to local legislatures was fixed, not at an increasing rate according to population, but at the rate which existed at the census of 1861 – by this means, as the population increased, the subsidy would not increase with it ... If Upper and Lower Canada increased their population they would be obliged to resort to direct taxation; and he [Galt] thought they might trust the people themselves to keep a sharp watch over the local Governments lest they should resort to direct taxation. He thought no surer check could be put upon them than thus fixing the grants they were respectively to receive.[50]

Galt's explanation leaves little doubt that the reason the delegates chose to grant the primary sources of revenue to the federal government was not in order to maintain "fiscal integrity," as one historian has suggested,[51] but to restrict the activity of the provincial legislatures. Galt publicly acknowledged that the new constitution aimed to take from the provinces "a large share of the subjects previously legislated upon" by them. Thus, the most efficient way of doing this was to deny them sufficient funds. The deeper motives for providing grants-in-aid to the provinces clearly seem to have been political. Alexander Galt has given us every reason to suspect that the delegates at Quebec City were fully aware of the axiom about the power that goes with controlling the purse.

"The Running at Large of Swine"   An important conclusion emerges from studying the Quebec Conference proceedings and the seventy-two

resolutions adopted. The framers of the terms of union took pains to define the scope of federal legislative powers broadly, and took equal care *not* to define too precisely the character of the local or provincial governments. Charles Fisher and E.B. Chandler, two Maritime delegates, had challenged that approach, urging in an amendment to the third resolution that local governments also "be formed on the model of the British constitution."[52] It was a clever ruse, by which Chandler and his supporters attempted to win formal recognition of the parliamentary character of the provincial legislatures. But it failed, for the conference – led at this point by Charles Tupper and Leonard Tilley – voted down their effort to define even in general terms the character of government at the provincial level with the thoroughly unsatisfactory claim that it was "not judicious to fetter our actions by the passage of a resolution of a simply declaratory character."[53] Why was it "not judicious," and how would such a declaration "fetter" the actions of provincial politicians? We will never know. That such a line of reasoning could have prevented the conference from addressing the issue of the character of the local legislatures speaks volumes about the determination of leading delegates not to have strong provincial governments in the new nation.

Chandler was outraged at this turn of events and protested in no uncertain terms that the powers granted to the provincial legislatures were insignificant. "You are now proceeding to destroy the constitutions of the local Governments," he thundered, "and to give them less powers than they have had allowed them from England and it will make them merely large municipal corporations."[54] After attempting to win wider legislative authority for the provinces, Chandler tried to have the delegates reverse their earlier decision and bestow the residual powers on the provincial legislatures. John A. Macdonald trumped this proposal by retorting that adopting it would be equivalent to embracing "the worst features of the United States."[55] That was sufficient to rally the conference against Chandler's motion; labelling anything as smacking of the American style of federalism was the kiss of death, as Chandler and other proponents of provincial powers quickly found out.

Beyond listing the eighteen rather insignificant areas over which the provinces would have legislative authority, then, the delegates made no effort to determine the composition of the provincial governments. In fact, resolution 42 explicitly provided that "[t]he local legislatures shall have power to alter or amend their constitutions from time to time." Be it noted that the delegates were careful not to make a similar provision for the federal Parliament, in order to guarantee that it could not readily be changed. In addition, resolution 41 stated, "The local government and legislature of each Province shall be constructed in such a manner as the existing legislature of each Province shall provide." These resolutions would later permit Charles Tupper and Leonard Tilley to raise the question of union among the Maritime provinces even after the terms of Confederation went into effect. It is difficult not to conclude – in view of the opposition from Chandler and Fisher, among others – that the delegates deliberately attempted to leave the character of the local legislatures as vague and imprecise as possible. It comes as no surprise that anti-confederates in the respective legislatures were to find such designs unsatisfactory.

Both the resolutions and minutes indicate that the main focus of the Quebec Conference was on the new central legislature and government. As we have seen, the former testify that the national government was to possess the residual powers; it was to be composed of upper and lower chambers, with membership in both houses carefully stipulated; and it was to have power to disallow provincial legislation. Moreover, it was to be given the authority to appoint lieutenant governors, who would possess the power of reservation in its name. It short, the resolutions reveal that by absorbing certain important areas (e.g., agriculture and immigration) and by possessing the wide authority to legislate for the "peace, order and good government of the federated provinces," the central government was unquestionably to be dominant in the most significant matters. They further show that the authority of the federal government to legislate was always to be accompanied by the possibility of expansion, whereas the powers of the local or provincial legislatures almost always contained explicit restrictions.

It is impossible to overemphasize the conclusion that the constitutional framers resolutely intended to establish a strong central government and at the same time to reduce the legislative authority of the provincial governments.[56] One Prince Edward Island anti-confederate concluded with exasperation after reading the Quebec resolutions that they gave the provinces little more authority than to "regulate the running at large of swine." The new constitutional proposals even stipulated that the provincial legislatures would be subordinate to the central government without direct access to the sovereign; henceforth, they would have to go through the governor general, who alone was the recognized representative of the Crown. The old provincial constitutions would effectively be repealed by the new constitution. From the time of union forward the provinces would derive their existence and legitimacy from the Confederation Act, which would specify the scope of their legislative competence. As we shall soon see, the deliberate dismantling of provincial powers raised the hackles of opposition forces when the resolutions were debated in the various legislatures after the delegates to Quebec City returned to their respective provinces.

THE NEW PARLIAMENT AND IMPERIAL SOVEREIGNTY

The foregoing review of the Quebec Conference proceedings has revealed how supreme the central government was designed to be vis-à-vis the provinces. An important question remains: How sovereign did the delegates intend the federal government to be vis-à-vis the British Parliament? The constitutional framers were not "embarrassed" by the necessity of discussing the question of sovereignty, according to D'Arcy McGee. Moreover, the advocates of union constantly promised that Confederation did not mean independence from Great Britain; on the contrary, it would lead to stronger, closer ties, which would help British North America resist the magnetic forces of American republicanism. John A. Macdonald stressed in his defence of the plan of union that the central government would be "sovereign" yet also "subordinate."[57] And when Lord Carnarvon introduced the Confederation bill in the British Parliament he declared, "The real object we have in view is to give to the central government those high functions and almost sovereign powers by which general principles and uniformity of legislation may be secured in those questions that are of common interest to all the Provinces."[58]

From Carnarvon's words it appears that the federal government was to be given "almost sovereign" powers for internal or domestic purposes. The context of Macdonald's remarks bears out the same intention, that is, the granting of almost absolute jurisdiction over domestic legislation, over "questions that are of common interest to all the Provinces." It is important to stress that the Fathers of Confederation never thought they should have jurisdiction over external affairs, such as treaties with other nations. McGee later made this point in a speech at Cookshire, Quebec: "There [i.e., in the British Crown], for us, the sovereign power of peace and war, life and death, receiving and sending ambassadors, still resides."[59] And there the framers of the constitution desired it to remain. There can be no doubt that they wanted their new nation to remain subordinate and dependent. They neither wished nor requested absolute control or jurisdiction even over domestic matters, since they desired the imperial right of disallowance to be continued; they did not have the power to terminate it, in any event. The British North American provinces were dependencies, subject to the sovereign authority of

Great Britain, incapable of severing the bonds of authority without imperial consent. It is important to understand, however, that the British government, while not disposed to grant the colonies complete independence, was at this time reexamining its colonial policy; many prominent British officials urged the termination of colonial bonds. The leading men of British North America, however, wanted no part of such independence and insisted on continued formal attachment to the mother country.

It is just as well that they held these sentiments, for in 1865, two years before Confederation, the British Parliament emphasized its sovereign rights over the colonies by passing the Colonial Laws Validity Act, which stipulated, among other things, that "[a]ny Colonial Law which is or shall be in any respect repugnant to the Provisions of any Act of Parliament extending to the Colony to which such law may relate, or repugnant to any Order or Regulation made under Authority of such Act of Parliament, or having in the Colony the Force and Effect of such Act, shall be read subject to such Act, Order or Regulation, and shall, to the Extent of such repugnancy, but not otherwise, be and remain absolutely void and inoperative." This law removed any doubt regarding not only the British Parliament's control over the internal or domestic legislation of the colonies but also their sovereignty. Macdonald and the other framers fully concurred; they meant their new central government to be sovereign, more or less, with respect to domestic legislation – that is, to such domestic legislation as was not "repugnant" to any "Act of Parliament."

The Canadians further acknowledged their dependence by insisting that their constitution would be subject to the jurisdiction of the British courts. Macdonald stated during the Quebec Conference: "Any question as to overriding sectional matter [will be] determined by 'Is it legal, or not?' The judicial tribunals of Great Britain would settle any such difficulties should they occur."[60] The framers did not view this as irregular, since their constitution was to be an act of the British Parliament and – after 1833 and the reconstitution of the Judicial Committee of the Privy Council – subject to the appellate jurisdiction of that Judicial Committee.

What is important to observe is the fact that the constitutional framers seemed to believe that they had effectively eliminated the necessity for appeal to the courts; they believed – some today would say "naively" – that they had successfully defined the limits of both the provincial and federal governments so as to avoid any major clashes of jurisdiction. Macdonald explained this to the Canadian legislature in the following manner: "We have given the General Legislature all the great subjects of legislation. We have conferred on them, not only specifically and in detail, all the powers which are incident to sovereignty, but we have expressly declared that all subjects of general interest not distinctly and exclusively conferred upon the local governments and local legislatures, shall be conferred upon the General Government and Legislature." In summary, Macdonald concluded, "We have avoided all conflict of jurisdiction and authority."[61] In Nova Scotia, Charles Tupper likewise explained to the Legislative Assembly that the powers conferred upon the provincial legislatures "were so arranged as to prevent any conflict or struggle which might lead to any difficulty between the several sections."[62]

In addition to the careful distribution of legislative powers, John Rose pointed to another feature of the Confederation plan that would eliminate the possibility of conflict between the central and provincial governments: "[T]he other point which commends itself so strongly to me is this, that there is a veto power on the part of the General Government over all the legislation of the Local Parliament."[63] A colleague of Rose in the Canadian assembly, John Scoble, came to the same conclusion later in the debates over the plan: "A careful analysis of the scheme convinces me that the powers conferred on the General Central Government secures it all the attributes of sovereignty, and the *veto* power which its executive will possess, and to which all local legislation will be subject, will prevent a conflict of laws and jurisdictions in all matters of importance."[64]

These statements tend to imply that the plan of union contained an automatic resolution of legislative conflict in favour of the central government. One anti-confederate, Quebec's A.A. Dorion, recognized this imbalance and objected strenuously on the grounds that the plan granted sovereignty to the central government, which nothing prevented from exercising full authority over the provinces. Dorion contended that it was not sufficient for advocates of the plan to claim that the federal government would not infringe upon those powers "distinctly and exclusively conferred upon the local governments"; an examination of the plan would demonstrate that no powers of any real significance had been "distinctly and exclusively conferred." Dorion concluded with these comments: "I find that the powers assigned to the General Parliament enable it to legislate on all subjects whatsoever. It is an error to imagine that these powers are defined and limited by the 29th clause of the resolutions, i.e., the clause outlining provincial powers. Were it desirous of legislating on subjects placed under the jurisdiction of the local legislatures, there is not a word in these resolutions which can be construed to prevent it, and if the local legislatures complained, Parliament may turn away and refuse to hear their complaints, because all the sovereignty is vested in the General Government."[65] In light of the foregoing discussion of the respective powers of the federal and provincial governments, it is difficult not to agree with Dorion's conclusions.

A "DREADFULLY TORY" CONSTITUTION

The results of the Quebec Conference are embodied most authoritatively in the seventy-two resolutions adopted by the delegates, which speak volumes as to the degree of agreement on general principles of both form and substance that pervaded the meetings. Those principles were derived from Hobbes. The later defences of the Quebec plan of union raised by its draftsmen in the legislature of the United Canadas and the Maritime provincial legislatures confirm the breadth and depth of that consensus. Men as widely divergent in their political views as George Brown and John A. Macdonald forcefully urged their legislative colleagues to adopt the plan of Confederation – the only matter of substance on which these two implacable political enemies ever agreed. Indeed, their agreement has left historians and other commentators puzzled ever since. How can we explain Macdonald's alleged "conversion" to federalism after he spoke so strongly against it and so strongly in favour of a unitary system modelled on Great Britain? And how do we account for Brown's enthusiastic support for a plan leaving so little autonomy to the provinces? Writing to his wife Anne from London during the constitutional conference, Brown conceded that "our Constitution is dreadfully Tory – and so it is – but we have the power in our hands ... to change it as we like. Hurrah!"[66]

In one important respect, Macdonald's shift to federalism is easier to explain. In a confidential letter written during the Quebec Conference to Isaac Buchanan, a Hamilton merchant, Macdonald revealed that the planned constitutional arrangement would have more in common with a legislative system, because of the strength of the central Parliament, than with a federal system, despite the use of the word "federal" in the first resolution. "We are very busily engaged in conference and things go on satisfactorily but slowly. – There are many interests and prejudices to be dealt with, but we shall arrive at a satisfactory solution. – My great aim is to strengthen the general legislature and government as much as possible, and approach as nearly to the legislative Union as is practicable and in this I hope to be successful."[67] Indeed, the ambiguous embrace of federalism that has plagued Canadian constitutional history since the Quebec Conference is evident in the third resolution, in which the delegates affirmed their desire to perpetuate their connection with the mother country as well as their "desire to follow the model of the British constitution so far as our circumstances will permit." Subsequent resolutions spoke of vesting the executive authority or government in the Sovereign of the United Kingdom of Great Britain and Ireland and of being "administered according to the well-understood principles of the British constitution."[68]

The resolutions and subsequent debates make it clear that the delegates' main focus was on the practice of government found in British constitutional history, not on the abstract theory of government. The government of the new Canada was founded not on theory but on practice: time-honoured British constitutional practice. But that does not mean that practice was not informed at some stage by theory. As we have seen, the British constitution, for all its boasting about the virtue of practice over theory, was founded on the theoretical foundations provided by Thomas Hobbes.

But neither were the delegates unschooled in the principles of government. And while no-one would ever suggest that John A. Macdonald was a political philosopher, he *was* a lawyer and learned in the law according to the standards of the day. In addition to formal instruction in the great works on Roman law, such as Cicero's writings and Justinian's Code, as well as in the classics of Anglo-Saxon jurisprudence, such as Blackstone's *Commentaries on the Laws of England*, he would have been acquainted with the developments of British constitutional history. Furthermore, if the list of books in his library is any indication of the range of his reading in the first principles of the English constitution, we can say that he was well-read, even learned, in that area.[69] His library contained a number of books that he certainly must have consulted before and during the great debates leading up to Confederation. The most noteworthy of the works Macdonald owned relating to the British and American constitutions were Lord Brougham's *The British Constitution* (2nd edition, 1861); Nathaniel Shipman's *Principles of Government* (1833), which contained a treatise on the United States; and George Curtis's *History of the Constitution of the United States* (1858), at the time one of the most celebrated studies of the origins and development of the American constitution. Also in his library was Christopher Reithmuller's *Alexander Hamilton and the Rise of the American Constitution* (1864), an extensive account of Hamilton's constitutionalism and his role in the formation of his country's constitution. In addition, Macdonald owned and presumably read Elliott's *Notes on the Philadelphia Convention* (1863), as well as Lord John Russell's *History of the English Government and Constitution from Henry VII to 1865*. Most important of all, he owned two works by Jean Louis DeLolme (1740–1806): *The Constitution of England* (1810)[70] and *The Rise and Progress of the English Constitution* (1838). DeLolme, a well-known and highly respected French authority on the English constitution, was referred to by many American and Canadian statesmen during the early years of the French republic. Alexander Hamilton called him "solid and ingenious" in *The Federalist Papers*.[71]

If any individual author more than another can be said to have introduced Macdonald to the Hobbesean character of the constitution of England, it was DeLolme. No-one, not even Brougham, presented the English constitution with as much emphasis on its core strengths and on the inherent weaknesses of republican government. It must have been music to Macdonald's ears to hear DeLolme, a French writer in republican France, sing the praises of English monarchy, not from the perspective of a loser in the French Revolution but as one who examined the history of the central institutions of the English constitution and saw much to admire. DeLolme presented nothing less than a "complete delineation of the advantages that result from the stability [of the Crown] in favour of public liberty."[72] He went on to explain that "the first peculiarity of the English government, as a free government, is its having a king – its having thrown into one place the whole mass, if I may use the expression, of the executive power, and having invariably and for ever fixed it there ... by making one great, very great man in the state, has an effectual check been put on the pretensions of those who otherwise would strive to become such; and disorders have been prevented, which, in all republics ever brought on the ruin of liberty, and, before it was lost, obstructed the enjoyment of it."[73] It was precisely this aspect of the English constitution that Alexander Hamilton admired most; it provided for "energy in the executive."

Drawing on a full range of English constitutional authorities, from Coke to Blackstone to Mill, DeLolme heaped unqualified praise upon the monarchical character of the English regime. The Crown aided especially the cause of stability and public order, without being dependent on the army. The character of the executive especially appealed to him as a means of securing the benefits of a genuine liberty. "The indivisibility of the public power in England has constantly kept the views and efforts of the people directed to one and the same object."[74] That one object was a secure public liberty. The English regime was pre-eminently stable and free of the internal defects of republican regimes. "The laws of England open no door to those accumulations of power, which have been the ruin of many republics."[75] Above all, British parliamentary government contained within its laws the proper means of responding to disorders. "A *representative* constitution places the remedy in the hands of those who feel the disorder: but a *popular* constitution places the remedy in the hands of those who cause it," DeLolme asserted.[76] It was perhaps on this basis that Macdonald argued in the legislature during the 1865 debates on the Confederation plan that to refer it to the people would be contrary to the English constitution.[77]

In DeLolme's view, the constitution of England was hierarchically structured so as to effect a stable, permanent political liberty whose blessings would accrue to the people at large. Liberty, he wrote, "consists in this, that every man while he respects the persons of others, and allows them quietly to enjoy the produce of their industry, be certain himself likewise to enjoy the produce of his own industry and that his person be also secure."[78] This is little more than a paraphrase of the reasons Hobbes gave for men entering upon the contract to leave the state of nature and construct civil society. Hobbes had written that men leave the state of nature and place themselves under the sovereign authority in order to secure peace, a peace where in each citizen is able to pursue "such things as are necessary to commodious living."[79] In brief, Hobbes saw the dual goal of civil society as peace and security. For DeLolme, no modern constitution provided these as well as the English constitution.[80] Monarchy tempered by representative government as it operated under the laws of England was the best constitution, preferable to republican government, which made popular disruption possible. There can be no doubt that DeLolme had his eye on what had happened in France following the revolution. Like Montesquieu, De Lolme wrote in the first instance with a view to instructing Frenchmen on the weaknesses of popular government and the virtues of the English constitution.

The Canadian constitutional framers were not as innovative as the American founders – beyond, that is, the attempt to wed a measure of federalism with the "well-understood principles of the British constitution." The essential Hobbesean features of the British constitution were accordingly embodied in the general plan of union from the very earliest stage and it is they, not federalism – the kernel and not the husk – that dominate. The executive government would be located in the House of Commons and would remain in power as long as it could command the support of the house. There was no need, therefore, to debate the merits or demerits of the doctrine of the separation of powers, as there was in Philadelphia in 1787 and later in the ratification debates. British constitutional practice had resolved the issue in favour of the fusion in the House of Commons.

Indeed, the Fathers of Confederation were preoccupied with the effective practice of government, not its theoretical justification. This focus explains the essential differences between the speeches justifying

the American constitution and those promoting the Canadian constitution. John A. Macdonald summed it up perfectly in a private letter
to Samuel Amsden of 1 December 1864: "I think that the Federation
scheme is a grand one and I hope to see it consummated ... It would
be unconstitutional and anti-British to have a plebiscite. If by petitions or public meetings Parliament is satisfied that the country do
not want the measure they will refuse to adopt it. If on the other
hand Parliament sees that the country is in favour of the Federation
there is no use in an appeal to it. Submission of the complicated
details to the country is an obvious absurdity. Fancy the worry and
expense of an election to vote for the constitution and then to dissolve
itself and a new election forthwith to follow for the united Parliament
and for both Parliaments of U. [sic] and Lower Canada."[81]

It would be difficult to imagine a similar statement coming from
the pen of an American founder. The republican spirit inspired by
Locke would never have countenanced it. The British monarchical
form of government, on the other hand, invited just such an attitude.
It comes as no surprise, therefore, to learn that Canada's constitution
was never submitted directly to the people for their consent, despite
the efforts of several prominent politicians in that direction. In fact,
it was debated formally in only one of the provincial legislatures, that
of the United Canadas. Where it was submitted indirectly to the
people in a general election, as in New Brunswick, it was roundly
defeated. But it has never been argued in Canadian constitutionalism
that, since the Confederation plan was not submitted to the people
for ratification, it lacked fundamental legitimacy. Under British constitutionalism the people of the provinces were not sovereign, as they
were in the United States; hence, legitimacy did not reside in the
consent of the governed. The act of union, or the British North
America Act, was an act of the sovereign British Parliament, and in
that fact alone lies the plenitude of its legitimacy, however stridently
this notion now strikes our ears.

CONCLUSION

The resolutions adopted at the Quebec Conference in 1864 became
the basis of the terms of the Constitution Act, 1867, by way of the
slight reformulation contained in the resolutions adopted in London
in 1866 which we shall encounter in the next chapter. There was no
substantive departure from the achievement of the delegates who set
down the terms of union; in every respect, the Constitution Act, 1867
reflected their aspirations and wishes. The British North America
Act was their achievement, not the British government's; it was a

made-in-Canada constitution. At no time following the formal enactment by the British Parliament of the Constitution Act, 1867 did any
of its framers complain that it did not reflect accurately the terms set
out in the Quebec Conference resolutions. Indeed, the Fathers of
Confederation saw it as a faithful rendering of their wishes, as for-
mulated at Quebec City in October 1864.[82]

While there can be no doubt that the dominant feature of the
constitution for Canada embodied in the seventy-two resolutions was
monarchy and attachment to the Crown, in time its most contentious
feature became its *federal* character. We shall therefore later examine
more closely the unique federal character of the Canadian constitution and see to what extent it has developed under the subsequent
impact of court supervision and political ingenuity. But first we must
see how its framers transformed the seventy-two resolutions into the
Constitution Act, 1867 at the London Conference.

4

An Object Much to Be Desired

You will at the same time express the strong and deliberate opinion
of Her Majesty's government that it is an object much to be desired
that all the British North American colonies should agree to unite
in one government.

Edward Cardwell to Governor General Lord Monck

The road from Quebec City to London and parliamentary approval
of the Confederation plan was strewn with the debris of heated
objections and failed efforts to scuttle the project. Following the
Quebec Conference, the delegates returned to their respective provinces and attempted to convince their legislatures to give formal
support to the resolutions for the plan of union. However, many of
the delegates themselves were of two minds about the plan, especially those from the Maritime provinces and Quebec. The leading
figures at the conference – John A. Macdonald, George-Etienne
Cartier, Alexander Galt, and George Brown from the United Canadas,
supported by Charles Tupper from Nova Scotia and Leonard Tilley
from New Brunswick and a scattering of others – were sufficiently
strong to have won formal approval for the Confederation plan at
the conference. It is when the delegates sought the consent of their
various legislatures that things began to go wrong.

Upon their return home, they were met with a volley of criticism
from their legislative colleagues, most objecting strenuously that the
delegates lacked authority to enter into an agreement to promote the
plan of union. Many members of the provincial legislatures of Nova
Scotia and New Brunswick, for example, were downright hostile to
the plan and gave bitter voice to their views. Joseph Howe of Nova
Scotia ridiculed the work of the Quebec Conference with the observation that after "three weeks of light labour" and "exhaustive
festivities" what was called "the Quebec scheme" of Confederation
was produced. Along with other vocal members of the legislature,
he viewed the plan as certain to deprive the province of its hard-won

right of responsible self-government. Indeed, the objections were so forceful in the Nova Scotia legislature that Charles Tupper dared not introduce a motion to approve the plan because it was certain to be defeated. In Prince Edward Island, the opposition was so great that its legislature was successful in winning the British government's approval to be excluded from any plan for colonial union.[1] Newfoundland, likewise, successfully asserted its ancient right to remain independent. The New Brunswick legislature formally rejected the plan after it was defeated in an appeal to the people; only after the concerted partisan involvement of the lieutenant governor, Arthur Gordon, was it eventually approved.[2]

In point of fact, the only legislature to give consent to the Confederation plan was the Legislative Assembly of the United Canadas. Even there, however, it met with hostility from several members, not the least vociferous of whom was Christopher Dunkin, who left the plan in tatters after a scathing four-hour line-by-line attack on its terms.[3] When the vote of approval did eventually emerge, it was noted that a bare majority of Quebec members had voted in support of the Quebec plan.[4] Thus, even in the very legislature that had supported colonial union so strongly there was deep division over the terms of Confederation.

Undeterred by the setbacks in the various Maritime provinces, the Canadian leaders, with the enthusiastic assistance of Governor General Lord Monck, pressed for and won approval to proceed to London with a view to laying a plan for the union of the North American colonies before the Imperial Parliament. The attitude of the British public and of many members of Parliament that greeted the delegates upon their arrival in the fall of 1866 helps to explain, in large measure, the official policy of the British government towards the Canadian colonies during the years immediately preceding Confederation. In general, that attitude was one of impatience; why could not the colonies look after their own affairs, especially such matters as defence, many in Britain asked. The feeling of men such as John Bright and the Manchester school of free-traders was that the colonies should be granted independence and be forced to fend for themselves. The London *Times* opined, shortly before the House of Commons gave third reading to the Confederation bill, that "We look to Confederation as the means of relieving this country from much expense and much embarrassment ... We appreciate the goodwill of the Canadians and their desire to maintain their relations with the British Crown. But a people of four million ought to be able to keep up their own defences."[5] It was time the youngsters grew up and left the comfort of home.

In addition, as C.P. Stacey showed years later, a spirit of anti-imperialism became strong in England after the American Civil War.[6] Many British citizens believed that the colonies constituted an "Achilles heel of England – the joint in her armour through which the sword of the resentful American republic might reach her."[7] The feeling that the colonies should assume independence pervaded the public in England.[8] Benjamin Disraeli wrote to Prime Minister Lord Derby in 1866 reflecting the pessimism prevalent among important members of the government: "It can never be our pretense, or our policy, to defend the Canadian frontier against the United States ... Power and Influence we should exercise in Asia, consequently in Eastern Europe; but what is the use of these deadweights which we do not govern?"[9]

There seems to have been no disposition among responsible Englishmen to conceal their unfriendly and unsympathetic feelings towards the internal affairs of the Canadian colonies. It was understandably disheartening for the Canadian delegation to encounter this attitude. George Brown had written to John A. Macdonald during a visit to England two years earlier: "I am much concerned to observe ... that there is a manifest desire in almost every quarter that, ere long, the British American colonies should shift for themselves, and in some quarters evident regret that we did not declare at once for independence. I am very sorry to observe this, but it arises, I hope from the fear of invasion of Canada by the United States, and will soon pass away with the cause that excites it."[10] But Brown was wrong; anti-colonialism increased in England after the American Civil War. Alexander Galt wrote of his disappointment over it following the London Conference in December 1866: "I am more than ever disappointed at the tone of the feeling here as to the Colonies. I cannot shut my eyes to the fact that they want to get rid of us. They have a servile fear of the United States and would rather give us up than defend us, or incur the risk of war with that country. Day by day I am more oppressed with the sense of responsibility of maintaining a connection undesired here and which exposes us to such peril at home. I pray God to show me the right path. But I doubt much whether Confederation will save us from annexation. Even Macdonald is rapidly feeling as I do. Cartier alone seems blind to what is passing around us."[11]

One of the most important consequences of such a dismissive attitude was that the plan of union was greeted with an almost contemptuous indifference. The delegates were treated politely but their cause was never embraced enthusiastically either during the conference discussions or later in Parliament when the Confederation Bill was discussed.

Despite this reception, the Canadian delegates, led by Macdonald, pressed on with their meetings with the British legislative draughtsmen. But even in London matters that had divided the colonies surfaced immediately. Apparently mindful of the disputes that arose in the legislatures after the Quebec Conference over the question of authority to enter into a union of all the provinces, the delegates from Nova Scotia and New Brunswick produced copies of the resolutions authorizing them to attend the London Conference. Charles Tupper wanted it to be understood that his legislature had clearly instructed him and the other Nova Scotia delegates to make certain that any Confederation Act would "ensure just provision for the rights and interests" of their province. For his part, Leonard Tilley was emphatic that the New Brunswick legislature insisted on the construction of an inter-colonial railway as essential to the success of the union movement. The Canadian delegation laid before the conference a resolution passed by their legislature asking the British government "to cause a measure to be submitted to the Imperial Parliament for the purpose of uniting the colonies of Canada, Nova Scotia, New Brunswick, Newfoundland and Prince Edward Island in one Government, with provisions based on the accompanying resolutions, which were adopted at a Conference of delegates from the said colonies, held at the city of Quebec, on the tenth of October, 1864." Thus, this resolution included Newfoundland and Prince Edward Island – both of which had by December 1866 received permission to remain outside the proposed union – and formally sought union of the provinces on the basis of the seventy-two resolutions adopted at Quebec, which so became the only basis for Confederation; no alternative scheme was ever presented. Even those from the Maritime provinces attending the London Conference understood that the Quebec resolutions would be the basis for their discussions. Both the Nova Scotia and the New Brunswick legislatures had instructed their delegates to attempt to press for more favourable terms for their provinces, but recognized that the Quebec Confederation plan would be the only one seriously discussed in London.[12] Certainly the leading Maritime confederationists, Tupper from Nova Scotia and Tilley from New Brunswick, supported the Quebec Conference terms of union.

This matter takes on great importance in light of William O'Connor's conclusion in his report that "it is demonstrably erroneous to say that the British North America Act is founded upon" the Quebec resolutions,[13] which set off an intense debate over the value of reflecting on them. O'Connor's shoddy report soon made it fashionable to say that the Constitution Act, 1867 was not the outgrowth of the deliberations of the constitutional framers at Quebec City in 1864. O'Connor claimed that it was the result of an entirely new process in London, under the guidance of the draftsmen of the British Parliament and a handful of delegates from the colonies. He took pains to distance the results of the Quebec Conference from the resolutions adopted in London in 1866. There can be no doubt that the imperial draftsmen contributed to the language of the British North America Act. But it nevertheless unequivocally expressed the form and substance of the seventy-two resolutions passed in Quebec City.

THE LONDON CONFERENCE

The London Conference of 1866, like the Quebec Conference two years earlier, was held in camera. Though it left even fewer notes, it fortunately also resulted in the adoption of sixty-nine resolutions, which became the basis for the British North America Act. No-one has ever disputed the connection of the London resolutions with the final constitutional document that emerged from the hands of the British Parliament in March 1867. The central question is to what extent the resolutions adopted in London incorporated those adopted in Quebec.

A first reading gives the impression that the only major difference between the two sets of resolutions is that seventy-two were pared down to sixty-nine. What happened to the three missing Quebec resolutions, and were they important? One was resolution 9, which read, "The Colony of Newfoundland shall be entitled to enter the proposed union, with a representation in the Legislative Council [Senate] of 4 members." It was struck out for the obvious reason that Newfoundland was not to be included in Confederation. It was replaced with the following: "The colony of Prince Edward Island, when admitted into the Confederation, shall be entitled to a representation of four members in the Legislative Council [Senate]. But in such case the Members allotted to Nova Scotia and New Brunswick shall be diminished to ten each, such diminution to take place in each province as vacancies occur." Three more resolutions, two dealing with Newfoundland and one dealing with Prince Edward Island, were later struck out for the same reason: that those provinces were not to be part of Canada.

The two other Quebec resolutions rejected at London were numbers 23 and 24. The first of them stated: "The Legislature of each Province shall divide such Province into the proper number of constituencies, and define the boundaries of each of them." Resolution 24 provided, "The local legislatures of each Province may from time to time alter the electoral districts for the purpose of representation in such local legislature, and distribute the representation to which the Province is entitled in such local legislature, in any manner such legislature may see fit." The London terms that replaced these two were numbers 24 and 25. London resolution 24 stipulated: "The number of members may at time be increased by the General Parliament, regard being had to the proportionate rights then existing." The new resolution 25 stated: "Until provisions are made by the General Parliament, all the laws which at the date of the proclamation constituting the Union are in force in the Provinces respectively, relating to the qualification and disqualification of any person to be elected, or to sit or vote as a member of the Assembly in the said Provinces respectively." The intent of the latter was to affirm that the provincial governments had authority to enforce the existing laws regulating elections until new provisions were made by the federal Parliament.

Confusion and debate surrounded Quebec resolution 24 long before the London Conference. The lieutenant governor of New Brunswick, Arthur Gordon, was the first to draw attention to a discrepancy between its wording in the official version adopted in Quebec and the version submitted to the Canadian legislature. In the form signed by Etienne Tache, the chairman of the Quebec Conference, it stated: "The local legislatures of each Province may from time to time alter the Electoral districts for the purpose of Representation in the House of Commons." The variant presented to the legislature of the United Canadas read: "The local legislatures of each Province may from time to time alter the electoral Districts for the purpose of Representation in such local Legislature." As Gordon pointed out, the difference was substantial and important. William McDougall, the provincial secretary of Canada, replied to Gordon's request for clarification on behalf of the governor general. McDougall cited the version signed by Tache, which included the words "for the purpose of Representation in the House of Commons." He went on to explain that the mistake was due to haste at the conclusion of the conference and that "it could never have been intended to destroy the independence of every Member of the General Parliament by giving power to the Local Legislature of his Province to 'alter' and thus practically to abolish his Constituency whenever by speech or vote he might happen to displease a majority of that Legislature."[14]

It is unlikely that the true intention of the Quebec Conference on this point will ever be known. There is little documentation on the issue. One thing is clear, however: McDougall's explanation is consistent with the intention of Macdonald and other leading constitutional framers to make the central government as free as possible of provincial interference. Macdonald himself noted the discrepancy in the two versions of resolution 24 and wrote to Charles Tupper in Nova Scotia about it. To allow local legislatures power to alter the federal electoral districts was, Macdonald wrote, "an obvious blunder, and must be corrected."[15] And corrected it was, at the London Conference.

The delegates in London expunged five existing resolutions and added two, bringing the total to sixty-nine. The two new resolutions, numbers 30 and 42, related to the powers and privileges of the House of Commons and to the education rights of Protestants in Quebec.

There were several other changes to or amplifications of the Quebec resolutions but none of them substantially affected the form of government as established in 1864. Indeed, the Quebec document constituted the working draft for the union of the provinces. All discussion in London centred on the Quebec terms; there was never any intention to scrap them and begin the process all over again, as O'Connor stated in his report. No-one put the matter more succinctly than Alexander Galt, a delegate to both Quebec and London and an avid confederate. Writing from London at the completion of the conference, Galt exclaimed triumphantly: "The Quebec scheme is adopted, very few alterations, and none that I regard as at all impairing it."[16]

THE DIVISION OF POWERS

The London Conference did not end with the adoption of the sixty-nine resolutions, however. Immediately afterwards the delegates, with the assistance of Colonial Office legal advisers, set about translating them into a bill to be presented to the Imperial Parliament. After seven drafts,[17] it was agreed that the plan of union was ready for the scrutiny of Parliament. Lord Carnarvon guided the bill through the House of Lords; Sir Charles Adderley, through the House of Commons. To the deep disappointment of the Canadians, who witnessed the proceedings from the parliamentary galleries, their bill drew very little attention or serious debate. Members of both houses greeted it with a supreme lack of interest that disheartened the delegates, who had worked so hard and with such excitement. Some years later, John A. Macdonald recalled how casually the Lords and Commons had treated their handiwork, claiming that they had shown as much interest as if the bill had been designed "to unite two or three English parishes."[18]

When we make our way through the minutiae of the act that brought about Confederation, we find the sixty-nine London resolutions firmly embedded. In fact, they, and hence the Quebec resolutions, form the very heart of the British North America Act. To this extent it is correct to say that the union of the British North American provinces was a "made-in-Canada" achievement.

All the London resolutions, then, found their way into the British North America Act, some varying slightly in language but none seriously altered – with one exception. London resolution 28, outlining the powers of the new central Parliament and government, read: "The General Government shall have power to make laws for the peace, welfare and good government of the confederation (saving the sovereignty of England) and especially the following subjects." Thirty-six subsections follow, spelling out the areas over which the federal government had authority to legislate. In the British North America Act, this resolution appeared as section 91 under "Powers of the Parliament," which stated: "It shall be lawful for the Queen, to make laws for the Peace, order and good government of Canada, in relation all Matters not coming within the classes of Subjects by this Act assigned exclusively to the legislatures of the Provinces; and for greater certainty, but not so as to restrict the generality of the foregoing Terms of this section, it is hereby declared that (notwithstanding anything in this Act) the exclusive legislative authority of the Parliament of Canada extends to all matters coming within the Classes of Subjects next hereinafter enumerated." Twenty-nine classes of subjects are then listed.

Before reflecting further on this important provision, it will be well to settle the discrepancy between the number of subsections contained in resolution 28 and in the British North America Act. The legislation did, in fact, include all areas of authority stipulated in the resolution, but because – in the eyes of the legislative draftsmen – some fitted better under other sections of the act, they were rearranged. Not only did the British North America Act include all the subsections of the London resolution without alteration, it also added a new one, subsection 8, which provided for the "Salaries and allowances of Civil and other Officers of the Government of Canada." This did not constitute a major change.

Finally, there was a slight change in the wording of the last subsection of resolution 28, which stated: "And generally respecting all matters of a general character, not specially and exclusively reserved for the local legislatures." The subsection was incorporated into section 91(29) of the Confederation act and read: "Such classes of Subjects as are expressly excepted in the Enumeration of the Classes of Subjects by this Act assigned exclusively to the legislatures of the Provinces."

The first difference of note appears in the head of section 91, where the act referred to those powers of legislation belonging "exclusively to the Legislatures of the Provinces." The idea of exclusivity did not appear in the head of resolution 28, which affirmed, "The General Parliament shall have power to make laws for the peace, welfare, and good government of the Confederation." However, the word "exclusive" *was* found in the equivalent Quebec resolution. The powers of the provincial governments were also termed "exclusive" in section 92 of the British North America Act, entitled "Exclusive Powers of Provincial Legislatures." The wording is an important issue, because the Quebec resolutions made it clear that the powers of the provincial legislatures were to be negligible. Was that ambition carried over into the Confederation Act? In other words, did the provinces accumulate more power by the time the original resolutions became the British North America Act? Or did the central Parliament stubbornly retain the preponderance of legislative powers stipulated in the Quebec and London resolutions?

The answers lie in the terms of the British North America Act that set out the respective powers of the federal and provincial governments, that is, in sections 91 and 92. But it is well to remember certain points. First, the British government adopted as government policy the plan of union espoused by the leading Canadian politicians and confederate Maritimers. Second, there was never any doubt in the minds of these principal players that the plan ought to be strong at the centre – that the preponderance of political power must reside with the new federal Parliament. Finally, the constitutional framers never at any time retreated from the terms adopted at Quebec whose intent was to produce a constitution that would bind the new nation together by way of a powerful central Parliament. This determination was reflected in sections 91 and 92.

Section 91 established the powers of the new Parliament, beginning with the forceful statement that it should have the power "to make Laws for the Peace, Order, and good Government of Canada, in relation to all Matters not coming within the Classes of subjects by this Act assigned exclusively to the Legislatures of the Provinces." The section then proceeded to list specifically the twenty-nine "classes of subjects" we considered earlier, but with the clear note that in designating these matters the act did not "restrict the Generality of the foregoing Terms [peace, order and good government]." Indeed, before listing the twenty-nine items, the act added the note "notwithstanding anything in this Act." Clearly, the intent was to grant broad legislative power to Canada's Parliament to make laws for the "Peace, Order and good Government" of the new federation, subject only to those limitations contained in the areas of jurisdiction granted "exclusively" to the provincial legislatures.

The critical question, therefore, is this: What legislative powers were granted *exclusively* to the provinces? The title of section 92, "Exclusive Powers of Provincial Legislatures," suggests an answer. A first reading of this important section of the constitution tends to convey the impression that the framers gave the provinces exclusive jurisdiction over sixteen categories of legislation. Section 92 began by granting to the provincial legislatures the authority to amend their provincial constitutions, with the exception of the office of lieutenant governor. After enumerating fourteen further specific areas of legislative jurisdiction the section concluded with the blanket statement, "Generally all matters of a merely local or private nature in the Province." But this first reading is troubled by the ambiguities – if not outright contradictions – contained in this list of "exclusive" powers, as contrasted with that in section 91, where the "exclusive" powers of Parliament were outlined emphatically. Subsection 2 of section 92 stated that the provincial legislatures should have power to levy "Direct taxation within the Province in order to the raising of a Revenue for Provincial Purposes." But how could this power be "exclusive," when section 91 already gave the federal government power to raise money "by any Mode or System of Taxation"? Parliament could move into direct taxation without the slightest scruple and so invade an "exclusive" area of provincial jurisdiction. Jurisdiction over "Local Works and Undertakings" was also granted to the provinces, except for the following matters: "Lines of steam or other ships, railways, canals, telegraphs, and other works and undertakings connecting the Province with any other or others of the province, or extending beyond the limits of the Province." Further, in the same section the provinces are prohibited from establishing "Lines of Steam Ship between the Province and any British or Foreign Country." The obvious intention of this part of the constitution (section 92(10)) was to affirm federal jurisdiction over interprovincial and international communications and transportation. The section concluded with the following puzzling provision denying to the provincial legislatures the authority to legislate for "Such works, as although wholly situate within the Province, are *before or after their Execution declared by the Parliament of Canada to be for the General Advantage of Canada or for the Advantage of two or more of the Provinces.*"[19] It shows how deeply the Fathers of Confederation desired to penetrate into the life of the provinces. Who would decide whether a provincial project was for the general advantage of Canada or one or more of the provinces? Obviously, the federal Parliament. In the end, the British North America Act made it clear (in section 95) that even "the running at large of swine" could be brought under the authority of Parliament!

When we look carefully over the items reserved "exclusively" for the provincial legislatures – hospitals, asylums, eleemosynary institutions, shops, saloons, taverns, and so forth – it is difficult to conclude that the matters assigned exclusively to their jurisdiction were very substantial. Even in matters relating to trade and commerce the Constitution Act, 1867 restricted the provincial power to incorporate to those "Companies with Provincial objects." This provision is narrower than the corresponding London resolution, which stated that the provinces would have power to incorporate "private or local companies, except such as relate to matters assigned to the General Parliament." The London resolution was stated in negative terms and contained the possibility for expansion of provincial authority; the act eliminated this opportunity by restricting power in the incorporation of companies to those with "provincial objects." Section 91 made it clear that Parliament was responsible for the "Regulation of Trade and Commerce." In addition, the federal powers of reservation and disallowance of provincial legislation abundantly illustrated that the constitutional framers were determined not to allow the provincial governments much room to manœuvre in legislative matters.

In general, then, the powers granted to the provincial governments were the same in the British North America Act as in the Quebec and London resolutions. If, indeed, any differences crept in at the London Conference they favoured the federal government, notwithstanding the use of the term "exclusive" in enumerating provincial powers. The act must be read in its entirety; no section can be read independently of a related section elsewhere. Above all, it must be read with due respect for the internal logic of the document as a whole.

An important point is that the framers of the constitution never swerved from the desire to be dependent on the British Parliament, under its final authority. The Constitution Act, 1867 was never intended to be a Declaration of Independence. Canada wished to remain just as much a colony as before Confederation, with the sole exception that the new country would be free to regulate itself with respect to most areas of self-government. As we have seen, not even the constitutional framers from Quebec wished to sever ties with the Crown.

A WORD ABOUT "PEACE, ORDER AND GOOD GOVERNMENT"

Many commentators on the Constitution Act, 1867 have drawn attention over the years to the all-encompassing phrase "Peace, Order and Good Government" found at the head of section 91. This phrase, it is frequently alleged, encapsulates the heart of Canada's constitution; it is generally cited as the Canadian equivalent of the American "Life, Liberty and the pursuit of Happiness." Moreover, Canada was founded from the "top down," not from the "bottom up" as was the

American regime; Canadians did not constitute themselves "a people" before striking for independence as Americans did. Indeed, they never felt any desire to do so. Without doubt, the phrase about "peace, order and good government" was intended to state the overall aims of the new Canadian regime. It therefore deserves our reflective attention. (It should be noted, parenthetically, that the wording appeared in the first four drafts of the act as "Peace, welfare and good government"; only in the final draft was the word "welfare" replaced by "order.")

Peace, order, and good government constitute an ascent from the necessity of certain conditions. Peace and order go together. Good government is a perpetual necessity requiring constant vigilance, as Hobbes reminded his readers. Peace and order can properly be taken for granted, once achieved and soundly established, like the foundations of one's home. Good government, however, can never be taken for granted, because government is subject to change with the change of the people who run it. This state of affairs underscores the essential feature of ministerial responsible government: the responsibility of the executive power of the nation to the elected representatives of the people. But the executive is not separate from the legislative power. The original word, "welfare," implied a condition of general sharing of the things necessary for life, such as private property: clearly a Hobbesian formula. The first essential condition – the *sine qua non* – is civil peace, to be followed by order [welfare], which implies some form of institutional arrangement designed to render permanent or secure the absolutely necessary condition of peace. The management of the public affairs of the nation resides in the executive in Parliament. Under the Canadian system of government there is no effective check on the power of the executive in a majority government. Opposition parties, theoretically, play an important role in the formulation of legislation, but they are toothless in the face of concerted determination under a majority government. Hobbes would be exceedingly pleased with this development.[20]

The practice of Canada's constitution has evolved since 1867. The powers of reservation and disallowance gave enormous authority to the federal executive – not to parliament – to superintend the provincial legislatures. These two provisions of the original constitution have fallen into disuse and would be impossible to resurrect.[21] They were to have been a powerful method of keeping the provincial legislatures and governments in line. There was to be only one sovereign authority in Canada: the executive in Parliament. This position flows directly from what Hobbes enunciated about the nature of the sovereign power; since the responsibility of the sovereign is to assure the conditions of civil peace, he or they[22] must have the power to enforce those conditions. One of the often overlooked intended consequences of the power of disallowance was the reduction of the role of the court in resolving disputes between the two levels of government. Given this power, the federal government needed to give no reason for disallowing an item of provincial legislation. Neither Hobbes nor Locke ever countenanced the existence of an independent judicial body with authority to sit in judgment over the acts of the sovereign Parliament. Under the British constitution the senior judicial officers sat as members of the second chamber of Parliament, the House of Lords, and actively participated in the making of laws.[23]

Hobbes would have us bear in mind that the opposite of civil peace is civil war, the worst of all kinds of war, with brother against brother and father against son and the attendant violent destruction of life and property. "Good government" is the mandate requiring those who control the levers of power to legislate *prudentially* on behalf of the citizens as a whole. Peace is not an end in itself; neither is order. Both are means to the end of good government. There is a tendency today to forget the unsettled conditions of European politics during Canada's Confederation period, to say nothing of the civil disorder south of the border.

The term "good government" implies an alternative to be avoided: "bad government," which for Hobbes meant a government that contained within itself the seeds of sedition;[24] one that could not permanently secure the conditions of a durable peace; one that could not eliminate the prospect of civil war. The Canadian constitution is therefore not indifferent to the quality of government. It implies that the only legitimate government is *good* government. But how do we distinguish between good and bad government? The answer to this important question is that the difference between good and bad government lies in the quality of the laws. And the standard by which we judge the quality of the laws passed by Parliament lies in the extent to which they preserve the conditions of peace and welfare of the people. Above all – and true to its Hobbesian foundations – the government of the Canadian confederation under it constitution has the power *to govern*. Canada's parliamentary system of government, adapted from Britain, contains the fusion of the legislative and executive. It is not confined by the separation of powers. A prime minister supported by a majority of members in the House of Commons can forcefully dictate the course of government … just as Hobbes would have it. For Hobbes, good government was strong government, and strong governments could govern effectively and with energy. The president of the United States does not have near the power to govern as the prime minister of Canada armed with a parliamentary majority. Such are Canada's foundations in the practice of English constitutional monarchy, buttressed by the theoretical underpinnings provided by Thomas Hobbes, one of England's greatest constitutional authorities.

The Canadian regime was based in the principles furnished by Hobbes to the extent that these provided the foundations in nature for the externals or the structure of the government. However, they did not provide its internal principles; those derived from the ancient English aristocratic tradition. Hobbes was formally indifferent to the substantive objectives of the regime. He viewed men's appetites and minds as prompting them in a variety of often conflicting directions, some religious, others commercial, still others political. So long as these forces contributed to the stability of the regime, Hobbes regarded them as acceptable to civil society. For Hobbes there could be no dichotomy between state and nation; the two had to fuse into what is today called *nationalism*, the love of one's country. Indeed, William Mathie has explained Hobbes in terms of "the belief that [nationalism] is the necessary, if not the sufficient, condition of a good political order ... State and nation coincide where the nation is in turn defined by a certain 'non-political similarity of similarities between men'."[25] In a departure from the Aristotelian teaching on friendship as the binding cement of community, Hobbes saw the state as providing the minimal conditions for peaceful living among citizens who, while pursuing their own ends, were willing to allow other citizens to pursue their interest in civil peace. In the first pages of *Leviathan*, Hobbes explains that "Commonwealth" or "State"

is but an artificial man; though of greater stature and strength than the natural, for whose protection and defence it was intended; and in which the *sovereignty* is an artificial soul, as giving life and motion to whole body; the *magistrates*, and other officers of judicature and execution, artificial *joints*; *reward* and *punishment*, by which fastened to the seat of the sovereignty every joint and member is moved to perform his duty, are the *nerves*, that do the same in the body natural; the *wealth* and *riches* of all the particular members, are the *strength: salus populi*, the *people's safety*, its *business; counsellors*, by whom all things needful for it to know are suggested unto it, are the *memory; equity*, and *laws*, an artificial *reason* and *will; concord, health; sedition, sickness;* and *civil war, death*. Lastly, the *pacts* and *covenants*, by which the parts of this body politic were at first made, set together, and united, resemble that *fiat*, or *let us make man*, pronounced by God in the creation.[26]

The state must guard against those things "that weaken, or tend to the dissolution of a commonwealth," chief among them the sovereign's contentment "with less power, than to the peace, and defence of the commonwealth is necessary."[27] For Hobbes, the new *polis* was a "city, which may be defined to be a multitude of men, united as one person by a common power, for their common peace, defence and benefit."[28]

Hobbes's commonwealth was not what we today would call an "ideological" regime. It was not committed to a set of theoretical abstractions from which it took its direction or drew its strength. Rather, it was deeply rooted in practice or experience, which in turn were deeply rooted in the selfish pursuits of radically independent individuals bound together in a community that guaranteed to each the maximum freedom to pursue his own self-interest.[29]

Finally, according to Hobbes, the sovereign authority of the state could not be divided. In *Leviathan* he wrote: "There is a sixth doctrine, plainly and directly against the essence of a commonwealth; and it is this, *that the sovereign power may be divided.* For what is it to divide of a commonwealth, but to dissolve it; for powers divided mutually destroy each other."[30] It was precisely this sentiment that hung over the deliberations on federalism at the founding of Canada. The abiding fear of men such as John A. Macdonald was that the federal principle was a Trojan horse which, once introduced into the constitution, would over time cause the nation to fracture and ultimately destroy it. Hobbes warned that the greatest evil was civil war and that the principle of divided sovereignty would lead inexorably to it. The constitutional framers read Hobbes's warnings in his writings and watched in horror as the federal republic of the United States convulsed in civil war. The 1860s were not the most auspicious times for either republican governments or federal constitutions.

5

The Ambiguous Embrace
of Federalism

A Federal Union, in short, must depend for its permanence, not on the
sentiment but on the reason of its citizens.

Edward Freeman, *History of Federal Government*[1]

If there is one feature of Canada's constitution that has been under
critical scrutiny from the very beginning it is the "federal" character
of the document. Domestic and foreign observers alike regarded the
British North America Act, with its dominant Parliament and weak
provincial governments, as inconsistent with the basic requirements
of a federal system. To the present day, federal and provincial politicians contest bitterly over the overbearing power of the Canadian
government and its encroachment on areas of alleged provincial
jurisdiction.

The preamble to Constitution Act, 1867 affirmed that it was the
desire of the British North American provinces to be "federally united
into One Dominion under the Crown of the United Kingdom of Great
Britain and Ireland, with a Constitution similar in Principle to that
of the United Kingdom." This was the only place in the entire act
where the framers expressed the intention that their constitution was
to be in some sense "federal." The laconic and puzzling formulation
of such a critical intention has long challenged constitutionalists. The
ambiguous formulation is compounded by the fact that the British
constitution is not federal in any sense of the term. After reviewing
the entire Constitution Act, 1867, Sir Ivor Jennings, one of the leading
British constitutional authorities of the past century, called its promise of a federal union a "vague doctrine" scarcely worthy of judicial
notice.[2] But it is clear from the language and logic of the constitution
of 1867 that the federal character was to be the husk and the monarchical character the kernel. The extant accounts by the principal
draftsmen of the document specify it was to provide the foundations

for a "monarchic federation." The implication is that the monarchical character of the constitution was to be its dominant characteristic. What was at work here is of considerable importance to our understanding of the principles built into our constitution from the earliest moment. The Constitution Act, 1867, in short, attempted to meld a unique, peculiar form of federalism with the British constitution, which was (and is) both unitary and monarchical but not federal. Reflection on this attempt may help to clarify the confusing manner in which the division of powers was enunciated. Above all, it may help in explaining the dynamics at work within the terms of the document, that is, the "logic of the constitution."[3] In other words, the British North America Act must be read in its entirety, as a document designed to lead the reader in a certain way towards specific conclusions. Section 92, for example, outlining the powers of the provincial legislatures, must be read in light of section 91, outlining the powers of the federal Parliament – not in the reverse order, as many "provincial rights" proponents have done.

From the earliest discussions of the new Canadian constitution, it was evident that the federal form of government embodied in it had little in common with the American federal system. Its defenders immediately set out to demonstrate that that was one of its chief virtues. They declared it unique, containing the best of the British and American constitutions. That was the official spin, which the school texts drummed into generations of young Canadians.

But if the constitutional framers were so proud of their unique federal system, why did they state their intentions on the federal character of the new constitution so awkwardly, even ambiguously? They repeatedly assured themselves that theirs would be superior to the American federal constitution by being a "monarchic federation." That ambition implied that they understood both federalism and the American constitution. But how well, indeed, did they understand these matters?

The very concept of federalism was still greeted with suspicion as late as the middle of the nineteenth century. After all, it had emerged out of the ashes of the French Revolution, during which the term *fédéralisme* was used in describing those radical Girondistes who attempted to detach certain *departements* from Paris and establish a *république fédérative*. It was a term synonymous with disruption.[4] As Alan Forrest reminds us: "In the summer of 1793 when the word first entered the everyday vocabulary of the French Revolution, there were few who were ready to lay claim to it. It was used almost entirely as a term of abuse by those who wished to belittle their opponents or to cast doubt upon their political credentials. To the critics of federalism, its central characteristic was a willingness to sacrifice national unity for selfish gain, to break up the political integrity of France in the interest of individual cities or regions."[5]

Federalism was not to lose its pejorative connotations till many decades after Confederation. Many people, especially Loyalists fleeing the American states, resented the use of the word, viewing it suspiciously as the back door to introducing the American system into British North America. The Fathers of Confederation were frequently called upon to explain its use and to defend its inclusion in the structure of their new constitution. It is not surprising, therefore, to learn that they were uncomfortable with the concept.

To whom did the leading Canadian constitutional draftsmen turn for instruction in the matter of federal governments? They found little guidance in the writings of the great nineteenth-century teachers on politics and political institutions.[6] They found none in ancient writings on political science or in Hobbes or Locke. Hobbes does not say a word about federalism, while Locke's "federative" power refers to foreign relations. Obviously, they turned to the United States, not only since it was close at hand and operating under a federal constitution, but also because the American founders had deliberated openly throughout the formative years about the pros and cons of the federal form of government. Their constitutional debates and other documents, especially *The Federalist Papers*, contained lengthy discussions about its advantages and disadvantages.

That source, however, was a dangerous one. The American federal system of government was republican, and republicanism was even more suspect to the Canadian constitutional framers than federalism. Many believed that it was not possible to import the federal husk of the American constitution without at the same time importing the republican kernel. Above all else, British North Americans were determined to retain monarchical ties and preserve the parliamentary system of government, complete with the fusion of the executive and legislative branches. There was very little dissent from that ambition. Moreover, the American federal union had erupted into civil war at the very moment that the union of the colonies was being contemplated. The result was both a theoretical and a practical quandary: both the available theory and the practice of federalism were positively discouraging. At the same time, a plan of union that openly espoused the abolition of the provincial legislatures was doomed to failure. The Canadian framers would never have been invited to Charlottetown if they had suggested such an arrangement, nor would the Quebec Conference have taken place.

For a long time, John A. Macdonald adamantly opposed a federal system for Canada. Along with several other leading men of the day, he actively supported a legislative union of the colonies as a direct replica of the British constitution. However, the determined resistance of Quebec and the Maritime provinces to being absorbed under one central legislature dominated by Upper Canada combined to frustrate that objective. Quebec chafed dreadfully under the Act of Union of 1841 and wanted a return of its own legislature. The Maritime provinces had fought far too long to achieve responsible self-government to throw it off casually. The federal form of government was, in a very real sense, reluctantly adopted at Confederation and the federal principle was seriously bent to suit the aspirations of the likes of Macdonald and Alexander Galt, who had never completely abandoned the hope of a more unified system of government. Galt went so far in a speech in the Eastern Townships of Quebec to promise that the "artificial boundaries that separate us into provinces would [if the new constitution were adopted] one day disappear."[7]

FREEMAN'S *HISTORY OF FEDERAL GOVERNMENT*

Fortunately, the Fathers of Confederation had one extensive English treatise on federalism to which they could turn. Known by its short title, *History of Federal Government*,[8] the monumental study was the work of a prominent Cambridge historian, Edward A. Freeman. Published in 1863 (the early days of the Civil War), Freeman's book was remarkable for several reasons, not the least of them the fact that it was a favourable treatment of federalism. Indeed, it was downright enthusiastic about the federal form of government. Not only that, it claimed that federalism and monarchy could coexist within the same constitution. Freeman even coined the highly felicitous term "monarchic federation," making it respectable for loyal British North Americans to talk about the subject without fear of being disloyal. In effect, he provided Canada's founders with a theoretical framework within which to countenance the prospects of some kind of federal union for British North America. For Freeman directly addressed a central concern of Macdonald's: the inherent tendency of federal systems to break apart or erupt into civil war. He cautioned his readers not to allow the civil war in the United States to lead them to condemn federalism, for "[t]o make a general political inference from a single example in history is not a very philosophical way of reasoning."[9] The alleged weakness of a federal system was, he acknowledged, a truism. But what was the alternative? "I freely admit, in a certain sense, the weakness of the Federal tie. But the real question is not whether the tie is weak or strong, but whether there are not certain circumstances in which a weak tie is better either than a strong tie or than no tie at all."[10] As well, Freeman continued, over time a federal union could lead to greater unity, a "complete union." This line of reasoning must surely have eased Macdonald's fears of federalism and made it easier for him to acquiesce in a federal union of the provinces. In any event, he owned a copy of Freeman's book and read it; and as we have seen he did change his mind and throw his support behind the Confederation plan.

Freeman showed a remarkable liberality for a nineteenth-century Englishman towards republicanism as well as federalism. Despite his generally favourable disposition towards republican government, however, he remained a staunch supporter of constitutional monarchy. Still, he had little patience with those who repudiated republicanism. "It shows simple ignorance, if it does not show something worse," he wrote in another work, "when the word 'republican' is used as synonymous with cut-throat or pickpocket."[11] There can be no question that that was precisely how it was viewed by many of his Canadian contemporaries. But while he persuaded few of the virtues of republicanism, Freeman did help several leading British North Americans, such as D'Arcy McGee, to appreciate federalism more than they otherwise would have. Let us, therefore, have a closer look at what Freeman had to say about federalism.

The complete title of Freeman's book was *History of Federal Government, from the Foundation of the Achaian League to the Disruption of the United States*. Despite the use of the word "disruption" in connection with the United States, Freeman spoke favourably of its federal system. By frequent references to *The Federalist Papers*, he demonstrated that he was thoroughly familiar with the major American constitutional documents, as well as de Tocqueville's famous commentary.

What is especially instructive for our purposes is the fact that Freeman devoted considerable space to a discussion of federalism in general. It is an impressive and sympathetic treatment of a full range of issues relating to federalism; indeed, it is nothing short of a comprehensive introduction to the subject. Anyone who before reading the book harboured reservations about the federal form of government would very likely be converted by the end. After defining what federalism meant, Freeman turned his attention to the differences between its ancient and modern forms, next to the "alleged weakness of the Federal tie" then to the "right and wrong of secession." He concluded with a comparative account of the American and Swiss federal systems.

In describing "a Federal Government in ... its most perfect form," Freeman declared: "On the one hand, each of the members of the Union must be wholly independent in those matters which concern each member only. On the other hand, all must be subject to a common power in those matters which concern the whole body of members collectively."[12] A little later he wrote, in language reminiscent of the British North America Act, "Each member is perfectly independent within its own sphere; but there is another sphere in which its independence, or rather its separate existence, vanishes. It is invested with every right of sovereignty on one class of subjects, but there is another class of subjects on which it is incapable of separate political action as any province or city of a monarchy of an indivisible republic."[13] However, Freeman made it clear that he was no visionary, that a perfect federal union was an ideal "so very refined and artificial, that it seems not to have been attained more than four or five times in the history of the world."[14]

Freeman's tome could scarcely have been written more directly for British North Americans. The topics he discussed specifically addressed the concerns of those political leaders who were genuinely fearful of federalism. The fact that the American union had erupted into civil war which concerned a large number of British North Americans, was brushed aside by Freeman. He asserted that the war was in no way a by-product of the federal union; in fact, a much greater war would likely have erupted had the Americans not chosen a federal form of government. "If the system has broken down at last, we may be sure that any other system would have broken down much sooner."[15] Freeman commended federal union as if he were intent on allaying the misgivings of the Americans' northern neighbours. For example, he wrote: "It is often said that the Disruption of the United States at once puts Federation out of court by proving the inherent weakness of the Federal tie ... The alleged weakness of the Federal tie is moreover, in a certain sense, a truism. The Federal tie is in its own nature weaker than the tie which unites the geographical divisions of a perfectly consolidated state. But what Federation ought really to be compared with is not perfect union, but the complete separation which has commonly been its only alternative."[16]

Freeman readily acknowledged that the bonds of sentiment formed over centuries that bind hereditary monarchies are stronger than those binding federal states. "A Federal Union ... must depend for its permanence, not on the sentiment but on the reason of its citizens," he concluded.[17] After praising the Achaian League and the constitution of the United States as "the most perfect developments of the federal principle which the world has ever seen,"[18] Freeman went on to make it clear that it was not simply the constitutional institutions that raised these constitutions to so high a level of esteem. Rather, for Freeman, "Federalism is essentially a compromise, an artificial product of an advanced state of political culture."[19] He cautioned that the federal system of government was one that was "likely to arise only under certain peculiar circumstances ... It requires a sufficient degree of community in origin or feeling or interest to allow the several members to work together up to a certain point. It requires that there should not be that perfect degree of community, or rather identity, which allows the several members to be fused together for all purposes. Where there is no community at all, federalism is inappropriate."[20] The most difficult task facing federalism was to create a willing desire to remain together in the interest of pursuing a common objective separately unattainable. It therefore called for a degree of statesmanship not required of other forms of government. For this reason it was also more vulnerable to dissolution. To the Canadian constitutional framers, monarchy was to be the unifying spirit that infused the several parts and bound them together into a general community without destroying those parts. It was to be the cementing force of the union, the centre of national coalescence.

Running implicitly throughout Freeman's discussion of federal constitutions from antiquity to the founding of the American republic was the theme of the consent of the governed. No federal union can be found in defiance of such consent or perpetuated in opposition to it. One thing is evident from a comparison of Freeman's thoughts on federalism and the Canadian framers' thoughts: both agreed that it is necessary to temper "democratic forms by aristocratic practice."[21]

Despite his praise of federalism, Freeman was not blind to the centrifugal forces constantly at work in all federal unions. But he viewed even this aspect of federalism with optimism. As if addressing John A. Macdonald and other Canadians who were holding out for a unitary state, Freeman mused upon a supposition: " Let us suppose that the members of a Federal Union, by long connexion and familiarity, by the habit of united action for many important purposes, have at last formed the desire for a still more complete union. To turn a Federation into a Consolidated state will be found at least as easy as to unite a group of isolated atoms into a Federation. The several States have already delegated a large portion of their rights to a common Government of their own choosing; all that is needed is to go a step further, and invest that common Government with rights more extensive still."[22] This very theme was widely propagated during the extensive public debates over confederation. Many of those who had previously held out for a legislative union of all the colonies, now argued that the Confederation plan allowed for later developments in that direction.

Monarchic Federation

Freeman saved his greatest encomium for "monarchic federation." In his view, nothing short of the future of the known world would be saved by this form of union. He even waxed eloquent over the prospects of a monarchic federation encompassing the Greeks, Serbs, Albanians, Roumanians, and Bulgarians. He considered a federal union of those ancient monarchies as the most practicable means of drawing them together in a peaceful bond, characterizing the region as "the grandest field that the world has ever seen for trying the great experiment of Monarchic Federalism."[23] But he was fully conscious that a "Monarchic Federation on such a scale has never yet existed, but it is not in itself at all contradictory to the Federal ideal."[24]

How these words must have fired the imagination of those British North Americans who were so enthusiastic about the prospect of uniting their provinces! Thomas D'Arcy McGee took up Freeman's implicit challenge and in a little book entitled *Notes on Federal Governments Past and Present*[25] sought to infuse the Canadian debate over Confederation with the Englishman's enthusiasm for monarchic federation. His defence of continued allegiance to the British Crown eventually led to McGee's assassination, but he saw the cause of confederation as his great historic ambition.

DELOLME'S *THE CONSTITUTION OF ENGLAND*

Not only was there a paucity of writings on federalism, there were few books available on the general nature of government to which the Canadian constitutional framers could turn for guidance. Of course, a number of works existed recounting the historical development of the British constitution without contrasting it with other forms of government. But there were very few examples of what one would properly call political science treatises on government. However, one such title did exist, and it appeared on almost all the library lists, both public and private, of the nineteenth century colonies. We have already encountered it in the library of John A. Macdonald: Jean Louis DeLolme's *The Constitution of England*. Originally published in France, by 1853 it had appeared in English translation with an introduction by John MacGregor, a member of the British House of Commons. DeLolme's book had two characteristics that made it important. First, it was essentially a lengthy encomium to the constitution of England; second, it was anti-republican, the one ingredient missing in Freeman. In a footnote to the English translation, MacGregor recounted the turbulent history of France since the late eighteenth century with every intention of demonstrating how the British constitution had been reformed peacefully during the same critical years: "Since that time [1789], there have occurred in that country, first a terrible and bloody revolution – then the abolition of monarchy, the execution of the

King and Queen and others of the royal family – then a republic – then an imperial and military despotism – then a restoration of the old dynasty – bloody attempts to overthrow that dynasty – then a revolution in 1848 – much bloodshed – then a revolution and a republic – then a *coup d'état* – the abolition of all civil, political, and religious liberty – and the reestablishment of the Empire by the nephew of Napoleon."[26] The none-too-subtle message was not lost on DeLolme's North American readers.

DeLolme began with an apology for commenting on the British constitution as a foreigner; but, said he, following his mentor Montesquieu he felt that a sympathetic and unbiased point of view might not be entirely unwelcome to his English readers. He certainly enjoyed an enthusiastic readership in British North America in the years preceding Confederation, judging from his book's popularity. As already noted, his anti-republicanism was especially welcome there because he spoke from within the camp of the enemy, republican France. In chapter IX of the book, "A Further Disadvantage of Republican Government," DeLolme warned that the people are almost always betrayed by those they trust. He therefore counselled that, whenever a people set out to write or revise their constitution, the leading men should be careful to incorporate the means of preventing the "conspiracy of wealth and power."[27]

DeLolme must surely have appealed to those British North Americans who were leaning in the direction of a more liberal regime. The influence of the Loyalists who appeared after 1783, armed with republican sentiments, upset the old monarchical mentality of the provinces. Not a few clashes arose between the old and the new subjects of the Crown. That there was certainly a flirtation with republican sentiments we learn from Premier James William Johnston of Nova Scotia, who wrote in 1864: "I was in my youth actuated by the Whig principles of English statesmen. I was early perhaps captivated, as many young men are, with the illusions of a republic – of a republic that was working out the great problems they had taken in hand; but reflection and observation have gradually sobered down this sentiment, and I feel that, however valuable a republic may be for giving energy to individual action, it is wanting in that power of elevation, of refinement, of enlargement and nobility of sentiment, and responsibility of action which can alone raise nations to that high toned condition which we desire to see, and our minds figure before us, as the object of our aspirations."[28]

As early as 1815 we find a preoccupation with the corrosive influence of "that republican disposition," as Bishop John Strachan called it. In a sermon preached at York (Toronto), Strachan went on to say that "in all essential points of a good government, our neighbours have completely failed ... Of the two experiments made in America and France to constitute governments productive of virtue and happiness only, both have completely failed. – In the former, the most base and wretched policy is pursued; and the latter ended in a military despotism. It is by peaceable and gradual steps, and not by revolutions, that the most solid improvements in the Science of government can be obtained. – It is in the power of God only to extract good from evil; and in his hands the revolutions and convulsions which are now terminating [throughout Europe], will be made the instruments of good."[29] The baseness of American attempts to invade Canada in 1812 while Britain was distracted by Napoleon, whom the Americans supported, drew the wrath of Strachan and many others. Catholics were no more favourably disposed to republicanism than Protestants, as we can see from a sermon delivered in 1810 by Joseph-Octave Plessis, bishop of Quebec. He reviled the very notion of popular sovereignty as most false, destined to promote irreligion and revolution.[30]

The determination of all the foremost Canadian constitutional framers and those who supported them, especially among the clergy, was to perpetuate the monarchical regime in British North America. They regarded it as in every way superior to the most undesirable alternative, a republican regime. It is extremely important for us to understand that the framers believed they understood the nature of the American regime and were fully competent to devise a system for the new Canada that would be superior to the American one. Theirs would embody the best aspects of the British system (the monarchic) along with the best feature of the American (the federal). The former was to be the substantive aspect of their achievement; the latter, the external or formal achievement.

"NO SERVILE COPY"

It becomes evident, in reading the speeches and documents from throughout the Confederation period, that Canada's founders were confident that their new constitution would produce a kind of citizen more virtuous and more civilized than the American constitution. They appear to have understood Montesquieu when he wrote that in the beginning men form the constitution, but in time the constitution shapes the character of the people. Whether they knew Montesquieu as well as their American counterparts is open to question; they did, however, recognize that the substance of the constitution was crucial to the regime. The substance had to be monarchical, and the institutions shaping the constitution therefore had to be such as to reinforce

that principal objective. We all too frequently tend to accept the determination to perpetuate a monarchical form of government as something to be expected of loyal nineteenth-century British subjects. But
our nation's founders understood it to mean a certain form of government that preserved the gradation of classes, with the Crown at
the pinnacle as both source of sovereign authority and symbol of
kingly virtue. Under such a constitution, honour flows down from
the Crown and all public service is service to the monarch.

It is this point that leads us to understand the kind of federal
structure embodied in the terms of Canada's fundamental constitutional document, the British North America Act. Just how did the
Canadian framers understand the federal character of their new constitution? One of the most terse summations came from Charles
Tupper, the leading pro-confederate from the Maritime provinces. In
defending the Confederation plan in a speech in Halifax in 1864,
Tupper drew attention to the differences between it and the American
constitution: "You have been told also that no servile copy of the
American Constitution has been made by us. I believe that in the
United States the question of slavery and the division of interest
would never have culminated in so great a trouble had it not been
for the doctrine of the sovereignty of each state. In our Constitution
you will find that the General Government has that general centralized power which will enable all the nation to be consolidated and
combined."[31] Tupper elaborated on these themes in an extensive
defence of the proposed union of the colonies in the Legislative
Assembly of Nova Scotia in 1865.

Far and away the most important contributor to the Canadian federal form of government was Alexander Galt of Canada West. In his
lengthy address in Sherbrooke in 1864, Galt described his conception
of federalism in detail. He began by outlining the defects of the "present
union" of the two Canadas, then proceeded to recount the recent steps
taken at Charlottetown and Quebec. He conceded at the outset that
the overwhelming preference of the delegates at Quebec was for a
legislative union, but that the idea was abandoned because of opposition from the Maritime delegates, who feared their "peculiar interests
might be swamped." "The term Federation was used," he informed
his audience, "because it was that [with] which the public mind is
most familiar." But, he cautioned immediately, "it must not be supposed, on account of the use of that term, that in the Union now
proposed to be established it was intended to imitate the United
States."[32] He next described how in the United States the federal government exercised only such powers as were delegated to it by the
states at the time the union was formed. "Each state," he continued,

"was regarded as a sovereign power, and it chose for the common interest to delegate to the general Government the right of deciding upon certain questions, which were expressly stated. All the undefined powers, all sovereign rights, remained with the Governments of the several states."[33] That was a decisive mistake, Galt said, and the cause of those "difficulties now convulsing the United States." British North Americans should learn from this failure and avoid the "states rights" principle in their new constitution. He went on:

[W]hen we had before us the lamentable results which we now witnessed, when we saw the evils which had arisen there, and perceived that there was apparently no remedy for them within the limits of the constitution, we might well hesitate to adopt any system that would be similar in its character. If we did so we should be lacking in that wisdom learned from the experience of others which was so peculiarly valuable. Therefore, in laying a basis for the union of these Provinces, it was not proposed that the General Government should have merely a delegation of powers from the Local Governments, but it was proposed to go back to the fountain head, from which all our legislative powers were derived – the Imperial Parliament – and seek at their hands a measure which should designate as far as possible the general powers to be exercised by the General Legislature, and also those to be exercised by the Local Legislatures, reserving to the General Legislature all subjects not directly committed to the control of the Local bodies. By this means it was believed we should escape the rock on which the United States had split and we should not have a sectional agitation springing up in one section of the country or the other, because each legislature, and especially each Local Legislature – acting within the bounds prescribed by the Imperial Parliament and kept within these bounds by the Court of Law – if necessity should arise for their interference – would find in the working of the plan of Federation a check sufficient to prevent it from transcending its legitimate authority.[34]

The American constitution, according to Galt, failed to meet the basic test devised by Hobbes: it failed to secure the conditions of peace. Put another way, its terms were insufficiently strong to prevent a civil war. The doctrine of states rights and the faulty division of powers between the central government of the federation and the members states were its chief weaknesses. These flows were carefully avoided in the Canadian federal plan of union by lodging the major legislative powers in the federal Parliament and reserving the residual powers to it as well.

Galt explained further that this assessment of the weaknesses of the American constitution led the delegates to decide that the best form of government for the British North American provinces would be one designed to protect the diversified interests of the several provinces and secure efficiency, harmony, and permanency; it would contain a "General Government charged with matters of common interest to the whole country, and Local Governments for each of the Canadas and the Provinces of Nova Scotia, New Brunswick and Prince Edward Island, charged with the control of local matters in their respective sections."[35] And while the lower house of the new federation was to be based on the democratic principle of representation by population, the Legislative Council, or Senate, was to be filled by appointment by the Governor General in Council. "It then became necessary to settle the number of members for the Upper House, and the more so because the Upper House was intended to be the means whereby certain local interests and local rights would be protected in the General Legislature."[36]

As for the powers of the general government: "It would have to deal with the public debt and all the means of sustaining the public credit. It would have the regulation of all the trade and commerce of the country, for besides that there were subjects in reference to which no local interests could exist, it was desirable that they should be dealt with throughout the Confederation on the same principles [as those covering taxes on imports etc.] ... It was most important to see that no local legislature should by its separate action be able to put any such restrictions on the free interchange of commodities as to prevent the manufacturers of the rest from finding a market in any one province, and thus from sharing in the advantages of the extended Union."[37] All the major means of raising general revenue were to be confined to the general Parliament, "and there was only one method left to the Local Governments, if their own resources became exhausted, and this was direct taxation."[38]

Concerning the constitution and powers of the local governments, "the first change he [Galt] had to draw attention to was with reference to the appointment of the Lieutenant-Governor who it was proposed should be appointed by the General Government. The reason why this was preferred to the appointment taking place as heretofore by the Crown was that it was intended that the communication between all the several Provinces and the Imperial Government should be restricted to the General Government. Inasmuch as the affairs the Local Governments had to administer were purely of a local character, not at all Imperial in their nature, it was felt that there was no necessity whatever for their being in communication with the Imperial Government, but that on the contrary very great mischief might arise, if they were permitted to hold that communication."[39] The office of lieutenant governor was to be viewed as an honour reserved for the outstanding public men of the provinces. At the present time, Galt noted, only the prize of "bench or bar" was available to such men. In his view, the office would provide

the links of connection between the Local Governments and the General Government, holding to that General Government the same relations as were now held by the heads of the Provincial Governments to the Imperial Government, and discharging the duties of their offices under the same local advice as that which the Governors now acted on ... Consequently we should always have the means of bringing about harmony, if any difficulty arose between any of the local bodies and the General Government, through the Lieutenant-Governor, and we should have a system under which, all action beginning with the people and proceeding through the Local Legislature, would, before it became law, come under the revision of the Lieutenant-Governor, who would be responsible for his action and be obliged to make his report to the Superior authority.[40]

Galt then proceeded to explain the federal government's powers of reservation and disallowance. He made it clear that a central feature of the new federation would be the role played by the central legislature; it was to serve as a check on the provincial legislatures. As a result, it was "proposed to take away from them every source of revenue they possessed except minor local revenues, and then to give them from the public chest a sufficient subsidy to enable the machinery to work." If this proved insufficient, then the local legislatures could resort to direct taxes which, Galt felt confident, would induce the people "to keep a sharp watch over the local Governments." It is interesting to note that he showed no similar concern about a need to check the operations of the federal government. He foresaw the prospects for considerable economy in the future because the provinces, having had "taken from them a large share of the subjects previously legislated upon,"[41] would no longer have the same financial needs. Is it any wonder that many members of the legislatures of the Maritime provinces complained that they were being reduced to the status of municipalities under the proposed union?

In concluding his marathon performance, Galt expressed the hope that in the not-too-distant future his audience "would find the system they were trying to inaugurate a basis of unity among the people, unity of government making the people more and more homogeneous till at length they might at no distant day be enabled to do away with those artificial boundaries which separated one province from another, and come together as one united people."[42] Galt's speech is reported to have elicited "loud cheers."

There can be no question that the framers of the Confederation resolutions concerned themselves with the jurisdiction of the provincial legislatures. But, as we have seen, the records of the Quebec Conference make it clear that they also skilfully avoided specifying in detail what those local powers were.[43] George Brown, for example, said at Quebec in 1864: "This matter received close attention of [the] Canadian government [i.e., of the government of the United Canadas] ... I would let the courts of each Province decide what is local and what [is] General Government jurisdiction, with appeal to the Appeal or Superior Court."[44] We must keep in mind that under the terms of the plan of union the judges of these courts were to be appointed by the federal government.

Likewise, John A. Macdonald resisted the efforts of a Nova Scotia delegate to specify in more precise detail the powers of the provincial legislatures. E.B. Chandler of Nova Scotia protested: "I object to the proposed system. You are now proceeding to destroy the constitutions of the local governments, and to give them less powers than they have allowed them from England, and it will make them merely large municipal corporations. This is a vital question which decides the question between a Federal and Legislative Union, and it will be fatal to the success of Confederation in the Lower Provinces."[45] To this Macdonald replied by drawing attention to the fact that Chandler's proposal smacked too much of the defective American constitution. "I think the whole affair," he countered, "would fail and the system be a failure, if we adopted Mr. Chandler's views. It would be adopting the worse features of the United States. We should concentrate the power in the Federal Government, and not adopt the decentralization of the U. States. [*sic*]. Mr. Chandler would give sovereign power to the local legislatures, just where the United States failed ... It would be introducing a source of radical weakness. It would ruin us in the eyes of the civilized world. All writers point out the errors of the United States."[46] Macdonald concluded with the observation that "[a]ll the failings prognosticated by De Tocqueville are shown to be fulfilled."[47] This rhetorical flourish does little to instill confidence in his reading of the Frenchman.

According to the report of the Newfoundland delegates to Quebec, Macdonald expounded convincingly on the weakness of the executive under the terms of the American constitution. Newfoundland delegates E.B.T. Carter and Ambrose Shea reported back to their colleagues: "In view of the framing of a constitution, the defects of the American system were fully considered. Though the wisdom of the men who framed that constitution had been attested by its success for three quarters of a century, it still embraced principles which rendered it unable to bear the strain of the crisis which lately arose, furnishing a most instructive lesson at the present time. The admitted great defect of the Federal system of the United States is the weakness of the Executive, which compelled them in their day of trial to resort to the exercise of power unknown to the law, placing private and public liberty at the mercy of arbitrary authority."[48]

INSPIRED BY ALEXANDER HAMILTON

Macdonald's preoccupation with the executive power was a Hobbesean legacy. According to Hobbes, governments must be able to govern in order to provide the state with the minimum condition of peace; they must also be armed with the strength sufficient to guarantee that condition. It is not an accident that the controlling phrase at the head of section 91 of the Constitution Act, 1867 reads: "It shall be lawful for the Queen, by and with the Advice and Consent of the Senate and House of Commons, to make Laws for the Peace, Order, and good Government of Canada." This is clearly a Hobbesean formula. The indispensable precondition of good government is a strong executive authority. Long before the term entered the lexicon, Canada's constitution implied "executive-dominant" government. No other kind would meet Hobbes's minimum conditions.

In these matters our founding fathers turned to Alexander Hamilton, whom D'Arcy McGee called "the very first intellect of all the authors of the American system."[49] It was Hamilton who had pointed to the virtue of the British constitution at Philadelphia. He made it clear that "in his private opinion he had no scruple in declaring, supported as he was by the opinions of so many of the wise & good, that the British Govt. was the best in the world: and that he doubted much whether any thing short of it would do in America."[50] Hamilton paid special tribute to the fact that the constitution of England united "public strength with individual security." What attracted him most was the fact that the British system contained "energy in the executive." Morton J. Frisch has written of Hamilton: "The central element in Hamilton's plan was the new executive, the element of monarchy which had been added to republicanism. Traditional republicanism lacked a source of energy, but Montesquieu, aware of this problem, incorporated executive power into republicanism through the substitution of executive power for monarchical power in Book XI of *Spirit of the Laws*. Following Montesquieu, Hamilton introduced into the Constitutional Convention a new form of republican government which was more energetic than the traditional republican forms by the introduction of an executive with certain of the characteristics of monarchy ... He wanted to *infuse* republicanism with the excellences learned from monarchy without departing from republicanism."[51] Hamilton made it clear that it was the British monarchical system that he had in mind, which was, as we have seen, especially attractive to the Canadian founders. They conceived their task as being easier than that of the American founding fathers; they wished to wed a semblance of republicanism to their inherited monarchical constitution.

There is considerable evidence warranting the conclusion that Hamilton's overtly pro-British disposition provided the main source of inspiration for the constitutional framers. The leaders among them – not simply John A. Macdonald – turned to the American founding and discovered in Hamilton's writings that mix of principles most conducive to their aspirations. There can be little doubt that Hamilton attempted to resuscitate the American republican form of government by appeal to British monarchical principles.[52] Canada's founders, for their part, attempted to adapt the British monarchical form of government through the selective appropriation of republican principles. This is not to forget that there are significant differences between monarchical and republican governments. One of the most fundamental is the principle of *limited government* that goes hand in glove with republicanism and affects the understanding of the judicial function, as we learn from Hamilton's essay on the judiciary in *The Federalist Papers*. It almost goes without saying that limited government is foreign to the Hobbesean British constitution and hence foreign to the Canadian constitution – at least until the adoption of the Charter of Rights and Freedoms in 1982.

Hamilton's published reflections on federalism and the virtues of the British constitution drew the serious attention of the foremost Canadian constitutional draftsmen. His writings enjoyed enormous popularity in both Britain and British North America in the 1860s. Christopher Riethmuller's *The Life and Times of Alexander Hamilton*, published in 1864, attested to the extent of the admiration for the American statesman. Riethmuller, himself British, characterized Hamilton as the one "who did the most to call it [the United States] into existence and to bring it into working order, while he foresaw its dangers from the beginning, and laboured incessantly to guard against them."[53] He went on to say that Hamilton understood the British constitution "with the instinct of a genius, and loved [it] with the enthusiasm of a high and generous nature." No other of the American founders, in Riethmuller's view, studied the world of politics as thoroughly:

Hamilton had an almost intuitive knowledge of European politics. He had studied the various forms of government and considered the relative position of the different nations of the old world, until they had all become familiar to him, and he spoke of them as if from personal experience. The result was, that he preferred the British constitution to every other, and held it to be the nearest approach to perfection of all governments past or present. Could he have found the materials for establishing such a form of polity in his own country, there can be no doubt, that he would have devoted all his energies to that end ... He saw that some kind of republican government was, at the period of the Convention, the only thing feasible in America, and his object was so to control and modify the democratic elements, as to render such a government safe and salutary."[54]

From contemporary European governments Hamilton turned to the ancients for guidance. "He showed that republics were no more exempt than monarchies from intestine discord, that jealousy of commerce begets hostility as well as jealousy of power, and that there had been as many popular as royal wars. He examined the constitution and history of the Greek republics, the Germanic Empire, the Swiss Cantons. He glanced from Sparta to Athens, from Rome to Carthage, from Venice to the Hanseatic League, and in this grand survey of the experience of centuries, in which he quoted all sorts of authorities, from Aristotle to Montesquieu, from Cicero to Neckar, he laboured to prove that every government, to be *strong*, must be *sovereign*."[55]

Riethmuller's assessment is consistent with the record of Hamilton's speeches at the Philadelphia Convention of 1787, where he openly confessed that he was an admirer of the British constitution because of its "executive energy." This sentiment must surely have fired the resolve of the Canadian framers to produce a constitution that preserved the British form of government on the northern half of the continent. Similar emotions must surely have been evoked by a statement Hamilton made in criticizing the New Jersey plan of union, that "no amendment of the Confederation, leaving the states in possession of their Sovereignty could possibly answer the purpose."[56] Again, in criticizing the strength of the states, he listed as the fifth in his "great and essential principles necessary for the support of Government" the matter of influence, by which "he did not mean corruption, but a dispensation of those regular honors and emoluments, which produce an attachment to the Government. Almost all the weight of these is on the side of the States; and must continue so long as the States continue to exist. All the passions then we see, of avarice, ambition, interest, which govern *most individuals*, and *all public* bodies, fall into the current of the States, and do not flow in the stream of the General Government. The former therefor will generally be an overmatch for the General Government and render *any* confederacy, in its very nature precarious. Theory is in this case fully confirmed by experience ... How then are all these evils to be avoided? Only by such a compleat sovereignty in the general Government as will turn all the strong principles and passions above mentioned on its side."[57]

For Hamilton, the senate was the key institution for stabilizing the new republic. In this matter he turned once again to Britain. He agreed with Jacques Neckar (1732–1804) that the British constitution

is the only Government in the world 'which unites public strength with individual security' – In every community where industry is encouraged, there will be a division of it into the few and the many. Hence separate interests will arise. There will be debtors and creditors etc. Give all power to the many, they will oppress the few. Give all power to the few, they will oppress the many. Both therefore ought to have power, that each may defend itself against the other. To the want of this check we owe our paper money, instalment law etc. To the proper adjustment of it the British owe the excellence of their Constitution. Their house of Lords is a most noble institution. Having nothing to hope for by a change, and a sufficient interest by means of their property, in being faithful to the national interest, they form a permanent barrier against every pernicious innovation, whether attempted on the part of the Crown or of the Commons. No temporary Senate will have firmness enough to answer the purpose."[58]

In Hamilton's plan, senators were to be elected to serve so long as they were of good behaviour. This body of more or less permanent representatives was "to have sole power of declaring war, the power of advising and approving all Treaties, the power of approving or rejecting all appointments of officers except the heads or chiefs of the departments of Finance, War and foreign affairs."[59]

Hamilton drew special attention to the fact that every republic lacking a senate suffered certain important inconveniences, and pointed out by historical examples that every republic that survived for a long time possessed such a body. In brief, he believed that the institution introduced duration and stability into a republican regime.[60] He observed that the long-lived ancient republics of Sparta, Rome and Carthage blended stability with liberty. In his view, republics were peculiarly in need of a stabilizing institution such as a senate for the same reason that they needed representative government: the collectivity or nation as a whole cannot govern. Senates serve as a check on the liberty of republican peoples. Accordingly, Hamilton contended at Philadelphia that the central problem for the founders was to establish good government, both *safe* and *secure*. He maintained that in every republic there should be some permanent chamber or body to correct the prejudices, check the intemperate passions, and regulate the fluctuations of a popular assembly, one that would – to use a Canadian expression – bring "second sober thought" to the deliberations.

Central to our purposes is an understanding of Hamilton's conception of federalism. Anyone who has taken the trouble to read *The Federalist Papers* carefully will discover that there is a deep division between Madison's and Hamilton's understanding of the subject. Madison's essays are contained in numbers 39 and 46; Hamilton's, in number 9. A review of their two perspectives reveals that Hamilton's is not only noticeably more laconic but also (I would argue) deliberately imprecise. His essay in number 9 noted: "The definition of a Confederate Republic seems simply to be, an 'assemblage of societies' or an association of two or more states into one State. The extent, modifications and objects of the federal authority are mere matters of discretion. So long as the separate organization of the members be not abolished, so long as it exists by a constitutional necessity for local purposes, though it should be in perfect subordination to the general authority of the Union, it would still be, in fact and in theory, an association of States, a confederacy."[61]

These words must surely have caught the attention of John A. Macdonald, even when Hamilton then proceeded to say that the "proposed Constitution, so far from implying an abolition of the State Governments, makes them constituent parts of the national sovereignty by allowing them a direct representation in the Senate, and leaves in their possession certain exclusive and very important portions of sovereign power."[62]

As noted, one of Hamilton's major preoccupations was the executive. He feared that the president (or governour, a term he frequently used) would not have sufficient power to govern. In the fourth item of his plan Hamilton said: "The supreme executive authority of the United States [is] to be vested in a Governour to be elected to serve during good behaviour – the election to be made by Electors chosen by the people in the Election Districts aforesaid – the authorities and function of the Executive to be as follows: to have a negative on all laws about to be passed, and the execution of all laws passed, to have the direction of war when authorized or begun; to have with the advice and approbation of the Senate the power of making treaties; to have the sole appointment of the heads or chief officers of the departments of Finance, War and Foreign Affairs, etc."[63] Finally, "All laws of the particular States contrary to the Constitution or laws of the United States [are] to be utterly void; and the better to prevent such laws being passed, the Governour or president of each state shall be appointed by the General Government and shall have a negative upon the laws about to be passed in the State of which he is Governour or President."[64] Macdonald must surely have been impressed and reassured by Hamilton's plan. If this kind of constitution could be called "federal," then Macdonald could have little difficulty accepting it. It appeared closely akin to his cherished goal of a legislative union.

The tendency today among Canadian political scientists is to view the federal character of the constitution as its major feature. However, this characteristic was evidently not intended to be anything more than minor. Indeed, the intention of the constitutional framers was to emphasize the monarchical or substantive character of the constitution – to make it primarily monarchical and only secondarily federal. The Canadian politicians must have been helped greatly by reading Riethmuller's account of Hamilton's efforts to reform the Articles of the Confederacy. "Hamilton and Hamilton alone," wrote Riethmuller, "saw the full extent of the peril [of continuing under the confederacy], and was prepared to devise a remedy. He entered into a complete examination of the principles of the existing Confederation, and condemned them as utterly impracticable, and incapable of adaptation or amendment."[65]

But Hamilton's contribution was not only as a critic of the Articles of the Confederacy. He took an active role in the constitutional convention and was the chief author of *The Federalist Papers*, acknowledged ever since as one of the most authoritative expositions of the constitution of the United States. Hamilton won the unalloyed admiration of most, if not all, of the early commentators on that constitution. George Ticknor Curtis, for example, in his *History of the Origin, Formation and Adoption of the Constitution of the United States* (1854), wrote: "The great ideas of a statesman like Hamilton, earnestly bent on the discovery and inculcation of truth, do not pass away. Wiser than those by whom he was surrounded, with a deeper knowledge of the science of government and the wants of the country than all of them, and constantly enunciating principles which extended far beyond the temporizing policy of the hour, the smiles of his opponents only prove to posterity how far he was in advance of them."[66]

For a time it appeared to the world, said Curtis, that "[t]he people of America, united for a season by the great struggle for independence, seemed about to split into a number of obscure and hostile factions, who only agreed in their devotion to republican forms, and in their antipathy to anything that resembled a strong government."[67] It took a bold – not to say visionary – man to recommend, as Hamilton did, a strong "[g]overnment, capable, both in peace and war, of making every member of the Union contribute in just proportion to the common necessities, and directing the forces and wills of the several parts to a general end."[68]

It is important to remember that all discussions of federalism, whether in Great Britain or in British North America, took place with an eye to developments in the United States. Edward Freeman accordingly drew a contrast between the success of the federal constitution of the United States and the many failed efforts in France to provide ordered government after the revolution of 1789. Americans, he wrote during the early years of the Civil War, "established, not the best of all possible constitutions, but the constitution which was the best possible in that particular time and place."[69] He then went on to list the succession of failed attempts in France to provide stable order and government: "When the American Constitution was drawn up, France was still under the absolute and undisputed sway of a Most Christian King. The American Union has been contemporary with a Constitutional King of the French, a Convention, a Directory, a Consulate for a term, a Consulate for life, an Emperor of a Republic, an Emperor of an Empire, a Constitutional King of France again, a King of the French, a Provisional Government, a Dictator, a President for four years, a despotic President for ten years, an Emperor for what period no one can foretell."[70]

It was an easy matter for Freeman to conclude that "[t]he constitution-making of Philadelphia has been at least more permanent than the constitution-making of Paris." But he did not simply write of the inability of the French to establish a constitution, but went on to praise the American efforts. "At all events," he concluded, "the American Union has actually secured, for what is really a long period of time, a greater amount of combined peace and freedom than was ever before enjoyed by so large a portion of the earth's surface ... [N]ever before has so large an inhabited territory remained for more than seventy years in the enjoyment at once of internal freedom and of exemption from the scourge of internal war."[71] And, as the republic was entering a civil war, insisted that its great achievement was "the direct result of the Federal System."

Unlike many of the Canadian anti-federalists, such as Christopher Dunkin, Freeman went to great lengths to reassure his readers that, far from being the cause of the "Disruption" of the United States, federalism had helped to stave off greater evil "for no inconsiderable term of years." These sentiments, rooted as they were in substantial historical documentation, must surely have given great comfort to the proponents of a federal union in British North America – especially since Freeman was so insistent that federalism and the monarchical attachment were not incompatible.

CONCLUSION

In light of more than a century and a quarter of history under the terms of what the late Eugene Forsey called "Macdonald's constitution," we find that Canada's history has been a constant series of wrangling over the division of legislative authority between the federal and provincial levels of government. In other words, the very *federal* character of the constitution has become a cause of discord. How did this happen? Did Edward Freeman mislead the Fathers of Confederation? The very institution that was supposed to ensure an orderly division of legislative responsibility between the levels of government and a national economic order has resulted in squabbling between increasingly stronger provinces and a correspondingly weaker federal Parliament. No observer, domestic or foreign, could characterize the years since Confederation in 1867 as peaceful. With the exception of the two main periods when Canada was at war, the relationship between Ottawa and the provincial capitals has been one long sequence of bickering. Contrary to what Alexander Hamilton promised, the Senate has not provided national stability. Indeed, if there is one institution of the constitution that has failed to serve the ends for which it was devised, it is the Canadian Senate. But the failure was in the original constitution. Unlike the American Senate, which represents the states equally, Canada's was designed to represent the propertied commercial class, and its members have been appointed by the government of the day. The Senate of the United States has served to draw the country together at the national level. The Canadian Senate has not played a corresponding role, since it is not a national forum for the expression of provincial interests. That function has been fulfilled by the extraconstitutional institution of the federal-provincial conference. Hamilton taught that no federal system could function properly without a senate in which the component parts were equally represented at the national level. In view of this, Canada's federal system has been structurally deficient from the very beginning, inasmuch as it failed to provide for a senate where the various parts would be represented at the national level *as representative of the various parts.*

More importantly, Canada's federal system has been interpreted by the courts in such a way as to give more power to the provinces, especially in economic matters. The provinces have become pitted against one another, when not arrayed against the central government. Hence, our federal system tends to divide, rather than unite, the nation.

We now turn to examine the effects of the courts and judges on the original constitution.

6

The Courts and the Rise of Judicial Power

In all wise nations the legislative power and the judicial execution of that power have been most commonly distinct, and in several hands; but yet the former supreme, the latter subordinate.

John Milton, *Eikonoklastes*[1]

By the nineteenth century, as we have seen, the English "Leviathan" had become "bridled"; kings became constitutional monarchs. The British Parliament emerged unchallengeable and all-powerful. The constitution of Britain conceded no room to an independent judicial power to overrule acts of Parliament. Judges were to be "lions, but ... lions under the throne." Neither Hobbes nor Locke envisioned a major role for the judiciary in the British constitution. When contrasted with contemporary republican constitutions, such as the American, where the judicial power is so dominant, the absence of a prominent role for the judiciary in the British constitution stands out. Indeed, so pervasive has judicial power become in our way of thinking that the absence of judicial review in Britain's constitution appears to us today a major defect. But was it by error or through a deliberate decision that the role of the judiciary was so reduced? And how, then, can we explain the prominent role the judiciary has come to play under the Canadian constitution, which professes to be "a constitution similar in principle to that of the United Kingdom"? If a dominant court is more characteristic of a republic than of a monarchy, how did Canada, a monarchic federation, acquire a Supreme Court with power to strike down acts of the Canadian Parliament?

The answers to these questions reside in the constitutional evolution of Great Britain. One of the most important events that occurred along the way towards the modernization of that nation's constitution was the struggle between Francis Bacon (Hobbes's teacher) and Edward Coke, one of the foremost common law jurists of British history. The battle between these two great minds represented that between those who resolutely upheld the absolute sovereignty of the Crown in Parliament and those, such as Edward Coke and his disciples, who championed judicial supervision of the legislative power of Parliament through reason embodied in the common law. It was the early manifestation of conflict between those who were determined to protect the intention of the legislature and those who favoured a judicial activism that would make up for its deficiencies. Bacon was explicit in his essay "Judicature" that "[j]udges ought to remember, that their office is *jus dicere*, and not *jus dare*; to interpret law, and not to make law, or give law ... Let judges also remember, that Solomon's throne was supported by lions on both sides: let them be lions, but yet lions under the throne; being circumspect that they do not check or oppose any points of sovereignty."[2]

Thomas Hobbes, Bacon's greatest student, challenged Lord Coke in his famous *Leviathan*. He struck directly at the heart of the common law, which is judge-made law rooted in the theory of precedent (*stare decisis*) – that is, in the authority of previous court judgments. He wrote: "though the sentence of the judge, be a law to the party pleading, yet it is no law to any judge, that shall succeed him in that office."[3] As for the role of judges in declaring the meaning of written laws, Hobbes heaped scorn on the commentaries, with an eye to Lord Coke's reputation for authority: "For commentaries are commonly more subject to cavil, than the text; and therefore need other commentaries; and so there will be no end of such interpretation."[4] For Hobbes the true interpreter of the law was the sovereign, either one man or an assembly of men. His purpose was clearly to define and confine the scope of the judicial function to a narrow field of activity, and his writings on the matter constitute the first explicit attempt to delimit the alleged duty of the common law judge to find equity in the abstractions of judicial reasoning. Equity, Hobbes maintained, was "the intention of the legislator." Joseph Cropsey has observed that "Hobbes considers the members of the legal profession, bench as well as bar, to be studiers of something that they do not make but in which it is their duty simply to become versed: lawyers are never rightly more than students of the law, a point that must be pressed emphatically in respect of the common law, which is thought by its hierophants to be generated by themselves out of their enriched reason."[5]

Hobbes restricted the judicial function by identifying the limits or the proper role of judicial reasoning. A judge's primary obligation was not to do "what is commodious, or incommodious to the commonwealth." Rather, the good judge "ought to take notice of the law from nothing but the statutes, and constitutions of the sovereign, alleged in the pleading, or declared to him by some that have authority from the sovereign power to declare them; and need not take care beforehand, what he shall judge; for it shall be given him what he shall say concerning the fact, by witnesses; and what he shall say in point of law, from those that shall in their pleadings show it, and by authority interpret it upon the place."[6] A judge clearly had no business resorting to the realm of reason, however enriched by the previous ruminations of commentators or the decisions of prior judges. "The things that make a good judge, or good interpreter of the laws, are first, *a right understanding* of that principal law of nature called *equity*."[7]

The good judge was not thereby deprived of his reasoning powers; rather, he was directed towards their proper use, with constant reference to the intention or authority of the sovereign. "[I]n the act of judicature, the judge doth no more but consider, whether the demand of the party, be consonant to natural reason, and equity; and the sentence he giveth, is therefore the interpretation of the law of nature; which interpretation is authentic; not because it is his private sentence; but because he giveth it by authority of the sovereign, whereby it becomes the sovereign's sentence; which is law for that time, to the parties pleading."[8] His guide should ever be the "law of nature" that guided him towards the proper conception of equity: that is, tempering the harshness of the law (arising from its universality) to suit the particular circumstances. True equity – not that of "the students of the common law" – was that "which depending not on the reading of other men's writings, but on the goodness of a man's own natural reason, and meditation, is presumed to be in those most, that have had leisure, and had the most inclination to meditate thereon."[9] Few men have had both such leisure and so much inclination to study "true equity" more fully or carefully than Hobbes himself. So it was that Hobbes, dismissing the authority of the likes of Edward Coke, explicitly replaced their commentaries with his own. He spoke out so forcefully in his own name in *Leviathan* so that there could be no mistake about it: true students of the common law, both lawyers and judges (who were always little more than students of the law), were best advised to study his book for instruction on the proper understanding of the judicial function. Judges must never be allowed unrestricted power to ruminate without limits, in the name of equity. Thus, the first duty of the sovereign was to make sure that judges knew the limits of their authority to preside in equity. In Hobbes's view, to allow judges an unrestricted role in equity was to invite civil discord and instability.

By the time the American Revolution was brewing, the single most authoritative legal text throughout the British colonies was William

Blackstone's *Commentaries on the Laws of England* (1770). Blackstone made it unmistakeable that he sided with Bacon and Hobbes on the question of restricting judges in equity. According to him, the best way to interpret a law was to enquire into the intention of the lawgiver at the time it was passed, using "signs the most natural and probable." He proceeded to enunciate five "signs": "the words, the context, the subject-matter, the effects and consequences, or the spirit and reason of the law."[10] Blackstone's remarks on equity make clear his view of the role of the judiciary. "The liberty of considering all cases in an equitable light must not be indulged too far, lest thereby we destroy all law, and leave the decision of every question entirely in the breast of the judge. And law, without equity, though hard and disagreeable, is much more desirable for the public good than equity without law; which would make every judge a legislator, and introduce most infinite confusion; as there would then be almost as many different rules of action laid down in our courts, as there are differences of capacity and sentiment in the human mind."[11]

THE ESTABLISHMENT
OF THE SUPREME COURT OF CANADA

In light of the British character of the Canadian constitution, it should come as no surprise that it did not contain a provision requiring the establishment of a supreme court.[12] The Constitution Act, 1867 simply authorized the Parliament of Canada to establish "a General Court of Appeal for Canada, and for the Establishment of any additional courts for the better Administration of the Laws of Canada." It was not until eight years after Confederation that Parliament enacted legislation establishing the Supreme Court of Canada. Even then, appeals could be taken from it to the Judicial Committee of the Privy Council in London. Indeed, the major constitutional cases that restricted the authority of the Canadian Parliament to legislate for "peace, order and good government" and expanded the scope of provincial legislative jurisdiction were decided by the Judicial Committee, not the Supreme Court. The bringing of appeals to the Judicial Committee was terminated only in 1949. To that time, therefore, it was effectively the "real" Supreme Court of Canada.

Two efforts were made to abolish appeals to the Judicial Committee.[13] The first bill died on the order paper when the Parliament of Canada was dissolved on 30 April 1949. The Liberal government of Louis St Laurent was returned on 27 June 1949. In the throne speech, it was noted that, with the inclusion of Newfoundland in Confederation, it was time to have all legal matters determined within Canada. On second reading Stuart Garson, the attorney general, asserted that it was time for Parliament to remove one of the "two badges of colonialism." The other "badge of colonialism," the requirement that all amendments to the constitution of Canada be made in the British Parliament, was not removed until the passing of the Constitution Act, 1982.

In a publex to the Secretary of State for Commonwealth Relations, British High Commissioner to Canada P.A. Clutterbuck noted that one of the principal reasons for terminating appeals to the Judicial Committee was "the tendency of the Privy Council, at any rate in the 19th century, to interpret the BNA Act in favour of the Provinces and against the central government."[14] Clutterbuck also reported on the previous efforts of the Quebec government to establish a "Court of Review" to act as an appeals court in provincial matters that might otherwise go to the Supreme Court of Canada. The proposed court never received the approval of the Quebec legislature.

The only major resistance on second reading came from George Drew, leader of the Progressive Conservative opposition. Drew did not oppose the termination of appeals at the Privy Council so much as the decision to terminate without consulting the provinces. His argument was that, since the bill proposed to abolish a tribunal that adjudicated disputes between the provincial and central governments, the provinces should be formally consulted. In place of the Judicial Committee, Drew urged the establishment of a "special constitutional tribunal." Prime Minister St Laurent responded by insisting that the Canadian constitution was not a contract and that amendments to it did not require consultation with the provinces. He also rejected out of hand the suggestion for a special court to handle constitutional questions.

When the bill came before the parliamentary committee, the Tory opposition tried to amend it to require the Supreme Court of Canada to adopt a strict adherence to Judicial Committee precedents. This effort, as well as a last-minute attempt to increase the number of Supreme Court judges from Quebec to four, was defeated by the Liberal majority with the aid of the CCF members, who had long favoured ending appeals to the Judicial Committee. When the bill was reported to the House of Commons unamended it was greeted by a one-man filibuster by the former mayor of Toronto, Thomas Church, who protested volubly on the grounds that termination spelled the end of Canada's place in the British Empire. The bill eventually passed both houses of Parliament and was proclaimed on

23 December 1949. The new legislation raised the number of Supreme Court judges from seven to nine, and made provision for three judges from Quebec instead of two.[15]

JUDGES AND THE DUTY TO REVIEW

In the first major study of judicial review in Canada, published in 1968, Barry Strayer drew attention to the fact that "[t]he concept of judicial review of legislation in Canada is not an inheritance from the common law." Despite this we "have come to accept it," Strayer observed, "as a fundamental, authorized by that unwritten law which is the source of so much of the judicial power."[16] It is important to note, however, that the expression "judicial review" is never used in Britain to describe a process in which judges pronounce as to the correctness or "constitutionality" of specific acts of Parliament. This is the case because British courts do not have the authority to strike down acts of Parliament. The term is American in origin but has become widely used in Canada.[17]

Strayer properly placed the concept of judicial review in the context of the struggle in seventeenth-century Britain over parliamentary supremacy and the limits of the judicial function. The most famous attempt to establish the higher authority of the courts emerged in Edward Coke's famous judgment in the 1610 *Dr Bonham* case.[18] He ruled that "it appears in our books, that in many cases, the common law will controul Acts of Parliament, and sometimes adjudge them to be utterly void: for when an Act of Parliament is against common right and reason, or repugnant, or impossible to be performed, the common law will controul it, and adjudge such Act to be void."[19] This view of the power of judges to exercise judgment in the cause of "common right and reason" was not to survive long. By the nineteenth century, when the Canadian framers were meeting to pen their new constitution, the matter had long been settled in Britain in favour of the unqualified supremacy of Parliament. But however it had been decided in Britain, the role of judges in reviewing legislation, both federal and provincial, emerged as controversial in Canada from the beginning because of the federal character of the constitution. Strayer wrote in his preface: "As in most other federal states, the courts in Canada perform important functions both in delineating the limits of federal and provincial legislative power and in adjusting those limits occasionally to meet changing social needs."[20] Thus, judicial review of legislation in Canada was regarded as essential because the federal nature of the constitution implied some form of authoritative adjudication between the two levels of government.

Strayer's general conclusion was that neither the common law nor the Constitution Act, 1867 formally granted the power of judicial review to Canada's courts. The power of the Canadian legislatures to strike down laws, he argued, was the by-product of British colonial practice. The function was "implicit in the royal instruction, charters, or Imperial statutes creating the colonial legislatures."[21] According to Strayer, the colonial courts were conscious "that they could supervise the exercise of limited powers granted under charters or statutes."[22] After observing that there was a studied reluctance to exercise that supervisory function, Strayer speculated: "Whether the courts in what is now Canada ever invalidated *ultra vires* legislation is not clear, but it may be assumed fairly confidently that at the time of Confederation they would have been prepared to do so in a proper case."[23] The fact that the Judicial Committee of the Privy Council exercised the power of judicial review over all colonial administrations was a powerful example to lower colonial courts. Indeed, it had acted as the highest court of appeal for all the colonies since 1833.

Strayer saw judicial review as emerging by default out of pre-Confederation practice and the federal character of the new constitution. He buttressed his position by pointing to the provisions establishing the courts in the Constitution Act, 1867 and related provisions concerning disallowance and reservation. In his view, Canada's constitution clearly resolved the age-old conflict between the legislature and the courts in favour of the legislature. The judiciary was not to be supreme over Parliament. Strayer's thesis led to the conclusion that judicial review of legislation in Canada involved a certain measure of usurpation by the judiciary.

W.R. Lederman took issue with Strayer's suggestion of usurpation. According to him, the central terms of the Constitution Act, 1867 – sections 96 to 100 – clearly imply the "intention to reproduce superior courts in the image of the English central royal courts."[24] Lederman's thesis rested on a review of the independence and the hierarchical structure of the British appellate court system. In his view, the terms of the Constitution Act, 1867 embodied the essentials of that court system, which was intended to provide a corrective for the judicial process in a series of appellate steps. He pointed to the similarity between section 99 of the Canadian constitution and the provisions of the Act of Settlement, 1701 stipulating tenure of judges during good behaviour and removal by joint parliamentary address. He also noted similarities between other provisions, such as those relating to salaries of judges.

In his rejoinder to Lederman, Strayer said he was not persuaded that the institutional similarities led to the power to review parliamentary legislation. Lederman's position ignored "the basic fact that the jurisdiction of the 'central royal courts' was subject to limitation by Parliament. Parliament could and still can prevent judicial review of the actions of public officers or agencies." Moreover, and more to the point, Strayer retorted further, the central royal courts "never had the power to review acts of Parliament for validity, in spite of the pretensions of Coke and others. It is therefore impossible to imply an inviolable right of judicial review in Canadian superior courts on the basis that this is an inherent characteristic of 'superior courts'."[25]

The debate between Strayer and Lederman was over which should have primacy: the intention of the legislature at a given moment, or the intention of the framers of the Constitution Act, 1867. Lederman gave no consideration to what the framers themselves said on these matters, while Strayer dismissed the extant historical records as inadequate.

RETURNING TO THE SOURCES

Jennifer Smith has noted of the exchange between Strayer and Lederman: "Whatever the force of their contending views ... they clearly owe little to evidence provided by the framers' opinions."[26] Smith properly directed attention back to an examination of those opinions, beginning with the records of the Quebec Conference. She noted that John A. Macdonald acknowledged the need for "some form of judicial review in his initial argument on the desirability of federal union."[27] Macdonald did, in fact, say at Quebec City in 1864 that the courts would be called upon to answer the question, "Is it legal or not?" But neither he nor anyone else at Quebec or later in the discussions on the Confederation resolutions ever used the term "judicial review." This is not mere quibbling over words. It is a dangerous anachronism to put the debate over the judiciary's role in the new Canadian federation in modern terms, which are weighed down with the baggage of recent American judicial activism. Furthermore, documents of the Confederation period make it abundantly clear that the focus was not on the judiciary but on the judicial resolution of jurisdictional disputes. The primary concern of the constitutional framers had to do with the legislative ability of the central government to superintend or "review" *provincial* legislation. For this reason, we must not place too much weight on Macdonald's cryptic words at Quebec. Smith portrayed Macdonald as a champion of "local partisans fearful of abandoning local autonomy."[28] Despite his rhetoric, nothing was further from his mind than protecting local autonomy. And nothing was more foreign to his way of thinking than judicial review, other than as an instrument by which the courts would give full recognition to the centralizing logic of the new constitution.

What do the early documents and debates tell us about the framers' thoughts on the important issues relating to the role of courts and judges under their constitution? Further, what can we learn about these matters from the debates on the plan of union that took place in all the provincial legislatures? Historic sources reveal that the provincial legislators focused their attention on the power of the central government to disallow and the prerogative authority of the provincial lieutenant governors to reserve provincial legislation for the approval or disapproval of the federal government. Not one member of any of the provincial legislatures spoke in favour of judicial adjudication of disputes between the two levels of government. The emphasis at every step of the process leading towards Confederation, from Quebec City to London, was on "legislative review" of provincial legislation. There was very little left over for "judicial review."[29]

The facts that our courts have since acquired enormous powers of judicial review of federal and provincial legislation and that the powers of reservation and disallowance have fallen into disuse do not give us reason to read into the historic record the roots of these newly acquired judicial powers in order to give them the respectability of historic validation. Our attention should more properly be focused on the strenuous efforts to construct legislative review in such a manner as to minimize judicial review, even render it unnecessary if at all possible. It is for this reason that the Fathers of Confederation claimed to have written a constitution superior to that of the United States and to have carefully eliminated or reduced to a minimum the possibility of conflict between the two levels of government. Their claim is frequently ridiculed as naive. But when we understand the full force intended for both disallowance and reservation it becomes more persuasive.[30]

Furthermore, it is important to observe how "non-federal" the judiciary was under the Constitution Act, 1867. The judicial process was radically centralized; the judges of the provincial superior courts were appointed and paid by the central government and could be removed only upon the joint address of both houses of the Parliament. R.B. Dickey of Nova Scotia joined with E.B. Chandler of New Brunswick at the Quebec Conference in warning that the resolutions on the subject were establishing a legislative union by centralizing all the major powers in the federal parliament and erecting a unitary court system. Their efforts to establish a "Supreme Court of Appeal to decide any conflict between general and states rights" was emphatically rejected by the rest of the delegates.

Dickey's compatriot Johnathan McCully vigorously espoused a legislative union over a federal union and therefore supported the efforts to establish a unitary judiciary. No-one at Quebec argued more strenuously against establishing courts with power to strike down federal legislation than McCully. He responded bluntly to George Brown's suggestion about the provincial courts being granted power to decide jurisdictional disputes by saying he wanted no part of a court system, such as the American, that would "set them over the General Legislature."[31] And no-one agreed more with McCully than John A. Macdonald. Indeed, Macdonald thought the judiciary could be the very instrument to give effect to the centralizing forces of the constitution. Accordingly, not long after assuming office as prime minister he set about to establish a "General Court of Appeal" for the new nation. He believed – not unreasonably – that the British North America Act had so arranged the powers between the two levels of government as virtually to preclude any conflict over jurisdiction. Contrary to Jennifer Smith, who has claimed that he changed his mind over the need for judicial arbitration when he came to defend the Quebec resolutions in the legislature, Macdonald was perfectly consistent.[32] Ironically, however, he required a judiciary to give formal endorsement to the dominance of the central government. He got what he set out to achieve: a constitution in principle embodying a legislative union while giving the appearance of a federal constitution. This deceptive constitutionalism was later to be called an "official mendacity" by Sir Ivor Jennings.[33]

Macdonald turned to Judge James Robert Gowan for advice on the prospect of judicial endorsement of the centralizing terms of the constitution. The judge informed the prime minister that the court was bound to enforce the principles of centralization so clearly enunciated in that document. However, the courts, especially the Supreme Court of Canada, were prevented from fulfilling this vital function because litigants could bypass the Supreme Court and go directly to the Judicial Committee of the Privy Council. A full fifty per cent of significant constitutional cases bypassed the Supreme Court of Canada in the critical early years of the nation's history. As a result, the controlling constitutional jurisprudence was formed in London, largely without the benefit of native Canadian judicial input.

THE INTERPRETATION OF CANADA'S CONSTITUTION BY THE JUDICIAL COMMITTEE

There is a voluminous literature on the role played by the Judicial Committee of the Privy Council in interpreting the terms of the

Canadian constitution throughout the early years of the new nation's history. But it is a seriously divided literature: there are almost as many who praise the work of the Judicial Committee as there are those who condemn it. The only point of agreement is that the "Law Lords" significantly altered the terms concerning the division in powers of the original constitution. Was the work of the Judicial Committee for the better or for the worse?

Many Canadian law professors and political scientists unleashed an avalanche of criticism when the Law Lords struck down federal legislation that attempted to meet the crisis of the Great Depression in the 1930s. They had ruled that the Parliament of Canada lacked the constitutional power, under "peace, order and good government," to adopt certain measures intended to ameliorate the Depression, despite the insistence of the provinces that the federal government do so. That chorus of critics was in short order supplanted by those who believed that the Judicial Committee had done the right thing in stripping Parliament of its dominant centralizing principles. These scholars (collectively called "the province builders") applauded the decentralizing thrust of the Judicial Committee's decisions; they favoured the emergence of strong provinces and the Law Lords had aided this cause by narrowing the range of the "peace, order and good government" clause of section 91 and expanding the "property and civil rights in the province" clause of section 92. W.P.M. Kennedy observed during the early years of this controversy that the Judicial Committee refused to see in the British North America Act "anything of a constitutional nature or to be guided by its historical origins ... They have applied to it arbitrary rules of construction which have at times robbed it of its historical context and divorced its meaning from the intention of those who in truth framed it."[34]

A review of the ongoing debate reveals several positions touching on the central issue of judicial review. More recent defenders of the Judicial Committee, led by Alan Cairns, have held that it ruled wisely by giving full cognizance to the "sociological realities" of the times. Others, such as V.C. MacDonald, Bora Laskin, and Eugene Forsey, have argued, on the contrary, that the Judicial Committee went well beyond its mandate and emasculated the centralizing terms of the constitution. It is their assertion, in particular, that the Law Lords had no business imposing their views of federalism on the Canadian constitution when it was clear that those views were not consistent with its original terms. Still others maintain that the British North America Act was so ambiguously written that the Judicial Committee had no alternative but to sort out the confusion inherent in terms that stipulated that both levels of legislative authority were "exclusive."

One thing is for certain: the effect of the Judicial Committee's work has been to weaken the powers of the federal Parliament and to increase the powers of the provincial legislatures.

"The Wicked Step-fathers"

The Judicial Committee's proponents have failed to take into account certain fundamental problems flowing from the quality of judicial construction it employed. Sir Ivor Jennings noted almost fifty years ago that the Law Lords "never seriously wavered from the principle that it was their function to interpret the 'intention of Parliament' as laid down in the Act."[35] Yet on several occasions we find a judgment by the Judicial Committee claiming, as Sir Montague Smith did in the *Parsons* case when confronted with an instance where the Constituiton Act, 1867 clearly demanded federal dominance, that "the legislature [i.e., the British Parliament] could not have intended that the powers exclusively assigned to the provincial legislature should be absorbed in those given to the dominion parliament."[36] He reached this conclusion despite the clear language of the Constitution Act, 1867. Why could this dominance *not* have been intended by the British Parliament? Smith's remarks seem especially disturbing when we consider that there are both specific and general provisions of the act pointing to the very possibility he dismissed out of hand. As well, the historic record of the four drafts through which the constitution passed were available to the Judicial Committee. The Constitution Act, 1867 is not contradictory, as many have claimed. Moreover, the historic account of the discussions about it, from Charlottetown and Quebec City to London, show that its centralizing terms were not the result of shoddy draftsmanship but of conscious effort by its framers.

But the question remains: How are we to understand the Judicial Committee's interpretation, which led it to conclude that the terms of our fundamental constitutional document were to be enclosed in "watertight compartments"; that the provinces were to be "autonomous"; that "peace, order and good government" ("notwithstanding anything in this Act") were to be restricted to times of emergency? The answer can best be found by first recognizing how the Law Lords themselves viewed their powers of adjudication in constitutional matters. There is a consistent disposition throughout the literature on the subject to assume that the Judicial Committee was performing a *judicial*, as opposed to a *political*, function when judging constitutional cases. Indeed, all criticisms take as a matter of course that the Law Lords were acting judicially in these instances. Unfortunately, courts rarely, if ever, set out explicitly how they understand the nature of their role. In the case of the Judicial Committee, however, we have several accounts that amount to statements about its members' perspective on their role as judges in constitutional cases. The first of these consist of verbatim transcripts of proceedings before the Judicial Committee in two constitutional cases: *Russell v. The Queen* of 1882[37] and the *Local Prohibition* case 1896.[38] The Judicial Committee set down important judicial doctrines in these two cases, doctrines that altered significantly and permanently the exercise of legislative power under the Constitution Act, 1867. In addition to these judicial sources there are the important nonjudicial statements by Viscount Haldane in which he explained the judicial function as it was exercised in the Judicial Committee.

It is immediately apparent from the transcripts of *Russell* and *Local Prohibition* that the Law Lords saw their function in cases arising under the Canadian constitution as essentially political, not judicial. Lord Watson went so far at one point in *Local Prohibition* to say that the Judicial Committee did not give judicial opinions at all. Also evident was a tendency on the part of its members to side with the provinces against the claims of the federal Parliament. Both transcripts disclose that the Law Lords viewed federal dominance as essentially a threat to viable provinces that was to be resisted. What is even more astonishing from the questions and objections raised throughout these cases is their complete disregard for the intention of the British Parliament itself, as expressed in the language of the British North America Act. What they attempted to do was identify areas of provincial power and place them beyond the easy reach of the Canadian Parliament. Contrary to G.P. Browne,[39] the Law Lords emerge as intent on giving effect to a conception of federalism which was clearly counter to that contained in the Constitution Act, 1867. They saw the function of the Judicial Committee as essentially political for the simple reason that they believed their role to be correcting the "deficiencies" of that act. In other words, they considered their function to be primarily legislative: redressing or correcting the mistakes made by British Parliament. What started as a not unreasonable proposition – determining the respective scope of federal and provincial powers – became a political mission, especially for Lord Watson and later for Viscount Haldane.

Far and away the most interesting comments on Haldane and his influence on the Judicial Committee have come from Stephen Wexler. Writing in the *McGill Law Journal*, Wexler presents a thorough and persuasive account of the main intellectual forces that moved Haldane to adopt a pro-provincial bias throughout his tenure as counsel before the Judicial Committee and later as a Law Lord.[40] The article confirms in intriguing detail that Haldane's was not a narrow perception of his function as formally judicial. His passion for the British Empire and for Home Rule are shown to have a profound impact on how he viewed the status of the provinces within the Canadian federal state. It also explains how "Haldane was able to misread the clear, unequivocal text of Canada's constitution."[41]

But it is a mistake to view this matter only through the eyes of Watson and Haldane. The *Local Prohibition* transcript makes it clear that other members of the board, especially Lord Herschell, were just as determined to make the terms of the British North America Act more consistent with a minimum federalism, that is, with clearly defined exclusive areas of legislative jurisdiction reserved to the provinces. In short, the overwhelming preoccupation of the Law Lords was with the very conception of federalism, however ill-prepared they were by training and experience to articulate it. They appeared institutionally unwilling to ask: What conception of federalism does the Constitution Act, 1867 itself contain? Indeed they seem never to have done so.

Haldane went to great lengths in a 1914 Australian case, *The Colonial Sugar Co.*, to reveal his understanding of federalism, especially Canadian federalism: "With reference to a great many people who talk on platforms just now of the 'the federal system' – in Canada there is no federal system. What happened was this: An Act was passed in 1867 which made a new state and divided certain powers of government, some being given to the Parliament of Canada and some to the Parliament of the provinces. The provinces were created *de novo*. The provinces did not come together and make a Federal arrangement under which they retained their existing powers and parted with certain of them, and an Imperial statute has got to ratify the bargain; on the contrary, the whole vitality and ambit of the Canadian Constitution was a surrender, if you like, and then a devolution."[42] His historical musings were further elaborated upon during his exchange in court with Sir Robin Finlay, the lead Australian lawyer, who attempted to set him straight about the origins of the Canadian constitution. Haldane's comments were sufficient to confirm that this learned Lord sitting on the Judicial Committee in Canadian cases was thoroughly out of touch not only with the historic record of the Confederation movement but also with the nature of the Canadian federal system, as contained in the British North America Act.

Haldane again expounded his views on the judicial function in a speech he gave at Cambridge in November 1921, while he was still active on the Judicial Committee. He said that the Law Lords were appointed for their qualities of past experience, for their "statesmanlike outlook ... the outlook which makes [them] remember that with a growing constitution things are always changing and developing, and that you cannot be sure that what was right ten years ago will be right today."[43] He returned to the subject five years later, in his introduction to the British edition of Mary P. Follett's book *The New State*, where he wrote: "The form of the state and the meaning of the resulting sovereignty may vary, following general opinion at different periods and under different conditions, and so may the mode of expressing the imperative."[44] True to his fundamental Hegelianism, Haldane insisted that "the will is no static thing but is a form of the dynamic activity characteristic of mind."[45] Above all, he agreed with Follett's statement that "the true state does not demand a merely submissive allegiance, for it is the outcome of a spontaneous and instinctive process of unifying manifold interests."[46] According to Haldane, the state is "a process." "The state is made," he maintained, "not by external acts, but by the continuous thought and action of the people who live its life. In this sense it is never perfect for it is a process that remains always unbroken in creative activity."[47] The art of statesmanship, even judicial statesmanship, lay in participating actively in the forward-looking process; there was to be no "submissive allegiance" to a founding vision. Hence, there was no need to ask what the intention of the constitutional framers was; rather, it was for the judge to use their document to respond to emerging demands – in Canadian terms, to the demands of the provinces for more autonomy.

Haldane praised Watson, a fellow Scot ("who came to London knowing nothing [and] became a great English lawyer"), for rendering

an enormous service to the Empire and to the Dominion of Canada by *developing* the Dominion constitution. At one time, after the BNA Act of 1867 was passed, the conception took hold of the *Canadian Courts* and *what was intended* was to make the Dominion the centre of government in Canada, so that its statutes and its position should be superior to the statutes and position of the Provincial Legislatures. That went so far that there arose a great fight, and as the result of a long series of decisions Lord Watson put clothing upon the bones of the Constitution, and so covered them over with living flesh that the constitution of Canada took *a new form*. The provinces were recognized as *an equal authority coordinate with the Dominion*, and a long series of decisions were given by him which solved many problems and produced a new contentment in Canada with the constitution they had got in 1867."[48]

On this basis the Judicial Committee went out of its way to set the Supreme Court of Canada straight. It overruled no less than fifty per cent of appeals emanating from it, while overruling only twenty-five per cent of appeals from other Canadian courts.

The *a priori* commitment of the Judicial Committee to a conception of federalism at variance with the Constitution Act, 1867 led it to "judicial statesmanship" and resulted in a political jurisprudence. We see this commitment at work when looking carefully at its judgments. By and large, the following pattern emerges. The Judicial Committee almost always (in the crucial Watson years) approached the question at bar by way of section 92. That is to say, the Law Lords began by asking whether the authority sought by the provincial legislature could be supported by an item listed in that section. The Constitution Act, 1867 was so drafted that if a judge approaches a dispute by first viewing it through the terms of section 92, then he or she will decide the issue in light of those provisions; the related provisions in section 91 will be read as subordinate to those in section 92. That is, if one posited a question such as, "Is this a matter relating to property and civil rights?" or "Is this a matter of a merely local or private nature?", the answer would in most cases be in the affirmative. The task for the court then became to diminish the force of the inevitably conflict-ing provision under section 91. This was precisely the procedure Judah Benjamin[49] recommended to the Judicial Committee in *Russell*. Benjamin pointed out that, a year earlier, *Parsons* had endorsed deter-mining an issue by first enquiring whether it was covered by one of the provincial powers enumerated in section 92. It was somewhat self-serving of Benjamin to urge this approach in *Russell*, because it was he who had convinced the Judicial Committee to adopt it in *Parsons*. In *Russell*, Sir Montague Smith expressed his agreement with Benjamin's approach succinctly: "According to the principle of con-struction there pointed out [in *Parsons*], the first question to be determined is, whether the Act now in question falls within any of the classes of subjects enumerated in section 92 and assigned exclu-sively to the Legislatures of the Provinces. If it does, then the further question would arise, viz., whether the subject of the Act does not also fall within one of the enumerated classes of subjects in section 91."[50] But this procedure erred on two counts. First, the general terms of section 91 came before section 92 and were clearly intended by the language of the Constitution Act, 1867 to control what followed. Section 91 gave the federal Parliament the wide power to make laws for "the peace, order and good government of Canada." It also left no doubt that the enumeration was not to be seen as restricting the full range of the "peace, order and good government" clause, "not-withstanding anything in this Act." Smith erred by interpreting the enumerated items as being detached from the controlling directives at the head of section 91.

The transcripts of *Russell* and *Local Prohibition* thus confirm the political character of the Judicial Committee's perspective, as well as the general entrance via section 92. The Law Lords are frequently reported as saying in response to counsel for the federal government: "There must be some restraint on federal power." In *Local Prohibition*, for example, Watson was disturbed at the prospect of "peace, order and good government" overriding "nearly all the clauses giving jurisdiction" to the provinces. Even he recognized that the terms of the British North America Act did just that, and he was unwilling to give effect to them. He thereby openly determined to rewrite the provisions of the Canadian constitution.

Lord Herschell, in *Local Prohibition*, likewise worried about federal power intruding into local matters. Edward Blake, a leading Canadian statesman and an outstanding lawyer, attempted to persuade the Law Lords that the Constitution Act, 1867 contained mutually exclusive and not concurrent powers. But Herschell resisted his efforts and led the Judicial Committee in favouring the provinces even more than Watson. Herschell had been co-counsel with Judah Benjamin in *Parsons*; it is not too much to say that he had a stake in maintaining the "principle of construction" he had helped to articulate in the earlier, controlling case.

There can be no doubt, however, that Watson was the principal proponent of "judicial statesmanship." Haldane wrote of him in the *Juridical Review*: "He was an Imperial judge of the very first order. The function of such a judge, sitting in the supreme tribunal of the Empire, is to do more than decide what abstract and familiar legal conceptions should be applied to particular cases. In this view, the function of a judge is to be a statesman as well as a jurist, to fill in the gaps which Parliament has deliberately left in the skeleton constitution and laws that it had provided for the British Colonies."[51]

Canadian commentators have, of course, been outraged by Watson's conception of the function of the Judicial Committee. Mark MacGuigan, for instance, recoiled at the "blatant judicial legislation" of the Judicial Committee.[52] Nevertheless, that body did not see its function as a purely judicial one in Canadian constitutional cases. If this is not sufficiently clear from the decisions of Watson, we have merely to turn to Haldane. For Haldane, the task of judicial statesmanship was even more compelling. He thought deeply about the duties of judges and wrote about them.[53] There can be little doubt that his commitment to Hegelian political philosophy influenced him at the bar; he himself admitted it. But it would be to overemphasize the influence of both Haldane and Hegel to say that it was of more than minimal effect, since Watson's views were well established by the time Haldane came to the bench. We have no way of knowing what philosophical influences prompted Watson in forming his ideas about the proper judicial function. Nor would Haldane's Hegelianism explain the views of Lord Herschell and others which were so compatible with Watson's own.

CONCLUSION

The reaction throughout Canada to the interpretation of the constitution of 1867 by Watson and Haldane was especially hostile in the accademic literature.[54] At the time, and until very recently, their understanding of the intention of the Canadian constitutional framers appeared condescending and wrong-headed. But ironic as it may seem, the exercise of *judicial* statesmanship by the judicial Committee was clearly consistent with the exercise of imperial power over the colonies. It must not be overlooked that Canada remained in a position of formal colonial dependence until 1931 and the Statute of Westminster. Nor should it be overlooked that no opposition arose in the British Parliament over the decisions of the Judicial Committee, that is, over the misuse of judicial authority. A parade of Canadian constitutional authorities might rail against the Judicial Committee, but there is no evidence that the British government or Parliament itself was at any time critical of the committee's judgments in Canadian cases. And if any body had a right to object to the legislative function of the Judicial Committee, it would be the British Parliament. The only conclusion is that it concurred in the perception of the judicial function as exercised by the committee.

However troubling judicial legislating may appear to us today, in the nineteenth century it had its proponents. John Austin, for example, wrote in *The Province of Jurisprudence Determined*, published in 1885: "I cannot understand how any person who has considered the subject can suppose that society could possibly have gone on if judges had not legislated, or that there is any danger whatever in allowing them that power which they have in fact exercised, to make up for the negligence or the incapacity of the avowed legislator. That part of the law of every country which was made by judges has been far better made than that part which consists of statutes enacted by the legislative."[55] Austin's comment shows how far from the views of even Blackstone matters had evolved. Blackstone had taken pains in his magisterial *Commentaries* to outline five "signs the most natural and probable" that should guide the judge in his task. The fifth rule, "the most universal and effectual way of discovering the true meaning of a law, when the words are dubious, is by considering the reason and spirit of it; or the cause which moved the legislator to enact it."[56] According to Blackstone the judge, in construing statutes, was to correct the law in a manner consistent with what the legislators had intended and to adapt that intention to particular circumstances.

Critics of the Judicial Committee of the Privy Council have claimed that this is exactly what the Law Lords failed to do. Those critics, among them the late Eugene Forsey, assert that the Law Lords substituted their own views for those of the Canadian framers of the constitution. In other words, the critics side with Blackstone against the Law Lords and Austin.

Contemporary attitudes towards the judicial function have been influenced by the doctrine of the separation of powers. But there is no strict separation of powers under the constitution of Great Britain, where the lord chancellor, who often presides in the Judicial Committee, is a member of the House of Lords as well as the Cabinet., sits in the legislature, and so is a member of both the executive and the judiciary. There can be no doubt that the Judicial Committee always was and still remains an advisory body of Her Majesty's Privy Council, offering what in constitutional matters is political advice. That advice has never been rejected.

Functioning thus as an extension of the legislative process, the Judicial Committee viewed its role as compensating for the "negligence and incapacity" of Britain's Parliament and of the Canadian framers of the Constitution Act, 1867. What it did, in fact, was weaken the legislative power of the central Parliament so as to accord a greater degree of autonomy to the provinces. It thereby made the Canadian system of government more authentically federal. In so doing, it was responding to the provincial request that it restore a large measure of the self-government that the provinces had enjoyed before Confederation. At the same time, the Judicial Committee confined the federal government and Parliament to matters more clearly national in scope. In siding with the provinces, the members of the Judicial Committee became the real "fathers" of the Canadian federal system.

Finally, buried deep in the dustbin of Canada's constitutional history lies an intriguing question: What would Canada be like today if the Law Lords had followed Blackstone and had given full force and effect to the strong central government desired by the framers? Recalling the reaction that greeted the proposed constitution throughout the Maritime provinces in the 1860s and the public outcry immediately following its adoption, it would be easy to imagine that Quebec would not have been the only province to seek secession from the Confederation of 1867.

7

A Nation of Christians

Religious nations are naturally strong on the very points on which democratic nations are most weak; which shows of what importance it is for
men to preserve their religion as their condition becomes more equal.

Alexis de Tocqueville, *Democracy in America*[1]

Religion, especially Christianity, was one of the central targets of the
Enlightenment philosophers, notably in France.[2] The cluster of *philosophes* known as the "d'Holbachian clique," which included the likes
of La Mettrie, Diderot, d'Holbach himself, and Voltaire, mounted a
devastating attack on all revealed religion but reserved their sharpest
criticisms for Christianity. Imbibing heavily of the old wine of Epicu-
reanism, these men became intoxicated and vicious in their assault.[3]
Gerhard Kruger has noted: "From Democritus through Epicurus,
Hobbes, Spinoza and Hume to Feuerbach and Marx there exists one
tradition whose classical representative is Epicurus," who banished
religion as the product of ignorance and fear.[4] This new natural philosophy, as it became known, wormed its way into the life of both
Hobbes and Locke. Michael Oakshott has commented that "never
before or since has the Epicurean tradition had so acute an exponent
or received so masterly a statement" as in Hobbes.[5] Hobbes consorted
with the leading French disciple of Epicurus of his day, Pierre Gassendi.
He not only absorbed the spirit of free enquiry unleashed by the new
natural philosophy prompted by Epicurus but also contributed to it.
According to Leo Strauss, "He gives that apolitical view a political
meaning. He tries to instil the spirit of political idealism into the hedo-
nistic tradition. He thus became the creator of political hedonism."[6]
Above all, Hobbes learned from Epicurus that religion was founded
in fear of "powers invisible," to use his own later words in *Leviathan*.
But Hobbes also recognized that a religion brought under the control
of the sovereign could aid the cause of civil stability. The Christian
religion, especially, stripped of its trappings of popery and theological
dogmatics, could when skilfully refashioned by the sovereign into

simple, clearly enunciated canons help the people do their duty of obeying the ruler: their one overwhelming duty.

John Locke imbibed Epicurean philosophy through association with François Bernier, another French disciple of Epicurus. Following Hobbes, he believed that Christianity properly rinsed of its traditional controlling characteristics, could aid the cause of civil order. Locke formally addressed its role in the state in *A Letter Concerning Toleration*, where he asserted that Catholics and atheists could not be tolerated because the former owed allegiance to a foreign prince and the latter were not to be trusted. "Those ... are not at all to be tolerated who deny the Being of a God. Promises, Covenants, and Oaths, which are the Bonds of Humane Society, can have no hold upon an Atheist."[7]

Beginning with Henry VIII, the sovereign became the head of the Church of England and Anglicanism was formally declared the religion of the realm (with the brief hiatus of the reign of Henry's daughter Mary). The views of both Hobbes and Locke eventually found their way into the English constitution, and soon thereafter travelled to the New World. A. James Reichley has observed that "Virginia, founded in 1607, thirteen years before the Pilgrims arrived on Cape Cod, maintained throughout its colonial existence an officially established Anglican church."[8] After the American Revolution, the political leadership of Virginia, headed by George Washington, John Marshall, and Patrick Henry, became convinced that state financial support for religion was necessary to strengthen social stability. And, once again, the American founders turned to Locke for support for this objective.[9]

In his "Speech on Conciliation with America," Edmund Burke took special note of the importance of religion, and particularly of Protestant denominations, in giving Americans a "free spirit" and reinforcing their opposition to "all that looks like absolute government." Where Catholicism had shown itself supportive of the civil authorities wherever it existed, dissenting Protestantism, he said, had "sprung up in direct opposition to all the ordinary powers of the world, and could justify that opposition only on a strong claim to natural liberty." The Church of England had also shown itself favourable to civil stability, but in America it was in "reality no more than a sort of private sect, not composing most probably the tenth of the people." Whereas the religion "most prevalent in our northern colonies is a refinement on the principle of resistance; it is the dissidence of dissent and the Protestantism of the Protestant religion."[10]

In continental Europe, by contrast, especially in France, religion became an object of public scorn and vilification. Church property was plundered. The *philosophes* rarely, if ever, addressed the political implications of the repudiation of religion. They did not see its use-fulness, as Hobbes and Locke had in England. Anti-clericalism swept France following the French Revolution, which was in effect the polit-ical explosion fuelled by the philosophical dynamite of the *philosophes*. In *Ancien Regime et la Revolution*, Alexis de Tocqueville noted the attack on Christianity in the eighteenth century and its impact on the French Revolution. "In France, the Christian religion was attacked with a sort of fury, without any attempt to put another religion in its place. Ardently and continually the effort was made to remove from the souls of men the faith which had filled them, and leave them empty ... The universal discredit into which all religious beliefs fell at the end of the last century doubtless exercises the greatest influence on all our Revolution; this is what gave it its distinctive character. Nothing contributed more to give to its physiogomy that terrible expression which it conveyed."[11]

With pointed reference to the United States, de Tocqueville noted, "There is no country in the world where the boldest doctrines of the *philosophes* of the eighteenth century, in matter of politics, were more fully applied than in America; it was only the anti-religious doctrines that never were able to make headway."[12] Alice M. Baldwin has shown persuasively that in colonial America the Christian religion permeated every aspect of life.[13] When the colonists of Massachusetts convened in 1779–80 to draft a new constitution, no fewer than thirteen of the sixty-two delegates were clergymen. The Reverend Ebenezer Parkman urged strenuously on one occasion that the new governor should be not only a Christian but a Protestant. The post-revolutionary constitutions throughout the former Thirteen Colonies made provision for the selection from among the Protestant clergy of an "Election Preacher" whose duty it was to preach widely on polit-ical matters, with a view to making sure that the legislators had due regard for the Christian faith before passing laws. One of the striking features of the election sermons, especially in New England, was the extent to which they appealed to John Locke – at least to his argument that governments are limited by the purpose for which they were founded, i.e., the good of the people. Positing that all government came from God, the election preachers concluded that "[a] govern-ment which did not have the good of the people at heart did not have the sanction of God."[14] And the Christian faith of the people was a primary public good.[15]

But even in the United States, where Christianity was so widely practised and was presumed to be the dominant faith of the people, a controversy arose almost immediately upon the adoption of the constitution in 1787. As Daniel L. Dreisbach has noted, "One of the most striking features of the United States Constitution of 1787 is the absence of a mention of the Deity or recognition of the Christian Religion."[16] These omissions caused much controversy during the ratification debates and continued to draw the fire of participants in the early constitutional life of the new nation. William Williams, for example, a signer of the Declaration of Independence and a member of the Connecticut ratifying convention, wrote to Oliver Ellsworth, a delegate to the constitutional convention and third chief justice of the United States Supreme Court, suggesting that the failure to mention God be corrected by "an explicit acknowledgment of the being of God, his perfections and his providence ... in the first introductory words of the Constitution."[17] The distinguished physician and devout Christian Dr. Benjamin Rush wrote to John Adams complaining that "many pious people wish the name of the Supreme Being had been introduced somewhere in the new Constitution."[18] Rush, another signer of the Declaration of Independence, knew that it explicitly stated that the rights justifying the rebellion against the British Crown were based on the "self-evident" truth "that all men are created equal, that they are endowed by their Creator with certain unalienable Rights, that among these are Life, Liberty and the pursuit of Happiness." Rush seemed to understand better than some of his contemporaries that the constitution could not be divorced from the Declaration of Independence, that the former was the completion of the latter. Richard G. Stevens noted recently that the Declaration "does not actually set up a government ... What is declared needs to be implemented. The Declaration needs to be complemented by another, a constructive, enactment."[19] The "constructive enactment" was the constitution of the United States, "which completes the work of the Declaration by actually establishing a government in order to secure rights."[20] Some commentators since the nineteenth century have argued that the American constitution's failure to mention God is misunderstood only because it has been divorced from the Declaration of Independence. There is no silence when the two documents are – properly – read together. What other authorities on American constitutional history have argued is that it was felt to be unnecessary to mention God because the founding fathers were well aware that "Christianity was recognized in virtually all state constitutions and manifested in the practices, usages and customs of all American civil governments of the Revolutionary period."[21]

The controversy was inflamed, rather than ameliorated, by the adoption of the first constitutional amendment shortly after ratification in 1789. The first amendment began with the words: "Congress

shall make no law respecting an establishment of religion, or prohib-
iting the free exercise thereof." It is noteworthy that the amendment
placed a restraint on the national Congress, not on the states. It
thereby acknowledged that the United States was a nation of states,
that certain things were formally left to the states; and – it would
appear – religion was one of them.[22] The controversy over the place
of religion in the public realm is far from over in the United States.
With the application of the Bill of Rights to the states by way of the
judicial interpretation of the fourteenth amendment, the display on
public property of Christian symbols has been ruled unconstitutional
on the grounds that it violates the "separation of Church and state."[23]
However, nowhere in the constitution of the United States is the
"separation of Church and state" mandated. The doctrine is a con-
coction of the United States Supreme Court and constitutes a major
modification of the constitution by the judiciary.[24]

RELIGION AND THE CANADIAN REGIME

Despite the major role played by the Christian faith in the life of
Canada, there has been strikingly little formal attention given to it as
a part of the core of the regime.[25] This is not to deny that every
historical discussion of Quebec has focused on the prominent role
taken there by the hierarchy and clergy of the Catholic Church. Nor
is it to detract from the attention confessional schools have received
over the years. But, by and large, the positive importance of Christianity's role in Canada has been neglected. For example, nothing
exists on the order of de Tocqueville's reflections in *Democracy in
America* on the importance of religion in the American regime.

This lack is all the more puzzling since Canada was founded as a
Christian nation: Quebec was established as a Catholic country and,
from 1627, Protestantism was by royal edict formally proscribed
throughout the colony.[26] All that changed in 1759. "For the conquest
of that Catholic colony by a Protestant country completely reversed
the order of things: Canada became officially a Protestant colony and
it was Catholicism, in its turn, that now came to be tolerated."[27] The
English military forces soon found that there were no Protestant
churches in Quebec and were obliged to ask the bishop of Quebec
City for permission to use a Catholic chapel. The bishop allowed
them to conduct a funeral service in the Ursuline chapel. On the
evening of 14 September 1759, the day after the Battle of the Plains
of Abraham, the first Protestant sermon was preached in Quebec. The
preacher was the Reverend Eli Dawson and he chose for his text,
"Therefore will I give Thanks unto thee, O Lord! Among the Heathen;

and sing Praises unto Thy Name." Dawson concluded this "indelicate discourse" with the peroration "that such Success may crown the Measures of Defence, which the Perfidy and Ambition of our Enemies oblige us to have Recourse to."[28] Needless to say, his sermon was not well received among the French Catholic inhabitants. But the occasion serves to remind us of the central importance of sectarian difference in the new order that was to follow the Treaty of Paris in 1763. The population of Quebec had little choice but to suffer the presence of their conquerors, but they fiercely defended their right to practise Catholicism and just as fiercely resisted the intrusion of Protestant practices and influence.

The treatment of Catholics in the North American colonies before the Treaty of Paris was openly and officially hostile. In Baltimore, for example, the Episcopalian Church was made the established church in 1702. Thomas D'Arcy McGee remarked in *The Catholic History of North America*, published in 1855: "The English revolution of 1688 was a disastrous event for the Catholic minority in British North America."[29] Upon King Billy's arrival in England, "things turned bad for Catholics in British North America ... The Governor and council of Pennsylvania had prohibited Catholic worship in 1734 and 1736; in 1740, Georgia had prohibited Catholics settling within her borders; in 1746, Fr. John Ury was executed in New York for the pretended 'Negro plot' to burn the city ... [and for being] a Catholic priest."[30] McGee also noted that "it is probable Canada [i.e., Quebec] might have been one of the original states of the Union but for the impolicy of General Arnold and the bigotry of a portion of the first Congress."[31] It was the Catholic, far more than the French, character of Quebec that aroused the ire of Americans during the debate over the Quebec Act of 1774. Governments took religious matters seriously, and the foundations of tension between Catholics and Protestants in North America were deeply rooted in English history. It is against this backdrop that we must come to understand the role of religion in the founding of Canada. In a certain sense, Christianity played a negative role in the form of this virulent and divisive anti-Catholic prejudice.

After the conquest, Canada was conceived with a specifically Protestant character. The Church of England arrived as soon as was expedient, not only as a formal counterweight to the Catholic Church in Quebec but also as an assurance that this essential element of the British constitution would be firmly rooted in His Majesty's new North American possessions. The imperial government set out to guarantee the position of the Anglican Church by designating and setting aside large tracts of land "to the Maintenance and Support of a Protestant Clergy ... and to no other Use of Purpose whatever" together with special Rectory lands "according to the Establishment of the Church of England."[32] The Constitution Act, 1791 accordingly set aside in Upper Canada 22,345 acres of land for the use of the Church of England, 1160 acres for the Kirk, and 400 acres for the Catholic Church. But the British authorities, under Prime Minister William Pitt, resisted efforts to extend the formal establishment of the Church of England in the new colony. "The Church of England might look for special favours from a friendly British government, but its real position was still a matter of politics for the provincial governors; the Church was not denied a claim to the whole endowment, but the Pitt government would not acknowledge that she held a right to it."[33] However contentious the reserved lands became – and they did become contentious – their purpose was to secure the stable foundations of civil society in the Christian religion.[34] The clergy reserves were finally secularized in 1854, but the Christian churches had become well entrenched and the Protestant leadership was a formal part of the civic government.

Despite the fact that the Anglican Church was never formally declared the "Church of Canada," its official presence was pervasive. Since the Test Act of 1678, Catholics had been proscribed from holding political or judicial office under the English constitution. Church and state were inseparable and all responsible offices of the state were vested in the hands of Protestants. "In theory, the Corporation Act of 1661, the Test Act of 1673 and the oaths of supremacy made it impossible for anyone who was not an Anglican to occupy any of the higher executive or judicial posts ... It was only the Catholics who were rigorously excluded, since an annual Indemnity Act was passed to cover Dissenters who broke the law."[35] The impact of the official status of Protestantism in British North America was reinforced by a flood of Protestant immigrants. A large number of Presbyterians from Northern Ireland arrived shortly after the Treaty of Paris in 1763 and many Protestants from New England arrived the following year.[36] These non-Anglican Protestants militated successfully against the efforts of some highly placed Anglicans to have the Church of England declared the established church. Moreover, their numbers served to intensify the animosity towards Catholics; many of the arrivals from Northern Ireland were more openly anti-Catholic than many Anglicans. We have only to read the inflammatory sermons from leading Protestant clergymen in the nineteenth century to appreciate the powerfully divisive role anti-Catholic feelings played in the life of the colonies. Needless to say, the large Catholic community in Quebec presented a formidable challenge to those zealots who were determined to make Canada safe for the Protestant religion and the constitution of England, one way or another.

Charles Daubeny remarked forty years before Confederation that, since 1688, "every British monarch must have known that the constitution of this country [Britain] was by the collected voice of the people declared to be essentially and exclusively Protestant. Every monarch of these realms must therefore have considered himself placed by divine Providence on the throne under solemn obligation to God and his country to preserve the constitution of it, so far as respected its fundamental principles of Protestantism, in the same state in which he found it."[37] These sentiments reflect the dominant thinking of British statesmen for more than a hundred years. A former solicitor general, Lord Ashburton, when speaking about the Quebec Act of 1774, explained his objections to extending toleration to Catholics in Quebec as follows: "My opinion of toleration is, that nothing can be more impolitic then to give establishment to that religion which is not the religion of our own country."[38]

In 1828, Henry Drummond wrote against the rising tide of republican sentiment: "Hence, too, the false opinion is sanctioned, that the people, not God, are the source of legitimate power; that power is delegated from the people to their rulers, and consequently may be resumed by the people, whenever the people shall deem such resumption to be for their benefit; whereas the true foundation of this, and of every Christian monarchy, rests upon the principle that 'powers which be, are ordained of God', and that, therefore, 'whosoever resisteth the power, resisteth the ordinance of God'."[39] J.C.D. Clark has comented in this connection, "This was in its essentials the doctrine which had provided the defense of the State against the American and Dissenting challenges in the 1770s and the French challenge in the 1790s; and as Burke saw, it derived inescapably from the Whig defense of the Glorious Revolution in the decades immediately after that event."[40]

Most discussions of religion are cast in terms of church versus state, that is, as a practical matter of power over subjects. But at root the conflict is more deeply theoretical – or, as Spinoza would have it, theological-political. Such early English modern philosophers as Hobbes and Locke viewed transcendent religion, as embodied in the Catholic Church, as fundamentally hostile to stable government. Allegiance to a higher or transcendent authority, one taking priority over state authority, clearly implied that the religious man would be, at best, a qualified citizen. He would be liable – was indeed, was commanded – to temper his loyalty to the civil law of the regime with the divine or revealed law of God. But both Hobbes and Locke saw that most men, especially the uneducated, could be induced to do their civic duty if their religion could be brought under the sway of the sovereign. So it was that the English constitution came to designate the monarch as both civil ruler and head of the Church of England. By the nineteenth century, the Protestant character of that constitution was indisputable, and those who emigrated to British North America wanted the benefits of its religious character – complete with its fierce rejection of Catholicism. Such a point of view set them on a collision course with the French Catholics of Quebec and Catholics throughout the other colonies. The British authorities had, from the time of the conquest, feared that Catholicism posed a threat in the newly acquired French territories. The Earl of Egremont wrote to Governor James Murray in 1763: "Watch the Priests very narrowly, and ... remove, as soon as possible, any of them, who shall attempt to go out of their sphere, and who shall busy themselves in any civil matters."[41]

Powerful Anglican clergymen such as Bishop Charles Inglis, first Anglican bishop of Nova Scotia, made their presence felt in public affairs. Inglis arrived from New York in 1787, where he had served as rector of Trinity Church, by far the most prominent and influential Anglican church in colonial America. He brought with him a distrust of republican government and a strong attachment to the British constitution, which he extolled from the pulpit. He believed that constitution to be the best example of good government, and that nothing short of continued connection with the mother country would do for God-fearing British North America. For him the principal benefit of the British constitution was its Christian character. Preaching before the Nova Scotia legislature in 1793, Inglis enunciated his belief in "government and religion as institutions of God, and the twin pillars on which society rests." He pressed his audience for a firm commitment to the principles of Anglicanism, as vested in the king and constitution of the realm.[42] If Inglis had had his way, the Anglican Church would have become formally established in Nova Scotia and throughout the other provinces, save Quebec. But in this ambition he was unsuccessful, for the British government remained unwilling to grant establishment to the Anglican Church in North America. This is not to deny that there was a *de facto* primacy given to the Anglican hierarchy and church throughout the old maritime colonies and the other British possessions. Anglican divines had a privileged *entré* into the counsels of civil government throughout British North America.

Thus Canada's religious foundations were formally Christian, but a Christianity at war with itself. The dominant Protestant voices were certain that Catholics could not be trusted to be loyal to the Crown. Nearly a century after the conquest, the Reverend J. Gilbert Armstrong announced in a sermon preached at Richmond Hill: "I am ready to show you that they [Catholics] cannot, to be true to their creed, yield to our most gracious Queen the allegiance which the Scriptures demand of her subjects – The Romish creed, lays down that the Pope is supreme – that he has universal authority."[43] These sentiments were, by 1855, long out of official fashion in England. The Emancipation Act of 1829 had repealed all laws that subjected Catholics to civil disabilities; all offices previously denied to them were opened to them throughout the United Kingdom, including British North America. Catholics could now, theoretically at least, sit in both houses of the imperial Parliament, though they were still barred from the positions of regent, lord chancellor, and lord lieutenant and lord chancellor of Ireland. The only requirement was to take an oath denying the power of the Pope in domestic affairs, recognizing the Protestant succession, and repudiating any intention to upset the Anglican Church. While the Emancipation Act brought official discrimination against Catholics to an end, it did not expunge the lingering animosity against the Church of Rome and its adherents throughout British North America, for such sentiments were deeply entrenched.

But to focus solely on the animosity between the Christian communities of the new Canada is to obscure the deeper implications of the religious question at the foundation of Canada. Despite their real confessional differences, there was a common agreement among them: Canada must be firmly rooted in the Christian religion. As Bishop Joseph-Octave Plessis of Quebec and Bishop John Strachan of Ontario, each in his own way, declared, its Christian foundations would contribute to the well-being of the nation as a whole. Indeed, there could be no enduring well-being without the strong public presence of the Christianity. Not surprisingly, leading Catholic clergymen, including Bishop Plessis, attempted to mollify the fears of Catholicism among their Protestant fellow citizens and to affirm loyalty to the British Crown. In 1810, more than a half-century before Confederation, he urged his listeners to give allegiance to the new government under which Providence had placed them.[44] He spoke forcefully of the virtues of monarchy and of the evils of the American form of government, founded on "the sovereignty of the people," a system he called "the most evil since it is the most false and most absurd."[45] He concluded his disquisition with a pledge of loyalty to the king and government of Great Britain and urged his congregation to follow his example. This was not a new theme for the Bishop of Quebec, for in 1799 he had preached a lengthy sermon on Lord Nelson's victory at Aboukir in which he drew attention to the replacement of the French criminal law by the English version, which he called "that masterpiece of human intelligence." The benefits for the French of Quebec flowing from Nelson's victory were clear, he announced: "Where is the good patriot, the loyal subject, I say, and more, even the true Christian, whose heart has not been gladdened by these happy tidings? Great Britain's command of the seas is assured; her colours fly majestically on all the oceans; her enemies are humbled and perplexed; the peace the whole world longs for is approaching. Do these considerations alone not suffice to bring cheer to all hearts? But here let us add that we have a special reason for rejoicing in this victory, for by consolidating Great Britain's power, it guarantees the peace and happiness of this Province."[46] The same theme was sounded frequently from the pulpits of Quebec long before and after Confederation. For the Quebec clergy, loyalty to the Crown and a corresponding hostility to republican government especially after the French Revolution – represented the means of ensuring the survival of the Catholic faith.

No Father of Confederation spoke as often or as forcefully on the subject of religion and the need for loyalty to the Crown as George-Etienne Cartier. Speaking at a banquet in honour of Alexander Galt in May 1867, Cartier contrasted the as yet unproclaimed new constitution of Canada with that of the United States. He noted pointedly that the American document did not take due account of religion, whereas the Canadian constitution was founded on religion. "Catholic or Protestant, the question of religion is in our eyes paramount," he concluded. Cartier never failed to remind his fellow Quebeckers that their "religion [was] the safeguard of the people," and that it was "the best means for French-Canadians to remain attached to the soil and by which to preserve their language and religion."[47] Speaking before the St Jean Baptiste Society in Ottawa one year after Confederation, Cartier said, to applause from his audience: "Since the conquest we have been saved from the misery and shame of the French Revolution. The conquest has given to us the beautiful and free institutions we possess today and under which we live happy and prosperous, because we are 'men of faith and progress'."[48] Cartier was an astute student of Montesquieu, who had written with admiration in *The Spirit of the Laws* of the commercial spirit of the British constitution.[49] Evidently with one eye on Lord Durham's report, Cartier bristled at the emerging reputation of French Canadians among English merchants as apathetic and lacking the entrepreneurial spirit of their Protestant counterparts. In 1849 he had urged support for the Montreal to Portland railroad upon his compatriots and enthused over its exceptional prospects of attracting foreign capital. He also spoke of the importance of private property, going so far as to say, "It is certain that property is the principal element represented in the House of Lords and it is the conservative element of the British constitution which has endured for such a long time."[50] Montesquieu had taught him that "[t]he spirit of commerce brings in its train the spirit of frugality, economy, moderation, work, prudence, tranquillity, order, and rule."[51] And further, "Commerce is a cure for the most destructive prejudices; for it is almost a general rule, that wherever we find agreeable manners, there commerce flourishes; and that wherever there is commerce, there we meet with agreeable manners."[52] In a speech to the delegates to the Quebec Conference, Cartier said: "For my part, I am ready to declare loudly today that the prosperity of the two Canadas is due primarily to the spirit of enterprise of the English race."[53] And in a speech delivered in July 1866, Cartier referred explicitly to "the spirit of the British constitution."[54]

Cartier, like his English-speaking colleagues, saw no conflict between entrepreneurial ambition and the spirit of religion. Cartier had become thoroughly assimilated to the new English regime, even to the extent that he saw virtue in the Conquest; it not only saved French Canadians from the evil of the French Revolution but brought all the benefits of the English constitution to Canada. Accordingly, he openly supported the monarchical spirit of that constitution and enthusiastically embraced its commercial spirit.

RELIGION AS EDUCATION

Religion, especially in Quebec, was intimately tied up with education. The Catholic hierarchy took strong measures to consolidate its hold over education, from childhood to university. Lord Durham took special note of the importance of Catholicism to the stability of the French community. "The Catholic priesthood of this Province have to a very remarkable degree, conciliated the good-will of persons of all creeds; and I know of no parochial clergy in the world whose practice of all the Christian virtues, and zealous discharge of their clerical duties, is more universally admitted and has been productive of more beneficial consequences ... they have been the promoters and dispensers of charity, and the effectual guardians of the morals of the people; and in the general absence of any permanent institutions of civil government, the Catholic Church has presented almost the only semblance of stability and organization, and furnished the only effectual support for civilization and order."[55] He went on to record that "it has been rightly observed, that the religious observances of the French Canadians are so intermingled with all their business, and all their amusements, that the priests and the church are with them, more than with any other people, the centres of their little communities."[56] Durham seemed to understand what some later observers could not, namely, that the Catholic religion was an essential defining part of Quebec nationality.[57] It destined to remain the pervasive binding force between Quebeckers until the middle of the twentieth century.

Janet Ajzenstat made the curious comment in her study of Lord Durham that the "French and English might be at war, but they were not quarreling about Protestantism and Catholicism." The absence of conflict between Catholics and Protestants in Quebec, was, she continued, "evidence that the Roman Catholic church had relinquished its role as support for the laws and institutions of the old French-Canadian way of life and was ready to accept the progressive reforms that he [Durham] was putting forward. The idea of 'virtue' defined by the church, was no longer at the centre of politics."[58] This was not the case; the Catholic Church in Quebec never abandoned the "idea of 'virtue' defined by the church." Indeed, its clerical support for the new monarchical regime was so considerable after the French Revolution precisely because it could continue to enjoy the benefits of the *ancien régime*. To suggest that it had abandoned the posture of censure toward the modern liberalism that arose out of the Enlightenment is to misread seriously the Catholic Church in Quebec during this period. It was not many years after Durham's report that Pope Pius X issued his famous encyclicals *Lamentabili* and *Pascendi*, in which he condemned "modernism." The hierarchy of the Quebec Church embraced the spirit and letter of both encyclicals. Inasmuch as modern liberalism was atheistic, it would never be embraced by Catholicism.

The Quebec hierarchy actively sought and welcomed French clerical *émigrés*, especially those from teaching orders that had been abolished in the wake of the French Revolution. Indeed, forty-five priests from France played a large role in establishing the foundations of the *colleges classiques* and parish schools throughout Quebec early in the nineteenth century. They brought with them a horror of all things connected with the Revolution and helped to consolidate the French Canadian attachment to monarchy.[59] Quebec was truly a homogeneous political community. Its central binding force was twofold: the French language and the Catholic faith. When Cartier returned from the London Conference in May 1867, he addressed a large crowd in St Hyacinthe. His report was received with outbursts of enthusiasm and support when he told them that Confederation was a *"revolution pacifique"* that assured all Quebeckers the continued enjoyment of their faith. The British government, he attested, had acted *"justement et genereusement"* in upholding the rights and privileges of French Canadians.[60] Speaking later the same month at the banquet in honour of

Alexander Galt, Cartier emphasized that the new constitution protected religion better than the American constitution.

THE PRIMACY OF THE CHURCH OF ENGLAND

As noted earlier, from the time of Governor Murray's appointment, official imperial sentiment and policy were far more sympathetic to the French inhabitants of Quebec, especially in matters of religion, than the English merchants wished. No-one reflected the official view more accurately than British Prime Minister William Gladstone. In a book published the same year as Durham's report, *The State in its Relations with the Church*, Gladstone made it clear that while primacy of place was accorded to the Church of England under the constitution of Great Britain, it was never Britain's policy or intention to drive out Catholicism in Quebec or indeed any of its possessions. Gladstone noted that "the principle upon which alone ... our colonies can be governed is that of preserving the good will of their inhabitants."[61] With special reference to Quebec, he said the Crown had entered into a contract with the French inhabitants:

It must also be observed, that there are real and important distinctions to be taken with respect to the varieties of relation between our several colonies and the mother country. Such of them as are only the adoptive children of the empire, and have been received into it when already adult, with their own fixed institutions, or at least with a prevalent religion other than that established at home, are very differently circumstanced from those which have gone forth from our own bosom, and have been reared by us from infancy. To refrain from rooting up what we have found enjoying an actual existence, both in law and in the formed convictions of the people, is very distinct from encouraging or assisting that which is newly proposed, and much more from being ourselves the authors of fresh diversities.[62]

But Gladstone demonstrated that there was no doubt in his mind that the Crown had a moral and religious mission to promote and extend the Christian religion. In support of this proposition, he cited a speech of the Lord Bishop of London to an assembly of "merchants, bankers and traders." The bishop had reminded the businessmen that the "true glory of a nation" lay in its duty to promote the happiness of mankind, and "that surely the happiness of mankind is to be measured by the place which they occupy in the scale of Christian knowledge and Christian practice."[63] The financial support afforded the Church of England and the establishment of clergy reserves was therefore no insignificant factor in the occupation of Quebec.

Gladstone spelled out in pounds and pence exactly how much was paid to the clergy throughout the British colonies, not only Quebec. He recognized that, though it was an anomaly, the Crown "provided that the Roman Catholic clergy should continue to receive tithe as theretofore, except that it was to be only payable to persons adhering to their own communion."[64] He justified this overt violation of the British constitution on the grounds that it was part of "the original contract" with the French following the Treaty of Paris: "The secular rights of the Roman Catholic Church in Lower Canada were a part of the original contract by which we hold the province, in this case a real treaty. And this admission does not involve any answer to the inquiry, whether such a contract ought to have been framed. The distinction in principle will not apply, where we have given State assistance as from ourselves to the Roman Catholic religion, or any other not included in the compact of the constitution."[65]

The British government took formal steps to ensure that Christianity became deeply rooted in the life of Canada. At no time did the novel doctrine of the separation of church and state take hold of the official mind. Few stated the matter more directly than William Knox, the highly influential undersecretary of state for the Colonial Department under Lord North. Echoing Hobbes, he declared, "The National Religion of any State may be presumed to be best adapted to the Civil Constitution of that State: [and] ... should be considered not only as a Matter of Piety and Prudence, but of the utmost Necessity in a Political View."[66] Nothing short of the "internal Peace of Society" depended on it, he argued. Accordingly, in the Constitution Act, 1791 the British Parliament provided for the establishment of the clergy reserves and rectory lands. However much this was a direct countermeasure to balance the ancestral privileges afforded the Catholic Church and clergy in Quebec,[67] its more fundamental purpose was to secure the place of the Christian religion, chiefly the Protestant denomination, in the life of the new community. Alan Wilson has pointed out that a principal means of supporting the Christian churches was land grants, a practice prevalent throughout the American colonies.[68]

Needless to say, the official British stance, as expressed by Gladstone, did not sit any better with the English colonists than Governor Murray's policy. Not only the merchants but also the leaders of the Protestant churches vehemently expressed their disapproval of the British government's generosity and tolerance. Nor was this the sole source of discord. In the early ninteenth century, Upper Canada became a battleground of sectarian politics within the Protestant churches whose bitterness was at times reminiscent of Northern

Ireland. The internecine battles arose over the ambiguity of the phrase in the Constitution Act, 1791 referring to lands for "a Protestant Clergy." The Anglicans – especially under the headstrong leadership of Bishop John Strachan – wanted the lion's share of the clergy reserves to go to the Church of England. It goes without saying that this attitude was not well received among Presbyterians or Methodists, who constituted a majority of the population in the early years of the nineteenth century. The only point on which the battling Protestant denominations agreed was their determination that the Catholic Church would benefit as little as possible from the reserves. They were singularly successful in achieving this aim.[69]

The Anglican Church in Upper Canada was admirably served by Strachan's powerful presence and influence. The fiery divine brooked no opposition to his conviction that the Church of England should benefit, if not exclusively, then at least predominantly, from the clergy reserves. Strachan took a back seat to no man in defence of the rights of the Anglican Church and the Christian character of Canada. A dominant force in the Family Compact, he did everything in his power to guarantee that British North America would develop in a manner loyal to both the Crown and the Christian – that is, Protestant – religion. To this end, he fought to keep education under the sway of the Anglican Church. Above all, he sought to establish university education as a Christian stronghold, with a measure of success. In 1827 he secured a charter for a university at York (Toronto), with himself as president. From the seeds thus sown in the form of what was called Kings's College arose the present University of Toronto. Strachan envisioned his university as a New World Oxford or Cambridge, under Anglican control and closed to Non-conformists and Catholics. His exclusionary intentions, not surprisingly, raised the hackles of other Protestant divines. The great Methodist leader and educator Egerton Ryerson erupted in fury at Strachan's pretensions and said so in the bluntest of terms. But Strachan persisted in his determination to achieve official pre-eminence for the Church of England. On one occasion, he even prevailed upon the more-than-willing Governor Peregrine Maitland to appoint an Anglican chaplain to the legislature and to have each session open with a prayer to be recited by him. The legislature balked, recommending instead that the prayer be led by clergymen of the various Protestant communities on a rotating basis. Neither Strachan nor Maitland would have anything to do with this proposal. The governor responded by suspending the prayer altogether, while defiantly retaining the Anglican clergyman on salary.

The effort to establish the Christian religion in Upper Canada was as closely tied to education as in Quebec. Strachan was not the only

Protestant leader to understand the religious mission of British North America. Egerton Ryerson, the leading spokesman for the Methodist community, was also active in promoting a form of public education that would be Christian and Protestant. This determination brought him into conflict with the hierarchy of the Catholic Church in Upper Canada.[70] The Catholic archbishop of Toronto, Armand-François-Marie de Charbonnel, wanted no part of a mixed public school system, which he perceived as dangerous to Catholic children, in agreement with the statement of the Catholic bishops of Baltimore that "teachers and texts in mixed schools endangered the souls of the faithful."[71] The ensuing conflict over the idea of a unified public school system became even more inflamed during the tenure of Archbishop John Joseph Lynch. Lynch refused any compromise with Ryerson's public system, even though his proposals included a strong role for religious supervision over school books with respect to "morals and religion."[72] These were years of hostile demonstrations against "Popery" and all things Catholic, led by the Loyal Orange Lodge. These unseemly outbreaks scorched the heart of the community well into the twentieth century. Rather than unify the community around the core principle of Christian charity, Christianity, through fractious sectarianism, became a source of public unrest and partisan discord in Upper Canada.

CONCLUSION

Despite the formal conviction of the leading political and ecclesiastical authorities at our nation's founding that the Christian religion should be one of its solid pillars, the ground of private and public morality, sectarianism produced protracted rivalry making Christianity more of a dividing than a stabilizing force in the community. In due course, the Christian character of Canada became weaker and weaker; the practice of the faith eventually became excluded from the public life of the country. The process began in Ryerson's public schools, when school boards became secular. This development took place long before Canada began to think of itself as a multicultural nation. Thus, the problem of sectarianism was resolved by importing into Canada's constitutional practice the doctrine of the separation of church and state. As we shall see in the Epilogue, today this doctrine is ever more pervasive. But it is thoroughly foreign to our constitutional heritage, both English and French. Its origins lie in the principles and practices of the French Revolution, the very forces Canada's early political and religious leaders wanted to exclude from the life of the nation. Those forces have especially taken hold in Quebec and have transformed the mores and religious practices of its people more profoundly than anyone would have thought possible in the nineteenth century. From being one of the most thoroughly religious societies in North America, Quebec has become the most radically secularized. While the forces of secularism have also become established in English-speaking Canada, no people has turned its back on its religious heritage as completely as Quebec. It has abandoned its religious faith, just as did France after the French Revolution.[73]

8

The Charter Court and
The Decline of Parliament

Judges must beware of hard constructions, and strained inferences; for
there is no worse torture, than the torture of laws.

Francis Bacon, *"Of Judicature"*

There is no doubt that the Judicial Committee of the Privy Council
radically transformed the constitution of 1867. But other economic
and political forces also contributed to the process. They included
two economic depressions, one lasting from 1873 to 1896, and the
Great Depression of 1929 to 1940. The first convinced many provincial politicians that the new federal government could not deliver the
promised economic prosperity, despite initial successes. Many began
to think that the country was too thinly stretched across a great
expanse of territory, sparsely populated and without adequate political structures. Despite Manitoba's entry into confederation in 1870
and British Columbia's in 1871, there remained a large tract of prairie
and mountain wilderness that appeared vulnerable to the expansion
of the rapacious Americans. The central government was able, for a
time, to support the great effort of nation-building in large measure
because it had the financial resources to undertake ambitious projects
such as a transcontinental railway. This iron rail was touted, to bind
the nation from coast to coast, at the same time laying the foundations for a vibrant national economy. East would provide West with
the finished products of manufacture, while the West would return
the favour with much-needed resources for the East's manufacturing.

These ambitions were dashed by the world-wide depression of
1873. Canada's grand national aspirations came virtually to a halt. The
provinces began to turn in on themselves to salvage what remained
of their traditional economic grounds of self-reliance. When the
depression ended in 1896 the nation itself was weak, but the provinces
were beginning to flex their muscles. Strong political figures began to

emerge who were determined to consolidate provincial self-reliance. Honoré Mercier in Quebec and Oliver Mowat in Ontario began to criticize the federal government's economic efforts. They also claimed that they, as premiers, spoke more authoritatively for their provinces than their federal counterparts. Armed with the strength of the Judicial Committee's decisions in favour of greater provincial legislative authority, Mercier and Mowat began to discuss their mutual problems in formal consultations. The federal government initially dismissed their efforts at cooperation, but it soon became apparent that they could not be ignored. In due course the federal government began to attend these conferences. So was born the Dominion-Provincial Conference, the first major extra-constitutional forum that was to shift the locus of dialogue from within the provincial legislatures to taking place between the leadership of the provinces and the national government. This simple – and on its face inconsequential – consultative device had the result of reducing the role of the federal Parliament and its members while simultaneously increasing the presence and role of the provincial premiers at the national level. In effect, if not in name, the conference became the *de facto* Senate of Canada, where the provinces appeared on an equal footing in a supra-national decision-making body. To this day, the provinces continue to meet in formal sessions and almost always demand a conference with the federal government to resolve matters of common interest, such as health care. The two levels of government now frequently hold dialogues at the ministerial level; for example, the federal minister of justice will meet with his provincial counterparts and thrash out their differences. These meetings most often end with the signing of formal agreements.

The Great War of 1914 commanded the attention of the entire nation and had the temporary effect of allowing it to forget its serious domestic economic problems. The artificial economy it produced and the distraction it provided permitted Canada to indulge for the first time in the sentiments of a nation at war. Canadians and their politicians (for the most part, even in Quebec) set aside their petty regional differences as their young men and women marched proudly off to war. Out of that experience arose the myth that, in the First World War "Canada came of age as a nation." For a time at least, Canadians were united in the conviction that their fighting sons were taking part in a grand world effort to stop the spread of tyranny once and for all. Besides, the war would not last long; the Allies would crush the Kaiser's armies after a few decisive skirmishes and it would be all over. So ran the mantra. But the war lasted four long and bloody years, with an unprecedented loss of life on both sides. After losing thousands of its best young men and watching those who survived return battered and broken in mind and body, Canada settled into a post-war mental and economic depression. It was not long until Canadians awoke to the realization that they had won the war but had lost the peace. The Treaty of Versailles of 1919 imposed an insuperable burden on the German nation and, many would later say, sowed the seeds of World War II.

The Great Depression shook Canada to its foundations. With the collapse of the manufacturing sector came the collapse of the resource sector; the nation's economy was ruptured. In an ironic twist bordering on the comic, the provincial governments turned to Ottawa and demanded that Parliament do something to ease the impact of the depression. Trekkers, unemployed workers who were mostly veterans of World War I from the hard-hit prairie provinces, boarded trains and headed to Ottawa to press their grievance before Parliament.[2] Several of the provinces asked the federal government to assume legislative control over matters that had been jealously protected as being of provincial jurisdiction. To the surprise of most observers, the federal government's efforts to oblige were struck down by the Judicial Committee on the grounds that the circumstances of the Great Depression were not sufficiently serious to warrant federal legislative intrusion into areas of exclusive provincial jurisdiction.[3] The judgment came in spite of the fact that both levels of government in Canada agreed that the widespread unemployment and homelessness were very serious indeed, and beyond the ability of the provincial governments to remedy. The economic terms of the 1867 constitution, specifically designed to provide a single national economy to be supervised by the federal Parliament, were recast by the Law Lords in such a way as to reduce Parliament's ability to act in times of critical economic dislocation.

Once again, war rescued Canada from economic problems. In 1939, Canadians responded to the call and put on uniforms for King and country. As in World War I, Quebec balked at the prospect of conscription into the military. Many Quebec intellectuals railed at the effrontery of being asked to send their sons to fight "England's war." Like the first, this World War lasted much longer than anyone had imagined. With victory finally coming in 1945, an exhausted Canada began to hobble back to the reality of the postwar reconstruction. Aided by the war economy arising from the United Nations "police action" in Korea barely a decade after the termination of hostilities in Europe, Canada regained a measure of economic prosperity. By this time the provinces had become so strong that the federal government had long abandoned the use of disallowance or even the power of reservation. No-one could pretend any more that Canada was governed by a constitution with a strong central Parliament.

Less than a decade after the end of World War II, the notion began to appear in the legal literature that the provinces were equal partners with the federal government. The new postwar federalism staked a claim for those who insisted that Canada was a nation of provinces in which there was to be a new arrangement of federal-provincial partnerships, of co-equal governments. The federal government could defiantly continue to dominate by using and abusing its power to tax and, above all, its power to spend. But the provinces had become too strong and independent to be overridden by it, or to be absorbed into a federal government-sponsored national vision. The new federalism would concentrate on building the provinces as separate economic units. Gone was the founding vision of the country as a single economic common market with central legislative authority.

The oil-rich western province of Alberta presently announced that it would develop its own resource policy and economic strategy independent of Ottawa. Alberta politicians, with the full support of the people, made it clear: Alberta's resources were for the benefit of Albertans. The response to this Alberta First policy was the National Energy Program of the second Trudeau mandate. The Liberal government defied Alberta in imposing the NEP, which robbed the Alberta treasury of millions of dollars in revenue from a natural resource located wholly within the borders of the province. The Trudeau government was determined to make the huge oil revenues redound to the benefit of the country as a whole, not simply to that of the province. The federal unprecedented intrusion into a provincial revenue source did much to solidify the power base of the western provinces, especially Alberta, where the people rallied around the protests of their provincial politicians. This act of the central government laid the foundation for "Western alienation," which festers to the present day and which spawned a powerful political force, the Reform Party of Canada, now known as the Canadian Alliance Party.

When we factor in the interprovincial trade restrictions put in place by the provinces, the result of "province-building" federalism, we see Canada entering the twenty-first century as a nation of squabbling principalities. Canada's federal system has become transformed from being – at least on paper – the most centralized to the most decentralized in the world. The one institution that could, to some considerable degree, have prevented this fragmentation, the Senate, is hampered because it does not represent the provinces in any meaningful sense. That role is played by the Dominion-Provincial Conference, which has, in turn, prompted the rise of "executive federalism," that hybrid extra-constitutional institution operating outside the formal political institutions of the constitution. The direct result of this development is the reduction of the role and importance of the Parliament of

Canada. Canada's constitutional process has been profoundly altered over the years since Confederation, in large measure by judicial fiat combined with the political ambitions of provincial premiers and their legislatures.

Added to these internal forces reshaping the constitutional life of Canada is the powerful presence next door of an aggressive republican nation that began after the Second World War to burst the seams of the old industrial order. Building on the latter-day industrial revolution of Henry Ford and others, the pace of American industrial innovation was breathtaking. Advances in technology fueled the post-war economy and vaulted America's industrial success to the forefront of the world. Telecommunications transformed the world into what Canada's Marshall McLuhan dubbed "the global village," with global markets. Almost overnight, everyone possessed a television set and became a witness to events on the other side of the globe. With the coming of mass television audiences came the American cultural juggernaut. Canadians were swept up in the tidal wave of American political and cultural values. Wave after wave of American television programs and movies made it increasingly difficult for Canadians to remain emotionally attached to the old monarchical symbols and institutions. It comes as no surprise that many, especially in the business community, began to call for closer ties, even political links, with the United States, so thoroughly Americanized had Canadians become midway through the twentieth century.

Along with courtroom dramas on daytime television, American television news vividly brought the civil rights movement into the living rooms of Canadians. In this way, Canadians became witnesses – often emotionally involved witnesses – to the cultural revolution that was taking place in the United States. Central to that dramatic series of events was the American judicial protection of rights. Canadians saw Americans, especially blacks and other underprivileged groups, successfully seeking relief in the courts thanks to a judicially enforceable bill of rights. Many Canadian commentators began to muse publicly about why Canadians did not have an equivalent document to provide them with a similar access to the courts. Eventually, Canadians began to call for the judicial protection of their rights – as if they had never been protected in law before.

The agitation resulted in the passage by Parliament of the Canadian Bill of Rights in August 1960. Hailed by its chief proponent, Prime Minister John Diefenbaker, as an important step towards the judicial protection of Canadians' rights and freedoms, the principal weaknesses of the legislation soon became apparent.

To begin with, the Bill's terms applied only to the federal areas of jurisdiction, thereby excluding the important provincial and municipal jurisdictions. Even its language was weak and unclear; it vaguely instructed the courts to "construe and apply" and "construe or apply" legislation so as not to infringe upon rights and freedoms. The ambiguous wording left Canadian judges uncertain of their role in the protection of the basic rights of Canadian citizens. As a result, the courts shied away from the Bill of Rights.

Above all, as an ordinary statute of Parliament, the Bill was not entrenched in the constitution; hence, it was regarded as too weak to live up to its promises. Canadians were not satisfied with it and increased the pressure for an entrenched bill of rights, one giving judges the power to strike down acts of Parliament and the provincial legislatures that restricted rights and freedoms.

TRUDEAU AND THE RIGHTS OF THE INDIVIDUAL

The call for a bill of rights for Canadians initiated the greatest event in the nation's recent history, one that reshaped the very kernel of its constitution and has altered the lives of the people like no other. Probably no event in the constitutional life of Canada was as dramatic, or caused greater bitterness in Quebec and more confusion in the rest of the country, than the one that occurred in June 1982. And no other single event in Canada's recent history is more directly traceable to the determination of one man to make a profound change in the way Canadians govern themselves. That event was the passage of the Constitution Act, 1982, and the man who was chiefly responsible for it was Prime Minister Pierre Elliott Trudeau.

In Quebec, political and intellectual elites had objected to having a new constitution imposed on the province without its consent. Other Canadians had wondered why Canada needed a new constitution at all. What was wrong with the British North America Act? Trudeau's reply was that Canada needed the right to amend its own constitution without going cap in hand to the Parliament of Great Britain, as it had since 1867. Moreover, Canadians needed a bill of rights by which they could secure the judicial enforcement of their fundamental rights as citizens. The new constitution fulfilled both these needs, since its two main parts were a set of formulas for amending the constitution within Canada, and the Canadian Charter of Rights and Freedoms. The amending formulas have had little direct effect on the lives of Canadians. The Charter, on the other hand, has already had and will continue to have profound effects. So Trudeau had taken on all contenders and the Constitution Act, 1982 was enacted at a solemn ceremony in Ottawa attended by Queen Elizabeth II, who personally gave Royal Assent. The new constitution, which included the British North America Act and the 1960 Bill of Rights as well as the Charter, became the fundamental law of the land. The responsibility of enforcing it was entrusted to the judiciary.

As federal minister of justice, Trudeau had issued a document in 1968 entitled *A Canadian Charter of Human Rights*. The intention behind the publication was, as Prime Minister Lester Pearson noted in the Introduction, "to entrench firmly in our constitution those fundamental rights and liberties which we possess and cherish."[4] Trudeau saw an entrenched bill or charter of rights as a means of uniting a nation comprising regional diversities and linguistic cleavages made more pronounced by the decentralized federal system that resulted from province-building. He had little interest in reforming federal institutions; he rarely spoke about Senate reform, for instance.[5] Trudeau characterized his view of federalism as "a functional, common-sense approach."[6] He took the Canadian federal system as he found it, complete with the federal-provincial conferences for purposes of mediation. His approach to it was conditioned by the mechanisms he found in place, which he attempted to shape as his personality and temperament prompted him. He believed with a passion that "Canada needed stronger bonds to hold the parts together."[7] Trudeau relished the give-and-take of the federal-pronvincial conferences, believing that the tension between the federal government and the premiers was good for the country. But he was uncompromising in his conviction that the "government of Canada is elected to seek the good of the whole country, and sometimes it will have to say no to one region in order to redistribute revenues or equality of opportunity."[8] He welcomed public sparring with the premiers, but boldly resisted those who he thought were reducing Canda to "a confederation of shopping centres."[9] "The National Energy Program, for example," he once explained, "was a conflict between the greater good of a region and the greater Canadian good. The premier of Alberta wasn't fighting for the benefit of any particular ethnic group, but he was fighting for his region against the federal government. That's always the problem of a federal state, because there were always inequalities between the various regions, and it is the job of the central government to think of the whole."[10] The Charter of Rights and Freedoms was fashioned to appeal to the people over the heads of both premiers and prime ministers. In a certain sense, it was meant to give the people the means of calling their political masters to account. "I invariably found that if our cause was right, all we had to do to win was talk over the heads of our adversaries directly to the people of this land."[11] Trudeau was convinced that "the glue that holds it [a country] together, the thing that makes nationhood, is the free will of a sovereign people to live together."[12]

There was resistance to the Charter both before and after it was enacted. One prominent academic asked scornfully: "Do you feel menaced by the prospect of the great Canadian majority, acting through its elected representatives in Ottawa, steam-rolling over your basic rights and liberties in pursuit of its own interests? Are you comforted by the possibility that soon the Canadian Bill of Rights may be 'entrenched' in the Constitution enabling our judiciary to veto these strident majoritarian demands and secure your liberty? If you can ... honestly answer in the affirmative, what you surely need is a psychiatrist, not a bill of rights."[13]

Other critics took a different tack. Charles Taylor, for example, opposed the Charter for the very reason that it propounded the liberal policy of "rights."[14] Basing a society on rights undermined all efforts to establish community, he warned. The Charter was destined to be a source of conflict and division in Canada; rather than bind the nation together, it would create greater divisions. According to Taylor, building a society on rights led to atomism, where individuals claiming "rights" frustrated all efforts to achieve "collective decision-making."[15] As an alternative to the "rights based society," Taylor advocated a "participatory society" where citizens lived together with a "recognized voice in establishing the 'general will'."[16]

Few observers appeared to realize that Pierre Trudeau's determination to bring about a fundamental change in Canada's constitutional monarchy was driven by a moral vision. It is necessary to understand the roots of that vision before we can truly understand the terms of the Charter. No man in Canada's history has come to the office of Prime Minister having pondered the ends of government and the principles of politics as thoroughly as Trudeau. There can be no mistake about it: his legacy was truly foundational; it altered the nation's character and became a permanent part of its life. His brain-child, the Charter, has been enthusiastically embraced by Canadians and has dominated the judicial process since its inception.

Fortunately for students of Canadian politics, Trudeau has left an extensive account of his political philosophy.[17] As a result, we are able to hear him speak directly to many of the fundamental issues underlying the adoption of the Charter. From his autobiographical writings, it is possible to acquire an insight into what motivated him to pursue politics in the first place. Trudeau has told us that his earliest teachers taught him that "authority came from God," but his innate rebelliousness led him to question the very foundations of all authority, both personal and political. He came early to the conclusion that as a "free man" he would bow only to those who could demonstrate superior knowledge. In politics, his distrust of authority brought him to the "study of liberalism and [to] conclude that democracy is the best vehicle because it permits all individuals together to choose the government."[18] He concluded, in a nutshell, that in political matters all "authority comes from the people."[19] Freedom of the individual was for Trudeau an absolute in human life, both in private realm and in politics. It is on this basis that he distinguished between "sin" and "crime". It is the distinct province of the state to regulate crime, but politicians must resist the temptation to conflate the two: "we were legislators, not priests or popes," he would thunder at his cabinet colleagues when discussing the thorny issues of abortion, homosexuality, and capital punishment. His famous statement that "the government has no place in the bedrooms of the nation" won him an avalanche of both approval and scorn.

Trudeau believed that the only restraint governing individual actions was the prohibition against harming another. The focus was on the "rights of the individual." But one was not permitted to force personal views on others or to prevent others from setting their own limits. Trudeau's vision of liberty was constrained only by the responsibility we all owe to one another. His passion for the liberty of citizens was to be extended to those of other cultures, which this cosmopolitan man professed to understand better than most Canadians because he had travelled so widely: to China, Russia, India, Cuba. The pluralism that flowed from his experience with other cultures became the foundations of Canadian multiculturalism. Under the umbrella of tolerance, all cultures became equally valid and could claim the protection of the Charter. Indeed, the Charter put in place "the culture of equality." It granted to everyone and every group an enforceable claim or right to equal access and to equal benefit under the law.

Politically Trudeau understood himself to be a liberal, as one who believed that the "first role of government is to create the conditions for, and to remove obstacles to, individual and collective freedoms."[20] The role of government was therefore to use its power by passing laws that would further this individual and collective liberty. For this reason, Trudeau believed that the "absolute liberal state" has been superceded by the "interventionist state which intervenes to make sure that the strong and the powerful don't abuse their strength and their power in order to take freedoms away from the little man."[21] This conviction explains Trudeau's defiant determination not to let one province, Alberta, hold the country to ransom during the energy crisis of the 1970s. His National Energy Policy was his way of championing the "collective liberty" of the nation as a whole over the "individual liberty" of one province's petroleum industry. In precise terms not to be misunderstood, Trudeau set himself and the governments he led against the abuse of majority power, whether commercial or political. "We believe," he once wrote, "that when majorities oppress minorities or the rich oppress the poor or the strong oppress the weak, 'no government' is bad government, because the state should be there to protect the weak against the strong."[22] In an effort to distance his brand of liberalism from libertarianism, he insisted that "some problems are better resolved by the state than by Adam Smith's invisible hand."[23] Trudeau spoke constantly of "the powerful," meaning principally those with corporate power, as well as of the need for governments to be ever-vigilant to make sure that "the powerful" did not encroach upon the liberty of individuals or the community. This all-consuming preoccupation set Trudeau in diametric opposition to his successor, Brian Mulroney, who courted and flattered corporate power in both public and private life. Following Montesquieu, Trudeau saw within civil society itself a tension, if not actual hostility, between government, the champion of individual and collective liberty, and corporate interests. This antagonism necessitated, in his mind, laws that would protect the people from the ambitions of the greedy. But he was not blind to the need to prevent governments themselves from oppressing individual and collective liberties; hence his passion for a judicially enforceable bill of rights.

Authority, or more precisely, the abuse of authority, in interfering with the private lives of citizens was the central preoccupation of this intellectual. "My approach was rooted in the theory of counterweights. At every moment in time, I believe that each conscious servant of the public good must ask himself or herself: In what direction should I be weighing in at this time? Should I be trying to weaken authority or should I be trying to strengthen it? For in a society, if everybody begins to follow a certain fashion, then that fashion becomes a tyranny. Those who don't follow it are looked down upon as being out of fashion and they lose their individuality. And when everybody starts to think or to do the same thing, we all lose our freedom."[24] This line of reasoning impressed a vast audience, especially prominent media figures such as Charles Lynch of the *Ottawa Citizen*, who trumpeted Trudeau's cause as profound and suited to the 1970s and 80s. At long last, in the minds of Trudeau's admirers, Canada had found its Philosopher King, a man who could cite the writings of ancient and modern philosophers while doing backflips off the diving board. It is certain that in 1968 Trudeau had swept the national imagination and became Canada's very own home-grown harbinger of popular culture's promise of a greater moral and political freedom. He was universally acclaimed by the media as "refreshing" when portrayed alongside his political rival, the solid but stodgy leader of the Progressive Conservative Party, Robert Stanfield. Later, on the international scene, Canadians contrasted him favourably with the bumbling Reagans and rigid Thatchers among whom he strode with a cavalier swagger.

In truth, Pierre Trudeau was Canada's most important prime minister and prime mover of national events since John A. Macdonald. For it was he who provided the theoretical basis for the new Canada, the new outward-looking Canada, the Canada that was urged under his direction to engage the world at large. Trudeau built upon the internationalism of his predecessor, Lester Pearson, Canada's most universally respected international public servant, a Noble Peace Prize winner, and the favourite son of the international diplomatic corps. Pearson had committed Canada to the international cause of world peace through the use of the Canadian military as peacekeepers. Pearson's internationalism, however, was institutional, involving as it did Canada's commitment to participate in the international organizations such as NATO and the United Nations. Trudeau's internationalism, on the other hand, was cultural; he cared less for international organizations and more for the diversity of international cultures. Trudeau showed his disdain for political and military alliances by reducing Canada's presence in NATO, to the consternation of the United States. He earned further scorn from the American Congress through his flirtations with Cuba and Fidel Castro, in defiance of the Organization of American States.

Trudeau exploded onto the Canadian scene as the only one capable of leading Canada on the international stage. It is ironic that in his cosmopolitanism he laid the foundations for the man he most disdained in politics, his polar opposite and successor, Brian Mulroney. The seeds of Mulroney's corporate continentalism were sown in the soil provided by Trudeau's openness to the world. However, where Mulroney saw the political narrowly in terms of business and the interplay of global economic forces, Trudeau saw people: rich and poor, young and old, sick and healthy, and, above all, culturally diverse. Pearson may well have opened the windows, but it was Pierre Trudeau who welcomed in the scented breezes of foreign cultures. If Canadians would not go out to the world, the world – with all its colourful customs and enchanting languages – would be brought to Canadians. Canada would become multicultural.

TRUDEAU AND REPUBLICANISM

Trudeau understood the role of government as being "to step in as a counterweight in order to regulate the economy by increasing taxes on the wealthy or giving subsidies to the poor or strengthening the power of the consumer."[25] Where Mulroney marvelled at the sight of corporate power, Trudeau saw its international concentration as a threat to the power of national governments to assist their peoples in important economic and social ways. For Mulroney, the benefits of the unregulated economy, achieved through formal free trade agreements that would create new business and new jobs, would "trickle down" to the people in the long run. For Trudeau, the benefits of "trickle down" came too late, governments had responsibilities to manage the economy at critical points in the ups and downs to make sure that the people as a whole did not suffer. In these leftist views he showed himself the attentive student of Harold Laski. They led him to impose wage and price controls, to the consternation of almost the entire field of business and economics in Canada. Trudeau firmly believed that governments could and should command the economic levers – hence controls. The "rough justice" that followed, he claimed, "was nothing like the gross injustices that would have been caused in the absence of controls, by an intolerable rate of inflation."[26]

Trudeau's resolute refusal to concede to what he considered unreasonable demands from the provincial premiers led many to view him as a centralist, as one who would take power from the provinces and concentrate it in Ottawa. But Trudeau was not a centralist, though John A. Macdonald most certainly had been. Macdonald had wanted to decrease the power of the provinces and thereby increase the power of Parliament; Trudeau believed that the provincial premiers should fight for their respective provinces. But, by the same token, he believed that the prime minister of Canada should fight just as hard for the things affecting the people of Canada as a whole. "I did object," he wrote at one point, "when a premier tried to get more power for his province in order to help a particular ethnic group."[27] His objections on these grounds included Quebec, a view of Quebec nationalism that earned him the reputation of being "out of touch" with that province.

Trudeau was also quintessentially a republican in his conviction that "the people" and "equality" are enduring values to which the institutions of government must offer obeisance. The nation-state must provide the institutional reinforcements sought by the aspiring bourgeois. It is for this reason that he could so easily become a member of the Liberal Party of Canada. Yet Trudeau himself, like Rousseau's *artiste*, was above the need for those same reinforcements. The bourgeois requires a certain kind of simplistic morality that keeps him both moral and civil. Rousseau's *artiste*, on the other hand, chafes at the restraints placed on personal action by bourgeois morality. This is the source of his dictum that both astonished and titillated Canadians: "The government has no place in the bedrooms of the nation." In uttering it Trudeau demonstrated how far distant he was from de Tocqueville, who had addressed the French Chamber of Deputies in 1848 to denounce just such a proposition. De Tocqueville condemned the idea that there were two moralities, public and private. He vigorously asserted that private mores affected public life, a matter "to cause disquiet and alarm to good citizens." He asked his political colleagues: "Do you know what is the general, effective, deep cause which makes private mores turn corrupt? It is the change in public mores. It is because morality does not prevail in the main acts of life, that it does not find its way down into the least important ones."[28] He feared that the consequences of this pernicious distinction would be "moral squalor and ruin."

Trudeau's republicanism is often thought to have been formed by his association with Harold Laski, the leading socialist guru at the London School of Economics and Political Science during Trudeau's tenure there. Laski, one of England's more prominent but forgettable socialist intellectuals of the 1940s and 50s, clearly had an influence on Trudeau. However, Trudeau's essays in *Cité Libre* and elsewhere reveal the even greater influence of John Stuart Mill; his writings are shot through with the doctrines enunciated in *On Liberty*. To this extent he was indeed a leftist. But Trudeau's political philosophy was a hybrid populism tinged with a distinct aura of historical paternalism found in Mill. There can be no denying that Trudeau to the end remained Canada's most intellectual prime minister, however much his political philosophy was a hodgepodge of incompatible sources. His most enduring republican legacy to the nation is the Charter, which has come to dominate the lives of Canadians in ways they might not have chosen. Indeed, it has become the new point of national coalescence, embraced by Canadians with enthusiasm: we are now like Americans because we, too, have a judicially enforceable bill of rights.

THE CHARTER OF RIGHTS AND FREEDOMS

The Constitution Act, 1982 was the instrument that, with one stroke, severed Canadians from their ancestral monarchical foundations. With the Charter, Canada began a new life as a nation, a republican nation. The Charter is based upon republican principles. It is the closest Canadians have ever come to a document that affirms the rights of the people. As everyone knows, the American constitution begins with the words, "We the people ..." The Constitution Act, 1982 explicitly acknowledges that "Canada is founded upon principles that recognize the supremacy of God and the rule of law." It does not say that the rights and freedoms enunciated in the Charter are grounded either in God or in nature, unlike the American Declaration of Independence, which formally rooted the basic liberties in "the laws of nature" and "nature's God." The framers of the Charter avoided the issue after lengthy discussion; they could not come to an agreement over the idea that the rights and freedoms enunciated in it owe their force to God or to nature. They also sidestepped Canada's Christian heritage under the conviction that to affirm it would offend against the multicultural nature of the nation in the twentieth century. The Charter simply declares: "Whereas Canada is founded upon principles that recognize the supremacy of God and the rule of law ..." It is obvious that if it had been written in the 1860s there would have been no reluctance to state that Canada was founded on "Christian principles" or "the rule of law informed by Christian principles." The document that emerged under the aegis of Pierre Trudeau makes no pretence of identifying Canada's Christian foundations as the bedrock upon which the rights and freedoms of Canadians rest secure. In so ignoring them, it would appear to deny those foundational principles. This departure from the old order did not displease the principal architect of the Charter, for it reflected his own personal universalism, which sought to identify the core similarities in all world religions without giving place of preference to any one of them.

Upon close inspection it becomes clear that the Charter is not a neutral document; that is, it is not founded on principles that are indifferent as to specific ends. It is founded on the principles provided by modern political thought, on post-Enlightenment republicanism which aims to "liberate" the autonomous individual from the hegemony of a higher law imposed either from below by nature or from above by God. The central, overriding principle that pervades every aspect of the Charter is the modern liberal promise of *equality*: all people – man and woman, child and adult – are *equal*. In what important respects people are equal is to be determined by the courts since the enactment of the Charter. The tradition prior to the Charter taught that it was the special province of the legislature to pass laws treating "equal people equally and unequal people, unequally." That meant that some people would not be treated in the same way as some other people. The pre-modern conception of equality rested on twin pillars. The first was the Judaic and Christian pillar of revelation, which taught that all men – male and female – were equal in the sight of God. The second pillar was the Platonic-Aristotelian tradition, which taught that "equal should be treated equally," that "inequality is the basis of justice."[29] The pre-Enlightenment philosophers acknowledged the natural inequality among people. Justice under the legacy of the teaching of Socratic natural right called for the natural inequality that prevails among people to be recognized by the laws of the state; under this principle, some people deserved greater honour than others. The equality provisions of the Charter adopted the post-Enlightenment doctrine that all people are equal *vis-à-vis* one another. This conception is founded in the teachings of Thomas Hobbes, who claimed in *Leviathan* that by nature all men are equal insofar as all men have the means to kill one another. In Hobbes's teaching, the state becomes the indispensable institution by which human beings give up the original condition of the "state of nature" where all men are "wolves to one another" for the security to live in peace with one another. Ever since the Enlightenment severed the ties with the religious grounds of equality the West has been struggling to find a substitute, one that would give strength as well as authority to the equal treatment of fellow citizens.

The Canadian Charter of Rights and Freedoms states: "Every individual is equal before and under the law and has the right to the equal protection and equal benefit of the law without discrimination." The concept of equality before the law and equal protection are inherited from the English common law tradition. The third element, "equal benefit of the law," is an innovation based in nineteenth-century egalitarianism. It has emerged as the most troublesome provision of the entire Charter, for not only does it require judges to assess a law in terms of its inherent justice, it also obliges them to address whether every "individual" is receiving "equal benefit" from a given law or policy. The obvious difficulty is that it is almost always impossible to make sure that people *are* receiving "equal benefit." More to the point, it is fundamentally impossible to measure or judge issues in terms of their benefits, to say nothing of their equality. How, for example, could the courts ever rule that all Canadian children must have "equal benefit" from education? Circumstances of economy and geography vary drastically throughout the country; so too do educational facilities. Inasmuch as these things vary they will be unequal – as will their benefits.

The Charter professes to nod in the direction of legislative supremacy with this statement: "The Canadian Charter of Rights and Freedoms guarantees the rights and freedoms set out in it subject only to such reasonable limits prescribed by law as can be demonstrably justified in a free and democratic society." While this provision would appear to reaffirm the traditional prerogatives of the legislatures in Canada, section 24 makes it clear that, with the adoption of the Charter, the Canadian judiciary has assumed a supervisory role unprecedented in the nation's history. "Anyone whose rights or freedoms, as guaranteed by this Charter, have been infringed or denied may apply to a court of competent jurisdiction to obtain such remedy as the court considers appropriate and just in the circumstances." It is evident that the Charter, which encompasses the activity of both Parliament and the provincial legislatures and their bureaucracies, gives judges great power in striking down any legislation or government directive that, in their view, offends its terms. Even the introductory provision purporting to uphold the supremacy of the legislatures is itself subject to judicial determination. It is for judges to say what a "reasonable limit" is and whether it "can be demonstrably justified." Parliament can declare that such-and-such piece of legislation is reasonable and justified and hence will prevail over a specific right or freedom listed in the Charter. The justices of the Supreme Court of Canada can – and have – defeated the efforts of the legislatures to circumvent the Charter by such means, for it is their unique responsibility to enforce its terms. Small wonder that some Canadians fear the Charter has introduced "judicial supremacy" into Canada.

THE NOTWITHSTANDING CLAUSE

Contrary to what the Charter appears to say, Canadian legislatures are not able to bypass its or the jurisdiction of the courts by means of section 33, which states: "Parliament or the legislature of a province may expressly declare in an Act of Parliament or of the legislature, as the case may be, that the Act or a provision thereof shall operate notwithstanding a provision included in section 2 [Fundamental Freedoms] or sections 7 to 15 [Legal and Equality Rights] of this Charter." Such a declaration lapses after five years but may be reintroduced for additional five-year periods. On its face, this section would appear to be easily invoked. In fact, it is rarely used, for reasons that the government of Alberta discovered when it announced its intention in 1998 to apply the "notwithstanding" clause to circumvent the Supreme Court's ruling on protection against discrimination based on sexual orientation. The public reaction against the use of the clause was too great.

Every term of the Charter, including the notwithstanding clause itself, is subject to definition by the courts, however clear it may appear to the average person. Thus, it is up to the courts to decide whether the legislatures or Parliament have validly invoked the notwithstanding clause. So too with highly controversial moral matters: the judges of the Supreme Court of Canada have already shown that they are determined to read the Charter provision relating to "security of the person" as implying a right to abortion and hence as sufficient to negate the explicit prohibitions of abortion in the Criminal Code. To the extent that the Charter's terms cover a very wide range of issues – "freedom conscience and religion," "freedom of thought, belief, opinion and expression," the right to be "tried within a reasonable time," the "right to life, liberty and security of the person" – the broad mandate imposed on the courts has made judges dominant players in the lives of all Canadians. Since the adoption of the Charter, scarcely a day goes by without a judicial judgment making front page news. At the time of writing, a British Columbia court's striking down the Criminal Code provisions relating to the possession of child pornography has caused a flurry of critical reaction throughout the country. The court ruled that the Criminal Code provisions relating to the simple possession of pornography contravened the terms of the Charter guaranteeing the freedom of expression. The case in currently before the Supreme Court of Canada.

The Charter has therefore significantly altered the way Canadians govern themselves; judges have become more important than elected representatives, federal and provincial.[30] And while its explicit directives apply to governments, the way in which the courts have begun to interpret the Charter demonstrates that it has become a code of conduct regulating the private lives of individual Canadian citizens. The Charter has begun to replace human rights statutes, the laws whose object is to reduce the friction between individuals and groups in the community resulting from human prejudices. Under a judicially enforced code of conduct, the courts can order compliance under penalty of sanction. Where human rights codes attempted to soften the relations between people of different cultural or religious backgrounds through persuasion and education, the relevant Charter provision substitutes the power of the police to compel compliance.

As recently as 1971, the leading Oxford constitutional authority Geoffrey Marshall could write of "the three branches of government under the English constitutional system in which the legislature is held to be a supreme or sovereign organ to which the executive and judicial branches are subordinate, and which is not (as matters stand) subject to any substantive limitations on the ambit of its powers; the freedom and equality of citizens being maintained by legislative restraint and by the impact of political and constitutional conventions."[31] It is instructive to note that when the British government incorporated the European Convention on Human Rights in a new Bill of Rights, the British courts were not given the power to strike down legislation allegedly contravening the Convention on Human Rights. Rather, they have been instructed to draw it to the attention of Parliament, which will take whatever corrective action it deems appropriate in the circumstances.[32] The British Parliament has clearly retained its supremacy.

The entrenchment of the Charter in the written constitution of Canada has seriously circumscribed the sovereignty of Parliament in Canada. To all intents and purposes, Parliament and the provincial legislatures are restrained in their work by a "new yardstick of reconciliation between the individual and the community and their respective rights, a dimension which, like the balance of the Constitution remains to be interpreted and applied by the Court."[33] All acts of legislative bodies in Canada that fail to meet the approval of the highest judicial authority, the Supreme Court, will be nullified as unconstitutional.

The Charter has begun to sink deep roots into the consciousness of Canadians. Every poll on the acceptance of the Charter indicates that Canadians have largely embraced the expanded role of judges. It is almost certain that no politician could be elected anywhere in Canada today on a platform to repeal the Charter, so profoundly has it become a mark of being a Canadian. For many decades Canadians were told by some politicians, such as John Diefenbaker, that their rights and freedoms were not secure, that an instrument was required that would grant them judicially enforceable rights, that without a bill of rights they were not truly a self-governing people. The Charter has, in fact, served to bind Canadians together at a supra-legislative level of consciousness. In doing so it has judicialized Canada's politics and politicized its judiciary.[34] It has, in essence, changed the regime from a constitutional monarchy with parliamentary supremacy into a judicial republic trapped in the institutions of monarchy and parliamentary supremacy. Small wonder that Canadians have become indifferent to the role of the monarchy under the constitution.

THE NEW ROLE OF JUDGES

From Canada's earliest moments with the Charter, its judges have given every indication that they were prepared to meet the challenge thrust upon them. For example, in an apparent effort to win the support of the community at large, the justices of the Supreme Court of Canada have demonstrated an unusual willingness to speak off the bench about their new role. In former times, judges were rarely seen and heard only through their written reasons for judgment. Since the advent of the Charter they have been more than willing to talk about their new mandate and their new important. Chief Justice Beverley McLachlin said in a 1989 address to law students that "[t]he Charter

... has changed the life of judges dramatically." She went on to state that "the Court will take an expansive approach to defining the rights and freedoms guaranteed by the Charter and will not hesitate to tackle substantive issues even where limiting their role to procedural concerns is a viable alternative."[35] "An expansive approach" is a clear departure from the traditional one, in which judges tended to rest their judgments on the narrowest possible legal grounds.

McLachlin's views came as no surprise, since they echoed those of the late Chief Justice Brian Dickson. In a majority judgment in one of the earliest Charther cases, *R. v. Big M Drug Mart*, Dickson wrote that "it is certain that the Canadian Charter of Rights and Freedoms does not simply 'recognize and declare' existing rights as they were circumscribed by legislation current at the time of the Charter's entrenchment. The language of the Charter is imperative. It avoids any reference to existing or continuing rights ... [T]he *Charter* is intended to set a standard upon which present as well as future legislation is to be tested."[36] Dickson left no doubt that, in his view, Supreme Court justices were obliged to go beyond the mere intention of the legislature. He laid it down that the Charter would be interpreted with a view to the purpose and the effect of an impugned statue: "Either an unconstitutional purpose or an unconstitutional effect can invalidate legislation."[37] Justice Bertha Wilson elaborated on this theme in the same case: "In my view, the constitutional entrenchment of civil liberties in the Canadian Charter of Rights and Freedoms necessarily changes the analytical approache the courts must adopt in such cases ... While it remains perfectly valid to evaluate the purpose underlying a particular enactment in order to determine whether the legislature has acted within its constitutional authority in division of powers terms, the Charter demands evaluation of the impingement of even *intra vires* legislation on the fundamental rights and freedoms of the individual."[38]

Further to this, Marc Gold has written, " The Charter enthusiast does not see the meaning of the Charter as limited by what the drafters may have intended."[39] Gold cited Wilson, one of the most "enthusiastic" Charter advocates, as stating explicitly that it was appropriate for judges to "go beyond the legislative text"; in the *Big M Drug Mart* case it was therefore proper for the Supreme Court to acknowledge the "socio-cultural content" of the right in dispute and to go beyond "mere due process."[40]

While the *Big M Drug Mart* case was important for setting out the new guidelines delineated by Dickson and Wilson for the adjudication of disputes under the Charter, it was also disturbing. In it, the Supreme Court ruled that the federal Lord's Day Act violated the drug company's religious freedom by requiring its store to remain closed on Sunday. It reached this conclusion despite the open admission that the legal fiction (i.e., the corporation) "cannot be said to have a conscience or hold a religious belief."[41] In the Supreme Court's eyes, the central defect of the Lord's Day Act was that it mandated the observance of a holiday on a day that is universally acknowledged to be a Christian day of rest, and that doing so was tantamount to requiring the drug company to perform a Christian religious act. In substance, the Supreme Court was saying that the Charter reduces the traditional role played in Canada by the Christian religion, though there is no doubt that the judgment in Big M Drug Mart would also prevent Parliament from mandating a Hindu, Muslim, or Jewish religious day of rest. The Supreme Court thus introduced the thin edge of the wedge leading to the separation of church and state, a concept completely at odds with the aspirations of Canada's founders. Nothing could be more foreign to Canada's constitutional history.

The Chretien government, for example, reinforced the secularization of public commemorative events by forbidding Christian clergy from mentioning the name of Jesus in their prayers at the Swissair 111 memorial service held at Indian Harbour, Nova Scotia in October 1998 – despite the fact that most of the victims were Christians. Likewise, the public service held in Ottawa in November 2001 to honour the victims of the attack on the World Trade Center in New York was pointedly devoid of any religious character. Many Canadians were puzzled by the Ottawa event, especially when contrasting it with the memorial service held in September 2001 at the National Cathedral in Washington or the moving religious service held the same month at Westminster Abbey in London.

The new willingness of Supreme Court judges to explain off the bench exactly how they understood their role under the Charter has aroused public concern over the "expansive" or "activist" nature of that role. Justice Dickson provided such explanations on several occasions. In the John Valentine Clyne address at the University of British Columbia in 1992, Dickson stated emphatically that "the Charter has altered our constitutional landscape." He blamed the media for creating the impression that "there has been a radicalization of our courts over the last decade."[42] But he did not deny that the Charter had drawn the courts into "new 'rights' oriented issues." However, he protested, this development was not, in fact, a radical new direction. The Charter itself was part of a long process from the uncertain times of the "implied bill of rights" through the 1960 Bill of Rights to the present day. Dickson was quick to note, however, that "the failure of the Canadian Bill of Rights to act as a real obstacle to the will of the legislature can be traced back to the deference our courts have long shown to legislatures."[43] This statement bore several revealing implications. First – apart from the aside that the Bill of Rights had been a "failure" – it suggested that an act of Parliament could be viewed by the courts as a "real obstacle" to the will of the democratically elected legislature. The further implication was that the courts could somehow know what the true will of the legislature was, better than the legislative body itself. Moreover, under Canada's inherited British parliamentary system, deference is properly accorded to the wishes of the legislature. Dickson implies that this deference had to be set aside with the new mandate imposed by the Charter. Small wonder that, in later Charter cases, other members of the Supreme Court, such as Justice McLachlin, could make statements such as this: "The Charter means that judges are called upon to answer questions they never dreamed they would have to face, such as the right to abortion, the right to work after sixty-five and the right to practise one's profession as one wishes ... Rules of construction [such as] *stare decisis* and the doctrine of precedent are of limited value when one is not only confronted by the new issues, but required to make fundamental value choices in deciding them."[44] As far as "value choices" were concerned, Justice McLachlin noted that "the broad, general language of the Charter permits a variety of interpretations and leaves judges no choice but to infuse their own values in applying the provisions to the circumstances of the particular case."[45] Thus, for McLachlin the Charter was the broad avenue through which judges could and indeed had to "infuse their own values" into the public life of Canada. Where legislators would seek to discover the values of the community and enact laws consistent with those values, Justice McLachlin would have us believe that her private values must guide the development of important public policies. Such a position is tantamount to a declaration of judicial supremacy.

The Charter, in McLachlin's understanding, clearly propels judges into an arena formerly reserved to legislators. Her understanding of the judicial function is far removed from that of the traditional British judge, who see it as his or her duty to settle disputes between parties, not to expand the realm of values. But McLachlin evidently believed that "the Charter, by conferring on the *courts supremacy over Parliament*, limited only by the override provisions of s.33 has heightened the importance of judicial decisions and of the judiciary as an institution."[46]

Few Canadian judges have been as vocal both on and off the bench about the altered role of the Supreme Court as Justice Claire L'Heureux-Dube. Her interests have extended beyond meeting the new challenges posed by the Charter; she has left no doubt that, as a female judge, she should actively espouse the feminist cause. Speaking on the topic "Will Women Judges Make a Difference?" to a group of feminists in 1997, she claimed that there was a clear "gender bias in the law" and that it was a part of her "responsibilities as a woman to uproot those biases."[47] But she went even further. The feminist "concern must not stop at forming a representative bench. Rather, we must extend our efforts to transform the approach to judging taken by all the members of the judiciary."[48] Drawing on the writings and research of some of the most prominent Canadian and American feminists, L'Heureux-Dube concluded that women judges would "bring an approach to ethical choices which focuses on considerations formerly lacking in the law, such as the context of a particular dilemma or the importance of obligations and relationships."[49] Horeover, this approach should be reflected in the judgments of female members of the bench: "Thus, I recognize that women's diverse experiences have been sadly lacking in many areas of the law and I have continually emphasized the necessity of incorporating them in our judicial decisions."[50] Finally, L'Heureux-Dube emphasized that she was part of a larger feminist cause: "I believe it crucial to have more women in positions of power, whether they be judges, legislators, politicians or other important decision makers. Women make up half of the population and have a right to be included and respected in the all-important decisions which affect their lives."[51]

There can be no doubting that the Charter has made it much easier for judges such as McLachlin and L'Heureux-Dube to further the cause of women. While it is one thing for women judges to sensitize male members of the bar and bench on matters such as rape and the abuse of women, it is clearly another thing for them to be cause-pleaders on the bench. This development is troubling, because the feminist "legal realism" is open to serious theoretical challenge. Justice Bertha Wilson approvingly cited "Carol Gilligan who has described women's sense of morality as differing from men's. According to this theory, women tend to focus more on relationships, connection, and context in deciding what is just and fair. Through their unique approach to decision making, it is hoped that women judges will bring these elements into our general understanding of the law."[52] L'Heureux-Dube, for her part, made reference to the writings of Mari Matsuda, who has encouraged women judges to pursue a jurisprudence of "multiple consciousness." "The multiple consciousness I urge lawyers to attain," Matsuda explained, "is not a random ability to see all points of view, but a deliberate choice to see the world from the standpoint of the oppressed. That world is accessible to all of us. We should know it in its concrete particulars."[42] Such a doctrinaire approach to judging is replete with problems that cannot simply be ingnored. One thing is certain, this form of judicial advocacy changes both the nature of judging and the role of judges. Citizens in a democratic society ought to be aware of this important and troubling development.

Another disturbing result of the Charter is a distinct rise in vested interest litigation. Those who spearhead social causes, such as feminist and gay and lesbian groups, have found it more convenient and effective to go to court with a Charter challenge than to approache the legislatures or Parliament. Feminists, for example, have been able to mount publicly-funded court challenges under the Courts Challenge Program, which was originally designed to assist minority language groups in seeking redress through the courts. Through a quiet bureaucratic extension of the original mandate whose resulte has been the inclusion of feminist groups, including pro-abortion activists, feminist have been relatively successful in furthering their social objectives by way of the courts. They no longer attempt to influence the course of legislation as it is being formed in the legislative process.[54]

CONCLUSION

What has been lost in the quiet shift from Parliament making the laws to judges making the laws: Parliamentary politics as envisioned by the framers of Canada's constitution implied prudential or non-absolutist government. The prudential character of governing has been lost to us today, primarily as a result of the proliferation of claims on government stemming from the assertion of rights or entitlements. This new politics bypasses the legislature of elected representatives and goes directly to the courts, where judges armed with the Charter rule absolutely. There is a direct and proportionate relationship between rights-based government and prudential government whereby the latter is diminished in direct proportion to the dominance of rights-based politics. Prudential government gives due regard to circumstances. The restraints placed on a given proposed course of action are determined by the capacity of the community to absorb a specific – even just – objective or policy. Rights-based government implies – indeed, requires – an active judicial power, one demanding that the social circumstances give way *immediately* to the desired legal objective. We have not heeded Montesquieu's warning that "[i]t is very bad policy to change by law what ought to be changed by custom."[55] The framers of the constitution knew that the art of governing people is imperfect, prudential. The judicializing of politics renders political solutions definite and unbending.[56]

Clinging to the Wreckage

How can Canada preserve fragments of a way of life and of understanding whose public relevance is doubtful to our ruling elites?

Peter Emberley on George Grant's *Lament for a Nation*[1]

Alexis de Tocqueville, writing early in the nineteenth century, observed that democratic peoples tended to trade away their liberty or freedom for equality. As we have seen, the underlying principle of the Constitution Act, 1982, dominated by the Charter, is the modern conception of equality, which is far more aggressive than the older version. The new one is fired by the principle of entitlement, which is by its very nature insatiably aggressive inasmuch as it is based in the willful transformation of wants into needs. For while needs are by nature limited, wants are by definition infinite.[2] The modern principle of equality literally drives those seeking their rights or entitlements into the streets – a direct legacy of its roots in the French Revolution. But the coming of judicially enforceable charters or bills of rights drives them, in turn, from the streets into the courts. In an important respect, the Charter is unique among bills of rights section 24 formally invites citizens to have recourse to the courts. The section gives the courts the authority to impose financial costs or other remedies on governments and the agencies of government where warranted, in the opinion of the court. It would have been more consistent with Canada's parliamentary monarchy to refer an aggrieved party to the offending legislative body or agency for appropriate relief, as the new British bill of rights does.[3] Giving judges such authority takes away from the legislative process what properly belongs to it, and grants judges too much power.

It is precisely this shift from legislative to judicial relief that has characterized modern republican governments, as developments in the United States have shown.[4] Canada is following in the same direction, so much so that it is becoming ineffectual to pronounce against the trend. The late Eugene Forsey dedicated his entire public and academic career to restoring respect for the monarchical character of the Canadian regime. He saw more clearly than many that nations do not alter the core of their constitutional lives by accident but by conscious design, and not always for the better. Contrary to what many appear to believe, the times do not change anything; people change the times. Trudeau, for example, made an enormous change in Canada's constitutional life by persuading others to follow him in crafting and adopting the Charter of Rights and Freedoms.

The Fathers of Confederation consciously established a certain kind of constitutional order, which has undergone profound transformation over the course of more than 135 years as a result of the overt acts of influential men. This transformation, from constitutional monarchy to republican democracy, has been the result of both internal and external factors, as we have seen. It leaves Canadians with the remnants of a system that cannot support the new republican regime. As a result, Canada presents itself to the world today as a nation deeply contradictory at its core. The outward pomp and circumstances of monarchy conceal from the casual observer the deep commitment to republicanism. The country has maintained the external trappings of monarchical government, with the Crown visible in the office of the governor general. To become law, all acts of Parliament must be duly passed by Parliament after three readings, be confirmed by a majority vote of the Senate, and receive royal assent, i.e., the Queen's signature. The monarch, not the governor general, is the head of state in Canada. The governor general must accept the advice of the cabinet but theoretically retains a large reserve of prerogative power: for instance, to refuse to grant a dissolution of Parliament and to drop the writs for a new election. The last time a governor general exercised that prerogative was in 1926, when Lord Byng refused to grant Prime Minister William Lyon Mackenzie King a dissolution and a new election. That refusal became the central issue in the election that same year. King emerged the victor; the Canadian people did not approve of the governor general's use of his prerogative power, which has never been used since.

In addition to the remnants of monarchical institutions, Canada's political process has retained parliamentary responsible government, modelled after the British Parliament. Ministers of the Crown must sit in either the Senate or the House of Commons and must be held formally accountable to the people by being subject to the questioning of Her Majesty's Loyal Opposition. The system presently in place is, in appearance, the same as the one put in place in 1867. But it functions in a "irresponsible" way. Responsible government, so strenuously fought for by Joseph Howe and the Baldwins, called for the ministers of the Crown to be members of Parliament and for the ministry to be answerable to the elected representatives of the people. In theory, Canada's Parliament presently operates "responsibly," as it was intended. But an element of "irresponsibility" has crept into the day-to-day operation of government. The power accumulated by the prime minister's office has worked to rob parliamentary oppositions of their right to questioning; ministers frequently refuse to answer the questions of opposition members and routinely foil attempts to amend government-sponsored legislation. Narrow political partisanship has come to characterize all political parties in Canada. In the United States Congress, Democrats frequently support Republicans and *vice versa*. In Canada this virtually never happens, so strong and uncompromising is the partisanship. James Madison worried so much about the emergence of narrow political partisanship that he saw it as one of the major duties of government to "break and control the violence of faction."[5] Edmund Burke, on the other hand, viewed "party divisions, whether on the whole operating for good or evil, are things inseparable from free government."[6] But Burke was not blind to the abuse of political partisanship and would most assuredly disapprove of its abuse. He understood that political parties could work for the "good or evil" of "free government." Burke, unlike Madison, saw factions or partisan political parties as part of the human condition, but he also believed that it had to be watched carefully and be tamed in the interests of free government. Canada's partisan politics is clearly in need of Burke's advice.

The republican spirit that pervades the vestigial monarchical institutions in Canada surfaces frequently and in many forms. The Charter is the principal source of this spirit. Calls for the reform of Parliament are prompted today by the Charter's equality provisions, not by an appeal to responsible government. The electoral system of first-past-the-post currently practised in Canada has been called into question on the grounds that the parliamentary results distort the actual vote of the electorate. It is conceivable that a party could win a solid majority of seats in the House of Commons with no more than forty per cent of the total vote. Indeed, most seats are not won by a clear majority of votes in the constituencies. In a multi-party system, as in Canada, the party candidate who takes a plurality of the votes wins the seat. As a result, most majority Parliaments do not reflect the majority preference of those who cast a ballot. In recent years, following general elections, Canadians have begun to hear calls for "proportional representation," in which the seats in the House of Commons would be apportioned on the basis of the total popular vote garnered by each political party nationwide, and for "more democracy," which is little more than a demand for the greater republicanization of the regime.[7]

These cries were not heard in the period when Canada's leading statesmen were demanding responsible government.

The spirit of republicanism is like an ocean swell, broad and powerful and lifting everything in its wake. Unleashed by the French Revolution, that spirit is evident in the massive and disruptive protest movements that have come to haunt the efforts of national leaders to enter into formal global economic alliances. People protesting political and economic covenants arrived at behind closed doors take to the streets today, much as they did in France in 1789 and 1848. However much people may have been inspired initially by the American Revolution, it was the French Revolution that provided the incendiary rhetoric and disruptive tactics used by modern republican activists.[8] In the words of Keith Michael Baker, "[T]he invention of the French Revolution set in chain a cultural and political dynamic with implications we are still living today."[9] Modern revolutionaries have the same objective as those of 1789: not simply to protest against the efforts of political and business leaders, but to disrupt their proceedings in such a way as to prevent them from reaching agreements. It is clearly a preemptive strategy that is itself undemocratic. It is one of the greatest ironies in the nation's history that the tactics and objectives of that revolution should be visited upon Canadians in Quebec, the very place where the principles of the French Revolution were formally confronted and rejected almost a century and a half ago. But the intellectuals of Quebec have successfully overturned the legacy of the French Canadian constitutional framers, such as George-Etienne Cartier, and have drummed the ideals of the French Revolution into the minds of successive generations since 1960. The Quiet Revolution was addressed principally to the minds of young Quebeckers. It was given that name because it was a philosophical and preparatory revolution. But just as theory always precedes practice, in Quebec the theory at the heart of the French Revolution successfully infiltrated the minds of young men and women and prepared them to write and act on those principles. Central to that revolutionary mission was an anti-clericalism reminiscent of the anti-clericalism at the heart of the French Revolution. Elysée Loustalot wrote in justification of the French Revolution, "It is because despotism was made to descend from the heavens, and given a divine sanction, that it was so powerfully established. The rights of man would have been restored long ago, it had not been for the thick veil with which the priests of every god smothered reason or the stupor they inflicted upon it."[10] Secularist sentiments fired the imagination and resolve of intellectuals in Quebec during the Quiet Revolution.

In addition, Canada has seen repeated calls for the reform of parliamentary procedures. Opposition parties have called for less party discipline and more "free votes" in the House of Commons. Under the present system, a prime minister with a majority government can, and almost always does, command the unbending loyalty of his or her members. It is the prime minister who sets the parliamentary agenda and appoints members to cabinet and keeps them there as long as they remain loyal.[11] In brief, Canada's much heralded system of responsible government has become corrupted; indeed, it could now be called "irresponsible government." And it would scandalize the framers of the British North America Act. Canadians have forgotten what Abraham Lincoln said twenty-five years before the American Civil War: "[T]he most difficult task of statesmanship is that of providing, not for the foundation, but for the preservation, of political institutions."[12]

NO TURNING BACK

However much the Canadian regime has turned its back on monarchy, the direction cannot be reversed. The transformation to republican government has taken hold in the public mind and has been institutionalized by the new Charter mandate entrusted to the Supreme Court of Canada. Yet institutional reforms are urgently required to accommodate the constitutional alterations. In other words, the solution to the problems that have emerged with the advent of republican government is not monarchical institutions, as Eugene Forsey would have recommended, but more or better republican institutions. Accordingly, the first area of reform must be the Senate. The main requirement is a Senate that represents the provinces equally. This single, achievable reform would go a long way towards binding the nation by providing a central institution where the concerns of the regions could be formally and effectively addressed. It would serve to recover what Burke called a nation's "true centre of gravity, and natural point of repose."[13] Armed with the considerable powers already accorded by the Constitution Act, 1867, the reformed Senate could work to restore the lost prestige and authority of Parliament. It could also begin to address the "irresponsible" elements that have crept into the operation of the Canadian system of government. When parliamentary representatives of the people are denied the forum in which to do their duty to their constituents, the government of the nation has become corrupt; it robs the people of their right to self-government, which is the fundamental condition of liberty.

There are few Canadians who would applaud the recent concentration of power in the office of the prime minister and the diminution of Parliament. But there is one figure lurking in the constitutional shadows who would: Thomas Hobbes. But Hobbes was no friend to democratic government. At no point in history has the Canadian political system been more in tune with the radical concentration of power in one man or a group of men recommended by Hobbes that at the present. The supreme constitutional irony is that the courts have emerged as the only institution with the limited power to place a bridle on the Canadian "Leviathan." But, under Canada's system of government, even the courts cannot cross the line into the political precinct governed by political rules beyond the reach of the law. There is nothing unconstitutional or illegal about the concentration of power in the office of the prime minister. And unless the prime minister breaks the law, his or her actions are beyond judicial remedy. No court can enter the political precinct of the prime minister's office and command the office-holder to curb his or her exercise of power. The solution to the problem of concentration of power must be a political one. A first step in the process of reform could be achieved by granting power to the government caucus to call the prime minister to account, as in Great Britain. But what prime minister is going to preside over the diminution of his or her power? Not until such time as the general public becomes sufficiently agitated to demand them will the necessary parliamentary reforms come about.

Finally, the central issue in these reflections on the current state of the nation is the warning de Tocqueville issued about democratic peoples casting off their liberty for the seductive embrace of equality. The latter is so naturally exciting and alluring; the former, so cold and demanding. The former places limits upon our friendships; the latter excites and invites us to an endless revelry. Edmund Burke wrote in his "Observations on the Present State of the Nation": "He would, I conceive be a very indifferent farmer, who complained that his sheep did not plough, or his horses yield wool, though it would be an idea full of equality."[14] While this book is not a lament for the nation, it is perhaps an address to the political elites of what might be called a nation of "indifferent farmers."

Notes

PREFACE

1 Cruickshank, *Charles Dickens*, 4.
2 See Everdell, *The End of Kings*.
3 McGee, "Speeches and Address Chiefly on the Subject of British North American Union," Speech given at Cookshire, Quebec, 22 December 1864, 3.
4 Gibbs, *Parliamentary Debates*, 813.

INTRODUCTION

1 McGee, Cookshire Speech, 22 December 1864, 6.
2 Ibid.
3 Burke, *Reflections on the French Revolution*, 251.
4 For an account of the importance of the Crown in the constitutional life of Canada, see David Smith, *The Invisible Crown*.
5 McGee, "The Political Morality of Shakespeare," 43.
6 Pangle, *The Spirit of Modern Republicanism*.
7 Vipond, *Liberty and Community*.
8 De Tocqueville, *Democracy in America*, 417–18.

CHAPTER ONE

1 Bernadete, *Socrates' Second Sailing*, 203.
2 Cassirer, *The Myth of the State*, 176.
3 Strauss and Cropsey, *History of Political Philosophy*, 411.
4 Bacon, *A Selection of His Works*, 303.
5 See Cropsey, *Political Philosophy and the Issues of Politics*, 291.

6 MacPherson, *The Political Theory of Possessive Individualism*, 1.

7 For an instructive account of the rise of modern executive power, see Mansfield, *Taming the Prince*, 121–80.

8 Locke, *Two Treatises of Government*, # 143.

9 Ibid.

10 Marshall, *Constitutional Theory*, 102.

11 Hobbes, *Leviathan*, 225–8.

12 Wood, *The Creation of the American Republic*, 10–11.

13 See Hill, *God's Englishman*, 147.

14 De Tocqueville, *Recollections*, 17. "Even considering the difference in population figures – France in 1840, 32,000,000; England and Wales in 1840, 16,000,000 – the English additional voting figures do not imply such a strain on the political organization as must have been the case in France … The French Republic, based on universal franchise, produced its dialectical antithesis – to use, for once, the Hegelian term."

15 Montesquieu, *Spirit of the Laws*, 19:68.

16 Jones, *The English Revolution, 1603–1714*, 179.

17 Hobbes, *Leviathan*, 210.

18 See Locke, *Two Treatises*, chapter 14, 203–7.

19 Mansfield, *Taming the Prince*, 258.

20 Maurois, *Disraeli: A Picture of the Victorian Age*, 55.

21 Montesquieu, *Spirit of the Laws*, 20:7.

22 Voltaire, *Letters on England*, 51. For a good contemporary account of laws made during this period, see Ludlow and Jones, *Progress of the Working Class, 1832–1867*.

23 Locke, 124, 184.

24 Jones, *The English Revolution*, 180–1.

25 Ibid., 182.

26 Williams, *Letters on Political Liberty*, 9.

27 Russell, *Memorials and Correspondence of Charles James Fox*, 2:361.

28 Cobbett and Wright, eds, *The Parliamentary History of England*, 29:259.

29 Burke, *An Appeal from the New to the Old Whigs*, 9.

30 Montesquieu, *Spirit of the Laws*, 19:27.

31 Edmund Burke, *Reflections*, 2:362–3.

32 Blackstone, *Commentary*, 1:336–7.

33 Bagehot, *The English Constitution*, 82.

34 See Burke, *Works*, 2:36–7.

35 Bagehot, *The English Constitution*, 59.

36 Ibid., 62–3.

37 Ibid., 53.

38 Mansfield, *Taming the Prince*, 190–1.

39 See Wolfe, *The Rise of Modern Judicial Review*.

40 Bagehot, *The English Constitution*, 284.

41 Ibid., 236.

42 See Cooke, ed., *The Federalist Papers*, numbers 9, 10, and 14, where the republican governments of ancient Greece and Italy are discussed and distinguished from the American designs.

43 Ibid., 51.

44 Frisch, *Alexander Hamilton and the Political Order*, 78.

45 Ibid., 3.

46 Ibid., 2.

47 Ibid.

48 See Hobbes, *Leviathan*, chapter 21.

49 Scholarly views of the founding of the United States have undergone a number of noticeable transformations. The early reverence for the constitution and the work of its framers began in the twentieth century to receive critical attention prompted by an emerging ideological perspective. Charles Beard's *An Economic Interpretation of the Constitution* (1913) was followed in due course by other analyses, such as Clinton Rossiter's *Seedtime of the Republic* (1953) and Bernard Bailyn's *The Ideological Origins of the American Revolution* (1967). For a critical assessment of these authors, see John P. Diggins, *The Lost Soul of American Politics* (1984). By far the most vociferous of the revisionists has been prompted by J.G.A. Pocock's *The Machiavellian Moment* (1975), which unleashed a flurry of activity designed to dislodge John Locke as a major influence on the American founding, prompting a lively debate among such scholars as Thomas Pangle and Allan Bloom.

50 See, for example, *The Toronto Globe*, 1861 to 1865.

51 Canada, *Debates on Confederation, 1865*, 561.

52 Ibid.

CHAPTER TWO

1 See Shortt and Doughty, eds, Egremont to the Lords of Trade, Whitehall, 5 May 1763, *Documents Relating to the Constitutional History of Canada 1759–1791*, Part1:127.

2 For the documents relating to these matters, see Shortt and Doughty, 127–211.

3 Egremont to the Lords of Trade, 5 May 1763, 128.

4 Shortt and Doughty, eds, *Address of French Citizens to the King Regarding the Legal System*, 227.

5 Shortt and Doughty, eds, Report on Commissions for Governors, 6 October 1763, 159.

6 Ibid.,175.

7 Shortt and Doughty, eds, See "Petition to the King," 11 December 1773, 495. See also "Case of the British Merchants Trading To Quebec," 512.

8 All references to the debates in the British Parliament on the Quebec Bill are drawn from Debates of the House of Commons in the Year 1774, drawn up from the notes of the Right Honourable Sir Henry Cavendish, Bart. (London: Ridgway, Piccadilly, 1839), 30. Henceforth all references will be to Cavendish.

9 Ibid., 32–3.

10 Ibid., 44.

11 Ibid., 47.

12 Ibid., 37.

13 Ibid., 52.

14 Baron Maseres, "Considerations on the Expediency of Procuring An Act of Parliament for the Settlement of the Province of Quebec," London, 1766. W.P.M. Kennedy, ed., *Statutes, Treaties and Documents of the Canadian Constitution 1713–1929*, 69.

15 Cavendish, 61.

16 Ibid., 88–9.

17 Ibid., 89.

18 Ibid., 192.

19 Ibid., 196.

20 Ibid., 289.

21 Ibid.

22 Commager, ed., *Documents of American History*, 1:74.

23 For a full account of the religious bigotry that swept the American colonies following 1774, see Charles H. Metzger, S.J., *The Quebec Act: A primary cause of the American Revolution*.

24 Boston *Gazette*, 11 April 1768.

25 Cited by Metzger, 197.

26 For a full account of the Articles of Capitulation, see Kennedy, *Statutes, Treaties and Documents*, 23–31.

27 House of Commons Debates on the Quebec Act; see Gourlay, *Statistical Account of Upper Canada*, 3.

28 Ibid., 8.

29 Ibid., 11.

30 Ibid., 15.

31 Ibid., 16.

32 Ibid.

33 Ibid., 19.

34 Ibid.

35 Ibid., 90.

36 Ibid., 68.

37 Morris, *Arguments to Prove the Policy and Necessity of Granting to Newfoundland a Constitutional Government*, 6.

38 Ibid., 76.

39 Howe, "Speech in Southampton," 14 January 1851, London: 1851, 10–11.
40 Lippincott, *Victorian Critics of Democracy,* 1.
41 London, *Times,* 17 May 1849, 11.
42 Beck, *Joseph Howe,* 22.
43 See Baldwin in Gibbs, ed., *Debates of the Legislative Assembly of the United Canadas,* I:790.
44 Wallot, "La Revolution francaise, le Canada et les Droits de l'Homme, 1789–1840," *Etudes Canadiennes,* 28:14.
45 See Wade, "Quebec and the French Revolution of 1789: the Mission of Henri de Mezière," *Canadian Historical Review,* 31:345–68.
46 See Oullet, *Le Bas Canada 1791–1840: Changements structuraux et crise,* 68.
47 Plessis, *Discours,* 42.
48 Plessis, Sermon preché par l'évêque Catholique de Québec Dans sa Cathédrale le quatrième Dimache du Carême, 1 Avril 1810. A la suite de la Proclamation de son Excellence le Gouverneur en Chef, du 21 Mars même année.
49 See Kennedy, 270.
50 Ibid., 271.
51 Ibid., 287–8.
52 Ibid., 287.
53 See Gates, *After the Rebellion,* for a fuller account of Mackenzie's radicalism.
54 Ibid.,163.
55 See Lower and Chafe, *Canada: A Nation,* 258.
56 See Ajzenstat, *The Political Thought of Lord Durham.*
57 Dion, "Tocqueville, le Canada francais et la question nationale," 7.
58 Morton, *The Kingdom of Canada,* 252.
59 Lord Durham, *Report on the Affairs of British North America,* 159.
60 Leacock, *Montreal: Seaport and City,*164.
61 Morton, *The Kingdom of Canada,* 281.
62 Toronto, *The Globe Extra,* 7 June 1849, 1.
63 Elgin to Grey, 30 April 1849, in Kennedy, *Statutes, Treaties and Documents,* 503.
64 Morton, *The Kingdom of Canada,* 281.
65 Barker, *Political Thought in England,* 1–2.
66 Agielhon, *The Republican Experiment 1848–1852,* 2.
67 See Hampson, *Saint-Just,* 237.

CHAPTER THREE

1 The title comes from Thomas D'Arcy McGee's comment that Canada's constitutional foundations were as "strong as the foundations of Eddystone." (*The Globe,* 31 October 1864, 4.) Eddystone is a group

of rocks off the coast of England southwest of Plymouth, on which there is an important lighthouse indicating the approaches to the English Channel.

2 See Pryke, *The Maritimes and Confederation*.

3 See Whitelaw, *The Maritimes and Canada before Confederation*, 128–48. For the Colonial Office reaction, see Gibson, "The Colonial Office View of Canadian Federation," *Canadian Historical Review* 35.

4 See Lytton to Head, 26 November 1858, *Journal of the Assembly* (Prince Edward Island, 1859), Appendix C.

5 See Lytton to Head, 10 September 1858, C.O. 42, Vol. 614, NAC.

6 Newcastle to Dundas, Confidential, 27 January 1860, C.O. 226, Vol. 92, NAC.

7 Minute of Manners-Sutton to Newcastle, Private and Confidential, 29 September 1859, C.O. 188, Vol. 132, NAC.

8 See *Journal of the Assembly* (Nova Scotia, 1861), 128, for Howe's resolution. See also Ibid. (1863) for Howe's 14 August 1862 letter to Dorion, Tilley, and Pope, explaining why the resolution was not sent earlier. NAC.

9 Newcastle to Mulgrave, 6 July 1862; reprinted in Pope, ed., *Confederation Documents*, 303.

10 Doyle to Dundas, 29 February 1864, *Journal of the Assembly* (Prince Edward Island, 1864), Appendix A, NAC.

11 Italics added.

12 Doyle to Dundas, 29 February 1864, *Journal of the Assembly* (Prince Edward Island, 1864), Appendix A, NAC.

13 Ibid., 42. (The vote of approval was 18 to 9). For the debate on this resolution, see *Debates and Proceedings of the Legislative Council* (Prince Edward Island, 1864), 109. NAC. See also Bolger, *Prince Edward Island and Confederation*.

14 Three members of this constitutional committee, John Scoble, John Sandfield Macdonald, and John A. Macdonald, dissented from the majority. They preferred a unitary form of government. See Careless, *Brown of the Globe*, II:129.

15 Trotter, *Canadian Federalism*, 57.

16 Monck to Dundas, 30 June 1864, *Journal of the Assembly* (Prince Edward Island, 1865), Appendix E, NAC.

17 Macdonald Papers, Vol. 46, NAC.

18 "Quebec Conference Minutes," Macdonald Papers, vol. 46, NAC.

19 Notes Taken at the Quebec Conference by A.A. Macdonald, Macdonald Papers, vol. 46, NAC. (Henceforth referred to as A.A. Macdonald Notes.)

20 See "Charles Tupper: Minutes of the Charlottetown Conference," *Canadian Historical Review*, 48, 101–12.

21 A.A. Macdonald Notes, 27.

22 Ibid., 30. The constitutional framers used the terms "federal" and "confederal" interchangeably.

23 Brown to Anne Brown, 17 October 1864, NAC.

24 A.A. Macdonald Notes, 28.

25 See Cartier's speech delivered at Charlottetown, September 1864, recorded in Whelan, *Confederation*, 8.

26 Cartier, "Discours sur la Confédération des Provinces de l'Amérique Britannique du Nord," 8 September 1864, Charlottetown, Prince Edward Island. Reprinted in Tasse, *Discours de Sir Georges Cartier*, 389.

27 See Skelton, *Life of Alexander Galt*, 371.

28 Gordon to Cardwell, 12 September 1864, C.O. 188, Vol. 141, NAC. See also Gordon to Cardwell, 26 September 1864, C.O. 188, Vol. 141, NAC.

29 Preserved in the National Archives of Canada, Ottawa.

30 A.A. Macdonald Notes, 28.

31 The term "Senate" was not used during the conferences or in the ensuing debates in the legislatures. British North Americans called the upper house the Legislative Council. Since the term was eventually used to describe the upper house in the new constitution, it is used here from the very beginning.

32 Pope, *Confederation Documents*, 11.

33 See A.A. Macdonald Notes, as well as Hewitt Bernard Notes, NAC. No explanation is given for not considering this suggestion.

34 Pope, *Confederation Documents*, 58; also A.A. Macdonald Notes, 31.

35 Pope, *Confederation Documents*, 58.

36 Pope, ed., *Correspondence of Sir John A. Macdonald*, 272.

37 Ibid.

38 Pope, *Confederation Documents*, 54.

39 Ibid., 84.

40 See Christopher Dunkin's withering four hour long denunciation of the plan of Confederation, Monday, 27 February 1865, *Canada Debates*, 482.

41 See the latest such attempt in Romney, "The Nature and Scope of Provincial Autonomy: Oliver Mowat, the Quebec Resolutions and the Construction of the *British North America Act*," 5. This article is significant for several reasons not the least of which is that the author never once cites the Quebec resolutions in support of his basic thesis. In this and other respects Romney's argument is seriously flawed.

42 Numbers in parentheses refers to subsections of resolution 43.

43 A.A. Macdonald Notes, 39.

44 Galt, "Speechon the Proposed Union of the British North America Provinces," Sherbrooke, 23 November 1864, 10, NAC.

45 Resolution 38.

46 A.A. Macdonald Notes, 59.

47 See the post-Confederation remarks of John A. Macdonald, *Provincial Legislation*, 105, where he stated that the lieutenant governors were Dominion officers and had to follow the instructions of the federal government. See also Galt, Sherbrooke Speech, 23 November 1864, 13.

48 *Canadian Debates*, 93.

49 Galt, Sherbrooke Speech, 23 November 1864, 18.

50 Ibid., 19.

51 See Creighton, *British North America at Confederation*.

52 A.A. Macdonald Notes, 33.

53 Pope, *Confederation Documents*, 56.

54 Ibid., 86.

55 Ibid., 84.

56 See Coles, *Journal of the Assembly* (Prince Edward Island, 1865), 56–71, NAC. Also Tupper, *Journal of the Assembly* (Nova Scotia, 1865), 208, NAC.

57 *Canadian Debates*, 27.

58 *Parliamentary Debates (Hansard)*. Reprinted in *Report pursuant to Resolution of the Senate to the Honourable The Speaker*, by the Parliamentary Counsel (O'Connor Report), 77.

59 McGee, Cookshire Speech, 22 December 1864, 7.

60 Bernard, *Notes of the Quebec Conference*.

61 *Canadian Debates*, 33.

62 *Journal of the Assembly* (Nova Scotia, 1865), 404, NAC.

63 *Canadian Debates*, 404.

64 Ibid., 911.

65 Ibid., 689. The *Times* of London wrote on 6 December 1864, after reviewing the Quebec resolutions: "We cannot find that the local legislatures have any exclusive power of legislation given them … Nothing is exclusively reserved to Local Legislatures."

66 Brown to Anne Brown, 17 October 1864, *Brown Papers*, NAC,1078.

67 Macdonald to Buchanan, 16 October 1864, Buchanan Papers, MG 24 D16 vol. 41, 33337, NAC.

68 See Vipond, *Liberty and Community: Canadian Federalism and the Failure of the Constitution*.

69 "Catalogue of Books in the Library of the Late Rt Honourable Sir John A. Macdonald: To be Sold by Public Auction at Earnscliff, Ottawa, about 17 or 18 May next." W.H. Lewis, Auctioneer, Ottawa, in the Macdonald Papers, The National Archives of Canada, Ottawa, Ontario.

70 The full title of this influential book reads: *The Constitution of England: or, an account of the English Government in which it is compared both with the Republican Form of Government and the other Monarchies of Europe*. More than 500 pages in length, it went through numerous expanded editions since first published in 1770 in French. Unlike Baron de Montesquieu's *Spirit of the Laws*, a work DeLolme criticized from time

to time in his book, DeLolme's work was widely respected throughout English and American circles.

71 See Cooke, ed., *The Federalist*, Papers, number 70, 479.

72 DeLolme, *The Constitution of England*, xv.

73 Ibid., 191.

74 Ibid., 211.

75 Ibid., 208.

76 Ibid., 266.

77 *Parliamentary Debates on Confederation of British North American Provinces*, 29.

78 DeLolme, *The Constitution of England*, 240.

79 Hobbes, *Leviathan*, 90.

80 The one subject on which DeLolme did not offer instruction was federalism. To his mind, the British constitution drew its greatest strength from being a unitary form of government, in no sense federal. Reverence for the unitary form of government went deep in DeLolme and Macdonald shared it. Macdonald would, however, change his mind on this matter (as we shall see in the next chapter) after reading Edward Freeman.

81 Macdonald to Amsden, 1 December 1864, Amsden Papers, MG24, B65, 42–4, NAC.

82 A debate has lingered over this issue ever since William F. O'Connor issued his Senate report, *Report pursuant to Resolution of the Senate to the Honourable The Speaker*, by the Parliamentary Counsel, relating to The Enactment of the British North America Act, 1867, any lack of consonance between its terms and judicial construction of them and cognate matters (Ottawa: The King's Printer, 17 March 1939). O'Connor's report purported to show that the framers of the Confederation Act, 1867 began *de novo* in London and that the terms of the constitution were devised at that conference; thus, there was no real relationship between the resolutions adopted in London and in Quebec. His conclusion simply does not pass scrutiny of either the relevant documents or the observations of the leading Canadian participants. See Reesor, *The Canadian Constitution in Historical Perspective*, 50: "Although some alterations were made, the Quebec resolutions emerged from the London conference, and following subsequent changes, basically unscathed."

CHAPTER FOUR

1 See Bolger, *Prince Edward Island and Confederation*.

2 See Creighton, *The Road to Confederation*.

3 Christopher Dunkin had been a professor of Greek at Harvard before coming to Quebec in 1836 and embarking upon a career in politics and

law. As a result of his tenure in the United States, Dunkin possessed a greater knowledge of both the theory and the practice of the American constitution than most of his colleagues. He was the principal cause of a "riot" at Harvard College in 1834. Students in his early morning freshman class resented his overbearing English manner and refused to take instruction from him. A disturbance broke out and the entire class was expelled. Among the students was Henry David Thoreau. See *Proceedings of the Overseers of Harvard University,* "The Report Accepted and the Resolutions adopted by them of the 25th August 1834, relative to the Late Disturbances in that Seminary."

4 See *Parliamentary Debates on the subject of the Confederation of the British North American Provinces,* 962.

5 Editorial, *The Times,* London, 1 March 1867.

6 Stacey, *Canada and the British Army,* 179.

7 Ibid.

8 See Viscount Bury, *Exodus of the Western Nations.*

9 Disraeli to Derby, 30 September 1866, quoted by W.F. Monypenny and G.E. Buckle, *Disraeli,* I: 476–7.

10 Brown to Macdonald, 22 September 1864, reprinted in Joseph Pope, *Memoirs of John A. Macdonald,* 273–4.

11 Galt Papers, 27, I D8, III, 1153, NAC. See also Cartwright, *Reminiscences,* 55.

12 The relationship of the Quebec resolutions to the London resolutions has been a minor thorn in the side of Canadian historians ever since William F. O'Connor, legal secretary to the Senate of Canada, wrote a report on the subject in 1939. O'Connor stated that Nova Scotia and New Brunswick had instructed their delegates to London to proceed on the basis of rejection of the Quebec plan of union. Further they were to begin the discussion *de novo.* See O'Connor, Annex 4, 40. But also see the discussions of this very point in several of the provincial legislatures: *Journal of the Assembly* (New Brunswick, 1866), Session 2, Smith, 20–35 and 69–75; and *Journal of the Assembly* (Nova Scotia, 1866): Campbell, 192, as well as Archibald, 193.

13 O'Connor, 41. The principal flaw of O'Connor's report was his failure to consult the appropriate Hansards in the Maritime legislatures. He almost studiously avoided the very debates that contradict his point of view. See also, Viscount Haldane in *Local Prohibition*: "The Act of 1867 was founded on the Quebec resolutions and expressions which came textually therefrom should be interpreted by the light of Canadian legislation." Olmsted, *Canadian Constitutional Decisions of the Judicial Committee,* 1: 346–7.

14 Pope, *Confederation Documents,* 299.

15 Pope, *Correspondence of John A. Macdonald,* 15.

16 Galt Papers, MC 27, I DB, III, 1152; letter written 28 December 1866; see also comment in Tupper Papers, MC 26, I (a), Vol. V, no. 247; also

Tupper to Dunkin, Tupper Papers, MC 26, I (a), Vol. V, no. 247, 25 June 1901, NAC.

17 The draft copies are preserved in the Macdonald Papers, MG 26, AI (a), Vol. 44, Part 2, NAC.

18 Cited by Dawson, *The Government of Canada*, 38.

19 Italics added.

20 In Great Britain the power of the prime minister with a majority government can be, and frequently is, checked by the "1922 Committee", that is to say, the caucus members without the cabinet, including the prime minister. This committee can unmake prime ministers – as Margaret Thatcher found out – and bring cabinet ministers to heel. No such check exists in the Canadian political system, where the prime minister keeps his caucuses separated into regional caucuses and thereby prevents the Members of parliament from mounting effective intra-party opposition.

21 Between 1867 and 1942, 122 provincial acts were disallowed. None has been disallowed since that time. See LaForest, *Disallowance and Reservation of Provincial Legislation*. See also Varcoe, *The Distribution of Legislative Power in Canada*. On the future use of disallowance, see Hogg, *Constitutional Law of Canada*, 4th ed., 112.

22 Hobbes speaks of the sovereign as one "Man or Assembly of men." See Hobbes, *Leviathan*, 121.

23 Britain's membership in the European Union and its incorporation of the European Convention on Human Rights has begun to alter the role of British judges. See Malleson, "A British Bill of Rights: Incorporating the European Convention on Human Rights," *Choices*, 1: 1999.

24 See Hobbes, *Leviathan*, chapter 29, which speaks of "the diseases of a Common-wealth" and the "poyson of seditious doctrines … Whereby the Common-wealth is distracted and weakened."

25 Mathie, "Political Community and the Canadian Experience: Reflections on Nationalism, Federalism and Unity," *Canadian Journal of Political Science*, 12:14.

26 Hobbes, *Leviathan*, 5.

27 Ibid., 210.

28 Hobbes, *Elements of Law*, 104.

29 See Macpherson, *The Political Theory of Possessive Individualism*, 72–4.

30 Hobbes, *Leviathan*, 213.

CHAPTER FIVE

1 Freeman, *History of Federal Government, from the Foundation of the Achaian League to the Disruption of the United States*, 114.

2 See Jennings, "Constitutional Interpretation: The Experience of Canada," *Harvard Law Review*, 51:37.

3 See Abel, "The Neglected Logic of 91 and 92," *University of Toronto Law Journal*, 19:487.

4 See *Dictionnaire de la Revolution et de l'Empire, 1789–1815*, 188.

5 Forrest, "Federalism," in Lucas, ed., *The French Revolution and the Creation of Modern Political Culture*, 309.

6 Jeremy Bentham, for example, said the federal form of government was like a "watch with two mainsprings." See "Anti-Senatica," *Works*, Vol. 4, 210.

7 Galt, Sherbrooke Speech, 23 November 1864, 4.

8 Freeman, *History of Federal Government, from the Foundation of the Achaian League to the Disruption of the United States*, Vol. 1. The projected second volume never appeared.

9 Ibid., 113.

10 Ibid.

11 Freeman, *The Growth of the English Constitution from the Earliest Times*, 224.

12 Freeman, *History of Federal Government*, 3.

13 Ibid.

14 Ibid., 4.

15 Ibid., 113.

16 Ibid.

17 Ibid., 115.

18 Ibid., 6.

19 Ibid., 90.

20 Ibid., 109.

21 Ibid., 324.

22 Ibid., 480.

23 Freeman, *History of Federal Government*, 712.

24 Ibid.

25 Thomas D'Arcy McGee, *Notes on Federal Governments Past and Present*, 25.

26 DeLolme, *The Constitution of England*, 39.

27 Ibid., 191.

28 *Journal of the Assembly* (Nova Scotia, 1864), 185, NAC.

29 See Strachan, "A Sermon on the Death of the honourable Richard Cartwright with a short account of his life," 27, 29–30. Preached at Kingston on 3 September 1815.

30 Plessis, "Sermon preché par l'évêque Catholique de Québec Dans sa Cathédrale le quatrième Dimanche du Carême, l Avril 1810. A la suite de la Proclamation de son Excellence le Gouverneur en Chef, du 21ᵉ mars même année."

31 Tupper Papers, M.G.26, FI(a) Vol. 1, document #23, 9 December 1864, NAC.

32 Galt, Sherbrooke Speech, 23 November 1864, 7.

33 Ibid., 8.

34 Ibid.

35 Ibid.

36 Ibid., 9.

37 Ibid., 10.

38 Ibid.

39 Ibid., 11.

40 Ibid., 14.

41 Ibid., 9.

42 Ibid.

43 See Hewitt Bernard minutes of the Quebec Conference, Macdonald Papers, vol. 46, NAC.

44 "Confidential Notes Taken at Quebec Conference, 1864," Macdonald Papers, vol. 46:17853, NAC.

45 Hewitt Bernard minutes of the Quebec Conference, Macdonald Papers, vol. 46, 32, NAC.

46 Ibid.

47 Ibid., 43.

48 *Journal of the Newfoundland Assembly,* 1865, 869.

49 McGee, Cookshire Speech, 22 December 1864, 14.

50 Farrand, ed., *The Records of the Federal Convention of 1787,* 1:288–9, 424.

51 Frisch, "Hamilton's Plan for Resuscitation of Republicanism," 4. I am grateful to Professor Frisch for providing me with several unpublished papers on Alexander Hamilton, which constitute a major portion of a forthcoming book on Hamilton by him.

52 Hamilton's view of the British constitution was not unique to him. Several of his contemporaries, especially among the anti-federalists, openly praised it and held it up as the litmus test of the proposed American constitution. Consider, for example, Patrick Henry's comments during the Virginia Ratifying Convention, 9 June 1788 when he was prepared "to pronounce the British Government, superior … to any Government that ever was in any country." Storing, ed., *The Complete Anti-Federalist,* 233–4.

53 Riethmuller, *The Life and Times of Alexander Hamilton,* 3.

54 Ibid., 185–6.

55 Ibid., l95–6.

56 Solberg, ed., *The Federal Convention and the Formation of the Union of the American States,* 141.

57 Ibid., 142.

58 Ibid., 145.

59 Ibid., 148.

60 See Flaumenhaft, "A Place for Duration in the Republic: Hamilton on the Senate," a paper presented to the Annual Meeting of the American Political Science Association, Washington, DC, August 1984. See also Flaumenhaft, "Hamilton on the Foundation of Good Government,"

The Political Science Reviewer, 6:143. The essentials of these two papers can be found in Flaumenhaft's recent book *The Effective Republic: Administration and Constitution in the Thought of Alexander Hamilton.*

61 Cooke, ed., *The Federalist Papers,* number 9, 55.

62 Ibid.

63 Solberg, ed., *The Federal Convention and the Formation of the Union of the American States,* 148.

64 Ibid., 149.

65 Reithmuller, *The Life and Times of Alexander Hamilton,* 131–2.

66 Curtis, *History of the Origin, Formation and Adoption of the Constitution of the United States,* Vol. I, 416.

67 Ibid., 185.

68 Ibid., 260.

69 Freeman, *History of Federal Government,* 111.

70 Ibid.

71 Ibid., 112.

CHAPTER SIX

1 Milton, *Eikonoklastes* (1649), in Hugh, ed., *Complete Poems and Major Prose,* 781.

2 Bacon, *The Essays or Counsels, Civil and Moral,* 110–14.

3 Hobbes, *Leviathan,* 26:182.

4 Ibid.

5 Cropsey, *Thomas Hobbes: A Dialogue between a Philosopher and a Student of the Common Law of England,* 10.

6 Hobbes, *Leviathan,* 26:184.

7 Ibid.

8 Ibid., 181.

9 Ibid.

10 Sharswood, ed., *Blackstone's Commentaries on the Laws of England,* I:212.

11 Ibid., 62.

12 The first comprehensive history of the Supreme Court of Canada is Snell and Vaughan's, *The Supreme Court of Canada: A History of the Institution.*

13 For a fuller account of the termination of appeals to the Judicial Committee, see Snell and Vaughan, *The Supreme Court of Canada,* 171–95.

14 Privy Council Office material re termination of appeals to the Judicial Committee of the Privy Council, P.C.8–1639. Dated 27 January 1949 (#109), 3.

15 See Hansard. The two new judges appointed were Gerald Fauteux from Quebec and John R. Cartwright from Ontario.

16 Strayer, *Judicial Review of Legislation in Canada,* 3.

17 For an excellent account of the origins of judicial review in Canada, see Gordon Bale, "The New Brunswick Origin of Canadian Judicial Review," *University of New Brunswick Law Journal*, 40:100.

18 8 CJo. rep. 113b, at 118a; 77 E.R. 646, 652 (K.B).

19 Ibid., 118a.

20 Strayer, *Judicial Review of Legislation in Canada*, 3.

21 Ibid.

22 Ibid., 9.

23 Ibid.

24 Lederman, "The Independence of the Judiciary," *Canadian Bar Review*, 24:805.

25 Strayer, *Judicial Review of Legislation in Canada*, 37.

26 See Smith, "The Origins of Judicial Review in Canada," *Canadian Journal of Political Science*, 16:1, 121.

27 Ibid.

28 Ibid.

29 See Bale, *Chief Justice William Johnstone Ritchie*.

30 See LaForest, *Reservation and Disallowance*.

31 Pope, *Confederation Documents*, 85–86

32 See Smith, "The Origins of Judicial Review," 122.

33 Jennings, *Harvard Law Review*, 51, 1:2.

34 Kennedy, "Law and Custom of the Canadian Constitution," in Kennedy, ed., *Essays in Constitutional Law*, 85.

35 Jennings, *Harvard Law Review*, 51, 1:35.

36 *Citizens Insurance v. Parsons*, (1881–1883) 7 AC 96.

37 Argument in Privy Council: *Russell v. The Queen* (Whitehall, 1882) [Transcript from the shorthand notes of Messrs. Martin and Meredith].

38 *Attorney General for Ontario v. Attorney General for The Dominion* (1896) AC 350.

39 See Browne, *The Judicial Committee and the British North America Act*.

40 Wexler, "The Urge to Idealize: Viscount Haldane and the Constitution of Canada," *McGill Law Journal*, 29:609–50.

41 Ibid., 650.

42 See *The Attorney-General for Australia v. Colonial Sugar Co.*, *Times Law Reports*, 30:203–9.

43 "The Work for the Empire of the Judicial Committee of the Privy Council," 22.

44 "Introduction by Viscount Haldane," in Follett, *The New State*, viii.

45 Ibid., vii.

46 Ibid., xi.

47 Ibid., xii.

48 Haldane, "The Work for the Empire of the Judicial Committee of the Privy Council," *Cambridge Law Review*, 1:148. Italics added.

49 Judah Benjamin remains one of the most intriguing "dark forces" behind
the scenes of Canadian judicial history. He became a distinguished bar-
rister in London, making a formidable reputation for himself as an
appeals court advocate after fleeing the United States following the
Civil War. Benjamin had been attorney general and secretary of war
under the Confederacy, and there was a warrant out for his arrest.

In Claudius O. Johnson's "Did Judah Benjamin Plant the 'States
Rights' Doctrine in the Interpretation of the BNA Act?" (*Canadian Bar
Review* 45:454–477) the author does not refute the claim that Benjamin
planted the seeds of states rights in the minds of the Law Lords.
Johnson's conclusion is that this assertion cannot be established by
the aid of *external* evidence. I am, however, persuaded by the *internal*
evidence that Benjamin did in fact exercise a far more powerful influence than Johnson was able to find by counting the number of judgments that Benjamin successfully argued on behalf of the provinces.
Johnson is correct in saying that Benjamin did not plant the doctrine
in the minds of the Judicial Committee. He did, however, help it along
in effectively reversing the order of sections 91 and 92 and thereby
paved the way for "autonomous" provinces. We might never be able
to mount a convincing case, since Benjamin destroyed his private
papers. The only full-length biography of Benjamin is Eli N. Evans,
Judah P. Benjamin: The Jewish Confederate.
50 *Russell v. The Queen* (1881–82) 7 ac 829.
51 Haldane, "Lord Watson," *Juridical Review,* 11:278.
52 MacGuigan, "Precedent and Policy in the Supreme Court of Canada,
Canadian Bar Review, 45:627.
53 See Robinson, "Lord Herschel and the British North America Act,"
University of Toronto Law Journal, 20:55.
54 See W.P.M. Kennedy, *Essays in Constitutional Law* (London: Oxford
University Press, 1934); Kennedy, *The Constitution of Canada 1534–1937*
(London: Oxford University Press, 1938); F.R. Scott, "The Special
Nature of Canadian Federalism," *Canadian Journal of Economics
and Political Science,* 1947, 13:22; Eugene Forsey, "In Defence of
Macdonald's Constitution," *Dalhousie Law Journal,* 1974, 22:38.
55 Austin, *The Province of Jurisprudence Determined,* 191.
56 Sharswood, ed., *Blackstone's Commentaries on the Laws of England,* 59–62.
57 Ibid., 62.

CHAPTER SEVEN

1 De Tocqueville, *Democracy in America,* 445.
2 For a full account of the rise of the new natural philosophy, see Hall,
The Scientific Revolution 1500 - 1800: The Foundation of the Modern

Scientific Attitude. See also Webster, ed., *The Intellectual Revolution of the Seventeenth Century*.

3 See Vaughan, *The Tradition of Political Hedonism: from Hobbes to J. S. Mill*, especially chapter 2, "The Revival of Hedonism."

4 Kruger, Review of Leo Strauss, *Spinoza's Critique of Religion* in *The Independent Journal of Philosophy*, 6/7:174.

5 Oakshott, "Dr. Strauss on Hobbes," *Politica*, 2:379.

6 Strauss, *Natural Right and History*, 169.

7 Locke, *A Letter Concerning Toleration*, 51.

8 Reichley, *Religion In American Public Life*, 85. See also Baldwin, *The New England Clergy and the American Revolution*.

9 See Kessler, "Locke's Influence on Jefferson's 'Bill for Establishing Religious Freedom'," *Journal of Church and State*, 25 (Spring 1983). See also Reichley, op. cit., 90: "The core tradition from which the Virginia liberals drew most of their social ideas was that initiated in England during the previous century by John Locke. The Virginians read Locke, who Jefferson said was one of the three greatest men in history (Francis Bacon and Isaac Newton being the other two), directly and encountered him indirectly through his influence on both Scottish realism and the French *philosophes*."

10 Burke, "Speech on Conciliation with America," *Works of Edmund Burke*, 2:187.

11 De Tocqueville, *Ancien Regime et la Revolution*, 243–4 and 248.

12 Ibid., 152–3

13 Baldwin, *The New England Clergy and the American Revolution*.

14 Ibid., 23.

15 See Ibid., Chapter III, "Concepts of Government," for a full account of this matter.

16 Dreisbach, "God and the Constitution: Reflections on Selected Nineteenth Century Commentaries on References to the Deity and the Christian Religion in the United States Constitution," a paper delivered at the American Political Science Association meetings, Washington, 2 September 1993, 1.

17 Cited by Dreisbach, "God and the Constitution," 4.

18 Ibid.

19 Stevens, *The Declaration of Independence and the Constitution of the United States*, 3.

20 Ibid., 4.

21 Dreisbach, "God and the Constitution," 26.

22 See Miller, *The First Liberty: Religion and the American Republic*. According to Miller, all state constitutions "included substantive statements reflecting a collective piety" (109). See also Goldwin, *A Nation of States*.

23 See Reichley, *Religion in American Public Life*, 115.

24 See Wolfe, *The Rise of Modern Judicial Review*, 315.

25 The recent writings of Reginald W. Bibby, a sociologist at the University of Lethbridge, has done much to correct this deficiency. See his *Restless Gods: The Renaissance of Religion in Canada*.

26 See Trudel, *L'Église canadienne sous le Regime militaire*.

27 Ibid., 175.

28 Ibid., 176. This sermon was published under the title "A Discourse, delivered at Quebec, in the Chapel belonging to the Convent of the Ursulines, September 27th, 1759; occasioned by the Success of our Armies in the reduction of that Capital; at the request of Brigadier General Moncton, and by Order of Vice-Admiral Saunders, Commander in Chief, by the Reverend Eli Dawson." It was termed an "indelicate discourse" by P.G. Roy in *À travers l'histoire des Ursulines* (Montreal: Bibliothèque nationale du Québec, 1939), 132.

29 McGee, *The Catholic History of North America*, 72.

30 Ibid., 72, 75.

31 Ibid., 71.

32 Wilson, "The Clergy Reserves of Upper Canada," Canadian Historical Association Historical Booklet (1969), 23:3. For a fuller account of the establishment of clergy reserves and the politics that eventually consumed them, see Wilson, *The Clergy Reserves of Upper Canada: A Canadian Mortmain*.

33 Wilson, "The Clergy Reserves of Upper Canada," 6.

34 Ibid., 9.

35 Wood, *Nineteenth Century Britain, 1815–1914*, 73.

36 See Haliburton, *An Historical and Statistical Account of Nova Scotia*.

37 Daubeny, *A Letter to the Right Honourable George Canning*, 5–6.

38 Debates of the House of Commons in the Year 1774 on the Bill for Making More Effective Provision for the Government of the Province of Quebec, Drawn up from the notes of Sir Henry Cavendish,18.

39 Drummond, *A letter to the King, against the Repeal of the Test Act, by a Tory of the Old School*, cited by Clark, *English Society 1688–1832*, 6–7.

40 See Clark, *English Society 1688–1832*, 352.

41 Egremont to Murray, 13 August 1763, in Shortt and Doughty, *Constitutional Documents*, 1:169.

42 MacDonald, "Steadfast in religion and loyalty: The Sermons of Charles Inglis, *Journal of the Canadian Church Historical Society*, Anglican Church of Canada, Toronto, 1990, 33:28.

43 Armstrong, "The Supremacy of the Sovereign," a sermon preached at Richmond Hill, 24 May 1855, 13.

44 Plessis, "Sermon preché par l'évêque Catholique de Québec Dans sa Cathédrale le quatrième Dimanche du Carême, 1 Avril 1810. À la suite de la Proclamation de son Excellence le Gouverneur en chef, du 21ᵉ mars même anée."

45 Ibid., 8.

46 Mgr. Joseph-Octave Plessis, "Sermon on Nelson's Victory at Aboukir," 10 January 1799, in Forbes, ed., *Canadian Political Thought*, 6–7.

47 Tasse, *Discours de Sir Georges Cartier*, Speech in Honour of Alexander Galt, 535.

48 Ibid., "Discours prononcé le 24 juin, 1868: A la fête St Jean Baptiste," Ottawa, 602.

49 See Young, "Dimensions of a Law Practice: Brokerage and Ideology in the Career of George-Etienne Cartier," in Carol Wilton, ed., *Essays in the History of Canadian Law: Beyond the Law, Lawyers and Business in Canada, 1830–1930*, 97: Cartier's "library of 890 titles was rich in French, British and American political economy, philosophy and history; Voltaire, Rousseau, Montesquieu, Chateaubriand, Bagehot, Mill, Macaulay, Bancroft, Hamilton, and Marshall had prominent places on his bookshelf."

50 Ibid., "Discours sur le Conseil Legislatif," (27 Mai 1853) à l'Assemblée, 41.

51 Montesquieu, *The Spirit of the Laws*, 46. For an excellent study of this work, see Pangle, *Montesquieu's Philosophy of Liberalism*.

52 Montesquieu, *The Spirit of the Laws*, 316.

53 Tache, "Discours sur les Institutions provincales," 405. Translated by the author. In this speech Cartier went on at length about the commercial spirit of the English.

54 Ibid., 495. Translated by the author.

55 Durham, *Report on the Affairs of British North America*, 72–3.

56 Ibid., 73.

57 See, for example, Silver, *The French-Canadian Idea of Confederation*, 130.

58 Ajzenstat, *The Political Thought of Lord Durham*, 35.

59 See Dionne, *Les Ecclesiastiques et les royalistes français refugiés au Canada, 1791–1820*.

60 Tasse, *Discours de Sir Georges Cartier*, 524.

61 Gladstone, *The State in its Relations with the Church*, 313. The two-volume treatise was so popular that it went into four editions in just three years.

62 Ibid.

63 Ibid., 314.

64 Ibid., 317.

65 Ibid., 313.

66 Wilson, "The Clergy Reserves of Upper Canada," 5.

67 See The Constitution Act, 1791, Article 35, *Canada 125: Its Constitutions 1763–1982*, 105.

68 Wilson, "The Clergy Reserves of Upper Canada," 3.

69 For a succinct account of the sectarian contest over the clergy reserves, see Ibid., 11 -16.

70 See Moir, *Church and State in Canada West,* especially chapter 7, "Religion and Elementary Education, 1852–1867."

71 Ibid., 151.

72 See Ryerson, *The Story of My Life.* See also Stortz, "Archbishop John Joseph Lynch and the Anglicans of Toronto," *Journal of Canadian Church History Society* (1980), vol. 27, 1:3.

73 For a penetrating work on the impact of the French Revolution, see Keith Michael Baker, *Inventing the French Revolution.*

CHAPTER EIGHT

1 Bacon, "Of Judicature," in *The Essays or Counsels, Civil and Moral,* 211.

2 See Liversedge, *Recollections of the On to Ottawa Trek.*

3 The so-called New Deal cases were *A.-G Canada v. A.-G Ontario* (Labour Conventions) [1937] AC 326; *A.-G Canada v. A.-G Ontario* (Unemployment Insurance) [1937] AC 355; *A.-G. British Columbia v. A.-G. Canada* (Price Spreads) [1937] AC 368; *A.-G British Columbia v. A.-G. Canada* (Farmers' Creditors Arrangement) [1937] AC 391; *A.-G British Columbia v. A.-G Canada* (Natural Products Marketing) [1937] AC 377; *A.-G Ontario v. A.-G Canada* (Canada Standard Trade Mark) [1937] AC 405. For a full discussion of these cases, see McConnell, "The Judicial Review of Prime Minister Bennett's New Deal," *Osgoode Hall Law Journal* (1968), 9:39.

4 Pearson, "Introduction," in Trudeau, *A Canadian Charter of Human Rights,* 8.

5 See Trudeau, *Federalism and the French-Canadians.*

6 Graham, *The Essential Trudeau,* 169.

7 Ibid., 175.

8 Ibid., 169.

9 Ibid., 170.

10 Ibid.

11 Ibid., 183.

12 Ibid., 176.

13 Russell, "A Democratic Approach to Civil Liberties," *University of Toronto Law Journal* (1969), 19:109. Russell has long since repudiated the views cited here and has become one of the most vocal supporters of the judicial activism under the Charter.

14 See Taylor, "Atomism" in Kontos, ed., *Powers, Possessions and Freedoms,* 61. See also Pocklington, "Against Inflating Human Rights," *Windsor Yearbook of Access to Justice,* 2:77–86.

15 Taylor, "Alternative Futures," in Cairns and Williams, eds., *Constitutionalism, Citizenship and Society in Canada,* 209.

16 Ibid.

17 Surprisingly, there has been very little written about Trudeau's political philosophy. One of the most penetrating enquiries into his thought is Samuel V. LaSelva's "Does the Canadian Charter of Rights and Freedoms Rest on a Mistake?", *Windsor Yearbook of Access to Justice* (1988) 8: 217.

18 Graham, *The Essential Trudeau*, 8. Unless otherwise noted, all references to Trudeau's writings will be drawn from this collection of his speeches and essays, which is a valuable contribution to Canadian studies.

19 Ibid.

20 Ibid., 46.

21 Ibid.

22 Ibid.

23 Ibid.

24 Ibid., 9.

25 Ibid., 43

26 Ibid., 44.

27 Ibid., 169

28 De Tocqueville, "Speech Pronounced in the Chamber of Deputies on January 27, 1848 During the Discussion of the Proposed Answer to the Speech from the Throne," in *Democracy in America*, Appendix III, 748.

29 See Artistotle, *Nicomachean Ethics*, V, ii, 267–80.

30 See Justice Rosalie Abella's comments on the superior place judges occupy in Canada since the Charter, "Judges and the public interest," *The Globe and Mail*, 14 April 2000, A 12.

31 Marshall, *Constitutional Theory*, 2.

32 See Malleson, "A British Bill of Rights: Incorporating the European Convention on Human Rights," *Choices: Courts and Legislatures*, 5.1:21.

33 Estey in *Law Society of Upper Canada v. Skapinker*, 1 SCR (1984) 366–7.

34 See Morton, "The Political Impact of the Canadian Charter of Rights and Freedoms," *Canadian Journal of Political Science* (1987), 20:31. Also Russell, "The Political Purposes of the Canadian Charter of Rights and Freedoms," *Canadian Bar Review* (1983), 61:30.

35 McLachlin, "The Charter of Rights and Freedoms: A Judicial Perspective," *University of British Columbia Law Review* (1989), 23:579.

36 Dickson in *R. v. Big M Drug Mart* (1985) 1 SCR 343.

37 Ibid., 295.

38 Wilson in *R. v. Big M Drug Mart* (1985) 1 scr 295, 359.

39 Gold, "Of Rights and Roles: The Supreme Court and the *Charter*," *University of British Columbia Law Review* (1989), 23:507, 513.

40 Cited by Gold, Ibid., 515.

41 Ibid., 312.

42 Dickson, "Has the *Charter* 'Americanized' Canada's Judiciary? A Summary and Analysis," *University of British Columbia Law Review* (1992) 26:195.

43 Ibid., 202.

44 McLachlin, "The Charter of Rights and Freedoms: A Judical Perspective," *University of British Columbia Law Review* (1989), 23:580.

45 Ibid., 585.

46 Ibid., 588. Italics added.

47 L'Heureux-Dube, "Making a Difference: The Pursuit of a Compassionate Justice," *University of British Columbia Law Review* (1997) 31:1.

48 Ibid., 6.

49 Ibid., 7.

50 Ibid., 12.

51 Ibid., 14.

52 *Société des Acadiens du Nouveau Brunswick v. Association for Parents for Fairness in Education* (1986) 1 SCR 626.

53 Matsuda, "When the First Quail Calls: Multiple Consciousness as Jurisprudential Method," *Women's Rights Law Report* (1989), II:7.

54 See Knopff and Morton, *Charter Politics*.

55 Montesquieu, *The Spirit of the Laws*, 19:299.

56 The Supreme Court of Canada has increasingly come under public scrutiny and criticism as a result of the judgments it has made under the Charter, and for the tendency of its judges to speak off the bench in defence of their rulings. See, for example, Knopff and Morton, *The Charter Revolution and the Court Party.*

EPILOGUE

1 Grant, *Lament for a Nation*, afterword by Peter Emberley, 104.

2 See Hirschman, *The Passions and the Interests.*

3 See Malleson, "A British Bill of Rights: Incorporating the European Convention on Human Rights" in Howe and Russell, eds, *Judicial Power and Canadian Democracy*, 27.

4 See Muncy, ed., *The End of Democracy*, 11.

5 Madison, *The Federalist Papers*, no. 10, 65.

6 Burke, "Observations on the Present State of the Nation," in *The Works of the Right Honourable Edmund Burke*, 271.

7 The daily press has taken up the cause of greater democracy. See, for example, Richard Gwyn, "Canadians fiddle while Democracy burns," *The Sunday Herald*, 22 April 2001, 10, and Michael Valpy, "Democracy demolished," *The Globe and Mail*, 21 April 2001, 12. John Manley and Brian Tobin, both cabinet ministers at the time, joined the fray by calling for an end of the ties with Great Britain; see, "Ministers Break Rank over Monarchy," *National Post*, 19 May 2001.

8 Marxism owed more to the French Revolution than Marx and Engels dared to admit; it was little more than the French Revolution encased

in a Teutonic rigidity. It is no accident that both the French and Russian Revolutions were followed by a tyranny; the Russian tyranny lasted longer and caused the deaths of more people because it was rigidly enforced by Germanic efficiency.

9 Baker, *Inventing the French Revolution*, 204.

10 Ibid., 221.

11 As leader of his or her political party, the prime minister is required to sign the nomination papers of those who wish to seek election under the party banner. If a member has not been loyal during a given session of Parliament, the prime minister can refuse to sign those papers, thereby preventing the person from running for election. Or the "disloyal" member can be evicted from caucus and the party. John Nuntziata suffered this fate in 1995. He was re-elected to Parliament in 1997 but lost the subsequent election.

12 Lincoln, "The Perpetuation of Our Political Institutions," Address before the Young Men's Lyceum of Springfield, Illinois, 27 January 1838. Cited by Harry Jaffa, *Shakespeare's Politics*, 113.

13 Burke, "Observations on the Present State of the Nation," in *The Works of the Right Honourable Edmund Burke*, 403.

14 Ibid., 369.

Bibliography

PRIMARY SOURCES

Public Documents (National Archives of Canada)

Canada: CO 42, Correspondence from Governor General to Colonial Office, 1864–1867; CO 43, Letter Books.

New Brunswick: CO 188, Correspondence from Governor of New Brunswick to Colonial Office, 1860–1867; CO 189, Letter Books.

Nova Scotia: CO 217, Correspondence from Governor of Nova Scotia to Colonial Office, 1860–1867; CO 218, Letter Books.

Prince Edward Island: CO 226, correspondence from Governor of Prince Edward Island to Colonial Office, 1860–1875; CO 227, Letter Books.

Newfoundland: CO 194, Correspondence from Governor of Newfoundland to Colonial Office; CO 195, Letter Books.

Despatches from Colonial Office to Governor General, Record Group 7, Series G 1.

Series G 2, Additional Despatches from Secretary of State for Colonial Office to Governor General; supplementary to G 1.

Series G 4, Despatches sent to Executive Council of Canada.

Series G 7, Despatches from Lieutenant Governors to Governor General.

Series G 8 B, Despatches between Colonial Office and Lieutenant Governor of New Brunswick.

Series G 8 D, Despatches between Colonial Office and Lieutenant Governor of Prince Edward Island.

Official Correspondence between Lieutenant Governors and Colonial Office, Record Group 9, B 2.

Private Papers (NAC)

Blake Papers

Brown Papers
Galt Papers
Howe Papers
MacDougall Papers
Macdonald, J.A.
Monck Papers
Tupper Papers

WORKS BY PRINCIPAL PARTICIPANTS
AT CONFEDERATION

Acadian. "A Letter to the Electors of Nova Scotia, Being a Reply to Confederation Considered on its Merits," Halifax, 1867.

Annand, William. "Confederation: A Letter to the Right Honourable The Earl of Carnarvon," London, 1866.

Archibald, A.G. "Letter to the People of Nova Scotia," London, 1866.

B–, Alphonse. "Contra-Poison: la confédération c'est le salut du Bas-Canada," Montreal, 1867.

Bolton, E.C. and H.H. Webber. "The Confederation of British America," London, 1866.

Bourinot, J.G. "Confederation of the Provinces of British North America," Halifax, 1866.

Buchanan, Isaac "The British American Federation a Necessity," Hamilton, 1865.

Cauchon, Joseph. "Étude sur l'union projetee des provinces britanniques," Quebec, 1858.

Dorion, A.A. "La Confédération couronnement de dix années de mauvaise administration," Montreal, 1867.

Galt, A.T. "Speech on the Proposed Union of the British North American Provinces," Montreal, 1864.

Howe, Joseph. "Confederation Considered in Relation to the Interests of the Empire," London, 1866.

– "A Speech on Union of the Colonies and Organization of the Empire," Pictou, 1855.

Macdonald, John A. *Provincial Legislation* (Ottawa: The Queen's Printer, 1869).

McCully, Jonathan. "British America: Arguments against a Union of the Provinces Reviewed; With further reasons for confederation," London, 1867.

McGee, Thomas D'Arcy. *The Catholic History of North America* (Boston: Patrick Donahoe, 1855).

– *The Irish Position in British and Republican North America* (Montreal: Longmoore and Co., 1866).

– "Notes on Federal Governments Past and Present," Montreal, 1865.

– "Union of the Provinces," Quebec, 1865.

Nova Scotia. "Confederation Considered on its Merits," Halifax, 1867.

Pope, W.H. "Observations Upon the Proposed Union of the British North American Provinces," Charlottetown, 1865.

Tache, J.C. "Des Provinces de l'Amérique du nord et d'une union fédérale," Quebec, 1858.

Tupper, Charles. "Letter to the Right Honourable Earl of Carnarvon," London, 1866.

Wilkins, M.I. "Confederation Examined in the Light of Reason and Common Sense and the British North America Act Shown to be Unconstitutional," Halifax, 1867.

OFFICIAL PARLIAMENTARY SOURCES

Province of Canada, Legislative Assembly, Journals, 1864–1867 (NAC)

Province of Canada, Legislative Council, Journals, 1864–1867 (NAC)

Province of Canada, Parliamentary Debates on the Subject of the Confederation of the British North American Provinces (Quebec, Hunter, Rose and Co., 1865).

Great Britain, Colonial Office, Question of the Federation of the British Provinces in America (London: The Queen's Printer, 1858).

– Correspondence Relative to a Meeting at Quebec of Delegates Appointed to Discuss the Proposed Union (London: The Queen's Printer, 1865).

– British North American Provinces: Correspondence Respecting the Proposed Union (London: The Queen's Printer, 1867).

Great Britain, Parliament, Hansard, 3rd Series.

New Brunswick, Legislative Assembly, Journals, 1864–1867 (NAC).

New Brunswick, Legislative Council, Journals, 1864–1867 (NAC).

Newfoundland, Legislative Assembly, Journals, 1864–1867 (NAC).

Newfoundland, Legislative Council, Journals, 1864–1867 (NAC).

Nova Scotia, Legislative Assembly, Debates and Proceedings, 1864–1867 (NAC).

Nova Scotia, Legislative Council, Journals, 1864–1867 (NAC).

Prince Edward Island, Legislative Assembly, Debates and Proceedings, the Parliamentary Reporter, 1864–1867 (NAC)

Prince Edward Island, Legislative Council, Debates and Proceedings, 1864–1867 (NAC).

Debates of the House of Commons in the Year 1774, drawn up from the notes of the Right Honourable Sir Henry Cavendish (London: Ridgway, Piccadilly, 1839).

Statutes, Treaties and Documents of the Canadian Constitution, 1713–1929 (Oxford: Oxford University Press, 1930).

Bernard, Hewitt. "Minutes of the Quebec Conference," Macdonald Papers, 46, NAC.

Shortt, Adam and A.G. Doughty, eds. *Documents Relating to the Constitutional History of Canada, 1759–1791* (Ottawa: The King's Printer, 1918).

SECONDARY SOURCES

Abel, Albert. "The Neglected Logic of 91 and 92," *University of Toronto Law Journal* 19.

Agielhon, Maurice. *The Republican Experiment 1848–1852* (Cambridge: Clarendon Press, 1983).

Ajzenstat, Janet. *The Political Thought of Lord Durham* (Kingston and Montreal: McGill-Queen's University Press, 1988).

– and Peter J. Smith, eds., *Canada's Origins: Liberal, Tory or Republican?* (Ottawa: Carleton University Press, 1995).

Aristotle. *Nicomachean Ethics*, V:11, translated by H. Rackman (Cambridge: Harvard University Press, 1926).

Armstrong, J. Gilbert. "The Supremacy of the Sovereign," a sermon preached at Richmond Hill, 24 May 1855 (Toronto: Thompson and Co., 1855).

Austin, John. *The Province of Jurisprudence Determined* (London: Weidenfeld and Nicolson, 1954).

Bacon, Francis. *A Selection of His Works*, Northrop Frye, ed. (New York: Macmillan Publishing Co., 1982).

– *The Essays or Counsels, Civil and Moral* (New York: Peter Pauper Press, n.d.).

Bagehot, Walter. *The English Constitution* (London: Fontana Press, 1963).

Bailyn, Bernard. *The Ideological Origins of the American Revolution* (Cambridge: Harvard University Press, 1967).

Baker, Keith Michael. *Inventing the French Revolution* (Cambridge: Cambridge University Press, 1990).

– "The New Brunswick Origins of Canadian Judicial Review," *University of New Brunswick Law Journal* 40 (1990).

Baldwin, Alice M. *The New England Clergy and the American Revolution* (New York: Frederick Ungar Publishing Co., 1958).

Bale, Gordon. *Chief Justice William Johnstone Ritchie: Responsible Government and Judicial Review* (Ottawa: Carleton University Press, 1991).

Barker, Ernest. *Political Thought in England* (London: Oxford University Press, 1959).

Beard, Charles. *An Economic Interpretation of the Constitution* (New York: The Free Press, 1913).

Beck, J. Murray, *Joseph Howe*, two vols (Montreal: McGill-Queen's University Press, 1982).

Bernadete, Seth. *Socrates' Second Sailing* (Chicago: University of Chicago Press, 1989).

Bentham, Jeremy. *Works* (Edinburgh: William Tait, 1843).

Biggar, C.R.W. *Sir Oliver Mowat* (Toronto: Warwick Brothers and Rutter, 1905).

Black, Edwin R. *Divided Loyalties: Canadian Concepts of Federalism* (Kingston and Montreal: McGill-Queen's University Press, 1975).

Blackstone, William, *Commentary on the Laws of England*, 4 vols (Chicago: The University of Chicago Press, 1979).

Bloom, Alan with Harry V. Jaffa, *Shakespeare's Politics* (New York: Basic Books, 1964).

– ed. *Confronting The Constitution* (Washington: The AEI Press, 1990).

Bolger, F.W.P. *Prince Edward Island and Confederation* (Charlottetown: St Dunstan's University Press, 1965).

Bourinot, John G. *Canada Under British Rule* (Toronto: Copp, 1901).

Brode, Patrick. *Sir John Beverley Robinson: Bone and Sinew of the Compact* (Toronto: University of Toronto Press, 1984).

Browne, G.P. *The Judicial Committee and the British North America Act* (Toronto: University of Toronto Press, 1959).

Brunet, Michel. "The French Canadians' Search for a Fatherland," in Peter Russell, ed., *Nationalism in Canada* (Toronto: McGraw-Hill, 1966).

Burke, Edmund. *Reflections on the French Revolution* (New York: Harvard Classics, P. F. Collier and Son, 1969).

– *The Works of the Right Honourable Edmund Burke* (Boston: Little, Brown and Co., 1866).

– "An Appeal from the New to the Old Whigs," in *Works* (New York: Harper Brothers, 1853).

Cairns, Alan C. *Constitution, Government and Society in Canada* (Toronto: McClelland and Stewart, 1988).

– "Constitutional Change and the Thee Equalities," in Robert L.Watts and Douglas M. Brown, eds, *Options for a New Canada* (Toronto: University of Toronto Press, 1991).

– *Disruptions: Constitutional Struggles from the Charter to Meech Lake* (Toronto: McClelland and Stewart, 1991).

– "The Judicial Committee and Its Critics," *Canadian Journal of Political Science* 4 (1971): 301–45.

– and Cynthia Williams, eds. *Constitutionalism, Citizenship and Society in Canada* (Toronto: University of Toronto Press, 1985).

Cameron, David R. "Lord Durham Then and Now," *Journal of Canadian Studies* 25 (1990).

Careless, J.M.S. *Brown of the Globe: Statesman of Confederation* (Toronto: Macmillan, 1959).

Carnarvon, Earl. *Speeches on Canada* (London: John Murray, 1902).

Cartwright, Richard J. *Reminiscences* (Toronto: William Briggs, 1912).

Cassirer, Ernst. *The Myth of the State* (New Haven: Yale University Press, 1961).

Cavendish, Sir Henry. *Debates of the House of Commons in the Year 1774* (London: Ridgway, 1839).

Clark, J.C.D. *English Society 1688–1832* (Cambridge: The University Press, 1985).

Cobbet, William and John Wright, eds. *The Parliamentary History of England*, 36 vols. (London: T.C. Hansard, 1806–20).

Cook, Ramsay. *Canada and the French-Canadian Question* (Toronto: Macmillan, 1965).

Cooke, Jacob E., ed. *The Federalist Papers*, (New York: Meridian Books, 1961).

Corry, J.A. *The Constitution and the Future of Canada* (Toronto: Richard De Boo, 1978).

Craig, G., ed. *Lord Durham's Report* (Toronto: McClelland and Stewart, 1963).

Creighton, D.G. *The Road to Confederation* (Toronto: Macmillan, 1964).

– *British North America at Confederation* (Ottawa: The Queen's Printer, 1939).

Cropsey, Joseph, *Political Philosophy and the Issues of Politics* (Chicago: University of Chicago Press, 1977).

– *Thomas Hobbes: A Dialogue between a Philosopher and a Student of the Common Law of England* (Chicago: University of Chicago Press, 1971).

Cruikshank, R.J. *Charles Dickens and Early Victorian England* (London: Sir Isaac Pitman and Sons, 1949).

Curtis, George Ticknor. *History of the Origin, Formation and Adoption of the Constitution of the United States* (New York: Harper and Brothers, 1854).

Cuthbertson, Brian. *The First Bishop: A Biography of Charles Inglis* (Halifax: Waegwoltic Press, 1987).

Daubeny, Charles. *A Letter to the Right Honourable George Canning* (London: John W. Parker, 1827).

Dawson, Eli, Rev. "A Discourse, delivered at Quebec, in the Chapel belonging to the Convent of the Ursulines, 27 September 1759; occasioned by the Success of our Armies in the reduction of that Capital; at the request of Brigadier General Moncton, and by Order of Vice-Admiral Saunders, Commander-in-Chief," (London: R. Griffiths, 1760).

Dawson, R.M. *The Government of Canada* (Toronto: University of Toronto Press, 1954).

DeLolme, Jean Louis. *The Constitution of England: or, an account of the English Government in which it is compared both with the Republican Form of Government and the other Monarchies of Europe* (London: Henry B. Bohn, 1810).

Dicey, A.V. *Introduction to the Study of the Law of the Constitution*, 10th ed. (London: Macmillan, 1959).

Dictionnaire de la Révolution et de l'empire, 1789–1815 (Paris: Libraire Historique, n.d.).

Dickson, Brian, "Has the Charter 'Americanized' Canada's Judiciary? A Summary and Analysis," *University of British Columbia Law Review* (1992) 26:195.

Diggins, John P. *The Lost Soul of American Politics* (New York: Basic Books, 1984).

Dion, Leon. "The Mystery of Quebec," *Daedalus* 117 (1988).

Dion, Stephane. "Le Nationalisme dans le convergence culturelle," in Raymond Hudon and Rejean Pelletier, eds, *L'Engagement intellectuel* (Sainte-Foy: Les Presses de l'Université Laval, 1991).

Dionne, N.E. *Les Ecclésiastiques et les royalistes français refugiés au Canada 1791–1820* (Quebec, 1905).

Driesbach, Daniel L. "God and the Constitution: Reflections on Selected Nineteenth Century Commentaries on References to the Deity and the Christian Religion in the United States Constitution," a paper delivered at the American Political Science Association meetings, Washington, 2 September 1993.

Durham, Lord. *Report on the Affairs of British North America*, Gerald M. Craig, ed. (Toronto: McClelland and Stewart, 1963).

Eberts, Mary. "The Use of Litigation under the Canadian Charter of Rights and Freedoms as a Strategy for Achieving Change, " in Neil Nevitte and Allan Kornberg, eds, *Minorities and the Canadian State* (Oakville: Mosaic Press, 1985).

Emberley, Peter. "Globalism and Localism: Constitutionalism in a New World Order," in Curtis Cook, ed., *Constitutional Predicament* (Kingston and Montreal: McGill-Queen's University Press, 1994).

Evans, Eli N. *Judah P. Benjamin: The Jewish Confederate* (New York: The Free Press, 1988).

Everdell, William R. *The End of Kings: A History of Republics and Republicans* (New York: The Free Press, 1983).

Farrand, Max, ed. *The Records of the Federal Convention of 1787* (New Haven: Yale University Press, 1966).

Flaumenhaft, Harvey. *The Effective Republic: Administration and Constitution in the Thought of Alexander Hamilton* (Durham: Duke University Press, 1992).

Follett, Mary P. *The New State* (London: Longmans, Green, 1926).

Forbes, H.D., ed. *Canadian Political Thought* (Toronto: Oxford University Press, 1985).

Freeman, Edward A. *The Growth of the English Constitution from the Earliest Times* (London: Macmillan and Co., 1872).

– *History of Federal Government, from the Foundations of the Achaian League to the Disruption of the United States*, vol. 1 (London: Macmillan and Co., 1863).

Frisch, Morton. *Alexander Hamilton and the Political Order: An Interpretation of His Political Thought* (Lanham: University Press of America, 1991).

Funston, Bernard W. and Eugene Meehan. *Canadian Constitutional Documents Consolidated* (Toronto: Carswell, 1994).

Gagnon, Alain-G., ed. *Québec: État et société* (Montreal: Éditions Quebec Amerique, 1994).

Gates, Lillian F. *After the Rebellion* (Toronto: University of Toronto Press, 1988).

Gerin-Lajoie, Paul. *Constitutional Amendments in Canada* (Toronto: University of Toronto Press, 1950).

Gibbs, Elizabeth, ed. *Debates of the Legislative Assembly of the United Canadas* (Montreal, 1970).

Gibbs, Thomas. *Parliamentary Debates on the Subject of Confederation of the British North American Provinces*, 3rd session, 8 Provincial Parliament of Canada (Quebec: Hunter, Rose and Co., 1865).

Gladstone, William. *The State in Relations with the Church* (London: John Murray, 1839).

Gold, Marc. "Of Rights and Roles: The Supreme Court and the Charter," *University of British Columbia Law Review* 23 (1989).

Goldwin, Robert. *A Nation of States* (Chicago: Rand McNally, 1974).

Gourlay, Robert. *Statistical Account of Upper Canada* (London: Simpkin and Marshall, 1822).

Graham, Ron, ed. *The Essential Trudeau* (Toronto: McClelland and Stewart, 1998).

Grant, George P. *Lament for a Nation* (Ottawa: Carleton University Press, 1989).

Gray, John Hamilton. *Confederation* (Toronto: Copp, 1872).

Gwyn, Richard. *The Northern Magus* (Toronto: McClelland and Stewart, 1983).

Haldane, Richard. "Lord Watson," *Juridical Review* 11 (1899).

– "The Work for the Empire of the Judicial Committee of the Privy Council," *Cambridge Law Review* 1 (1923).

Haliburton, Thomas Chandler. *An Historical and Statistical Account of Nova Scotia* (Halifax: Joseph Howe, 1829).

Hall, A. Rupert. *The Scientific Revolution 1500–1800: The Foundation of the Modern Scientific Attitude* (London: Longmans, 1962).

Hammond, M.O. *Confederation and Its Leaders* (Toronto: McClelland and Goodchild, 1917).

Hampton, Norman. *Saint-Just* (Oxford: Basil Blackwell, 1990).

Hill, Christopher. *God's Englishman: Oliver Cromwell and the English Revolution* (London: Weidenfeld and Nicolson, 1970)

Hirschman, Albert O. *The Passions and the Interests* (Princeton: Princeton University Press, 1977).

Hobbes, Thomas. *A Dialogue between a Philosopher and a Student of the Common Law of England*, Joseph Cropsey, ed. (Chicago: University of Chicago Press, 1971).

– *Elements of Law, Natural and Politic*, Ferdinand Tonnies, ed., (Cambridge: The University Press, 1928).

– *Leviathan*, Richard Tuck, ed. (Cambridge: The University Press, 1994).

Hogg, Peter W. *Constitutional Law of Canada*, 3rd ed. (Toronto: Carswell, 1992).

Howe, Paul and Peter H. Russell, eds. *Judicial Power and Canadian Democracy* (Montreal: McGill-Queens University Press, 2001).

Hume, David. "Of Parties in General," in *Essays Moral, Political and Literary* (Indianapolis: Liberty Fund, 1985).

Jaffa, Harry V. *Crisis of the House Divided: An Interpretation of the Issues in the Lincoln-Douglas Debates* (Chicago: University of Chicago Press, 1959).

– *A New Birth of Freedom: Abraham Lincoln and the Coming of the Civil War* (Lanham: Rowman and Littlefield, 2000).

Jones, I. Deane. *The English Revolution, 1603–1714* (London: Heinemann, 1931).

Keith, A.B. *Constitutional Law and the British Dominions* (Oxford: Basil Blackwell, 1935).

Kennedy, W.P.M. *Essays in Constitutional Law* (Oxford: Oxford University Press, 1920).

– ed. *Statutes, Treaties and Documents of the Canadian Constitution, 1713–1929*, 2nd rev. ed. (Oxford: Oxford University Press, 1930).

Kessler, Sanford. "Locke's Influence on Jefferson's Bill for Establishing Religious Freedom," *Journal of Church and State* 25 (Spring 1983).

Kontos, Alkis, ed. *Powers, Possessions and Freedoms* (Toronto: University of Toronto Press, 1979).

Knopff, Rainer and F.L. Morton. *Charter Politics* (Scarborough: Nelson Canada, 1992).

– *The Charter Revolution and the Court Party* (Peterborough: Broadview Press, 1999).

LaForest, Gerald. *Reservation and Dissallowance* (Ottawa: Department of Justice, 1955).

LaSelva, Samuel. *The Moral Foundations of Canadian Federalism* (Kingston-Montreal: McGill-Queen's University Press, 1996).

– "Does The Canadian Charter of Rights and Freedoms Rest on a Mistake?" *Windsor Yearbook of Access to Justice* 8 (1988).

Leacock, Stephen, *Montreal: Seaport and City* (New York: Doubleday, Doran and Company, 1944).

Lederman, W.R., ed. *Continuing Constitutional Dilemmas*, (Toronto: Butterworths, 1981).

– *The Courts and the Constitution* (Toronto: McClelland and Stewart, 1964).

– "The Independence of the Judiciary," *Canadian Bar Review* 34 (1956).

Levesque, Rene. "National State of the French Canadians," in F.R. Scott and Michael Oliver, eds, *Quebec States Her Case* (Toronto: Macmillan, 1964).

L'Heureux-Dube, Claire. "Making a Difference: The Pursuit of a Compassionate Justice," *University of British Columbia Law Review* 31 (1997).

Lippincott, Benjamin Evans, *Victorian Critics of Democracy* (New York: Octagon Books, 1964).

Liversedge, Ronald, ed. *Recollections of the On to Ottawa Trek* (Toronto: McClelland and Stewart, 1973).

Livingston, W.R. *Responsible Government in Nova Scotia* (Iowa City: University of Iowa

Locke, John. *A Letter Concerning Toleration* (Indianapolis: Hackett Publishing Co., 1983).

– *Two Treatises of Government*, with introduction and notes by Peter Laslett (Cambridge: The University Press, 1963).

Lower, A.R.M. *Evolving Canadian Federalism* (Durham: Duke University Press, 1964).

– and J.W. Chafe. *Canada: A Nation*, 2nd rev. ed. (Toronto: Longmans, Green and Co., 1948).

Lucas, C.P. ed. *Lord Durham's Report* (Oxford: Clarendon Press, 1912).

Lucas, Colin, ed. *The French Revolution and the Creation of Modern Political Culture* (Oxford and New York: Oxford University Press, 1988).

MacDonald, Corrine M.A. "Steadfast in Religion and Loyalty: The Sermons of Charles Inglis," *Journal of the Canadian Church Historical Society* (Toronto: Anglican Church of Canada, 1990).

MacGuigan, Mark. "Precedent and Policy in the Supreme Court of Canada," *Canadian Bar Review* 45 (1967).

MacKinnon, Victor S. *Comparative Federalism* (The Hague: Martinus Nijhoff, 1964).

Macpherson, C.B. *The Political Theory of Possessive Individualism* (Oxford: The University Press, 1962).

Madison, James, Alexander Hamilton and John Jay, *The Federalist Papers*, Jacob E. Cooke, ed. (New York: Meridian Books, 1961)

Malleson, Kate. "A British Bill of Rights: Incorporating the European Convention on Human Rights," *Choices*, 5, 1 June 1999 (Montreal: The Institute for Research on Public Policy).

Manfredi, Christopher P. *Judicial Power and the Charter* (Toronto: McClelland and Stewart, 1993).

Mansfield, Harvey. *Taming the Prince: The Ambivalence of Modern Executive Power* (New York: The Free Press, 1989).

Marshall, Geoffrey. *Constitutional Theory* (Oxford: Clarendon Press, 1971).

Masugi, Ken. *Interpreting Tocqueville's Democracy in America* (Savage: Rowman and Littlefield Publishers, 1991).

Maurois, André. *Disraeli: A Picture of the Victorian Age* (London: John Lane the Bodley Head Ltd., 1927).

Mathie, William. "Political Community and the Canadian Experience: Reflections on Nationalism, Federalism and Unity," *Canadian Journal of Political Science* 12, 1 March 1979.

McConnell, Howard. "The Judicial Review of Prime Minister Bennet's New Deal," *Osgoode Hall Law School* 9 (1968).

McLachlin, Beverely. "The Charter of Rights and Freedoms: A Judicial Perspective," *University of British Columbia Law Review* 23 (1989).

McWhinney, Edward. *Judicial Review in the English-speaking World* (Toronto: University of Toronto Press, 1965).

Meekison, J. Peter, ed. *Canadian Federalism: Myth and Reality* (Toronto: Methuen, 1971).

Metzger, Charles H. *The Quebec Act: A primary cause of the American Revolution* (New York: The United States Catholic Historical Society, 1936).

Mill, John Stuart. *Works* (Toronto: University of Toronto Press, 1967).

Miller, William Lee. *The First Liberty: Religion and the American Republic* (New York: Alfred A. Knopf, 1986).

Milton, John. *Eikonoklastes* (1649), in Merritt Y. Hugh, ed., *Complete Poems and Major Prose* (New York: Macmillan, 1957).

Moir, John S. *Church and State in Canada West* (Toronto: University of Toronto Press, 1959).

Monahan, Patrick. *Politics and the Constitution: The Charter, Federalism and the Supreme Court of Canada* (Toronto: Carswell, 1987).

Montesquieu, Baron de. *Spirit of the Laws*, translated by Thomas Nugent with an introduction by Franz Neumann (New York: Hafner Publishing Co., 1962).

Morin, Claude. *Quebec versus Ottawa*, translated by Richard Howard (Toronto: University of Toronto Press, 1976).

Morris, B.F. *Christian Life and Character of the Civil Institutions of the United States* (Philadelphia: George W. Childs, 1864).

Morris, Patrick. *Arguments to Prove the Policy and Necessity of Granting to Newfoundland a Constitutional Government* (London: Hunt & Clarke, 1828).

Morton, F.L. "The Political Impact of the Canadian Charter of Rights and Freedoms," *Canadian Journal of Political Science* 20 (1987).

Morton, W.L. *The Critical Years* (Toronto: McClelland and Stewart, 1964).

– *The Kingdom of Canada*, 2nd ed. (Toronto: McClelland and Stewart, 1969).

Muncy, Mitchell S. *The End of Democracy II* (Dallas: Spence Publishing Co., 1999).

Murphy, Charles, ed. *D'Arcy McGee: A Collection of Speeches and Addresses* (Toronto: Macmillan, 1937).

O'Connor, William F. *The Report pursuant to Resolution of the Senate to the Honourable The Speaker* (Ottawa: The Queen's Printer, 1939).

Olmsted, R.A. ed. *Canadian Constitutional Decisions of the Judicial Committee*, 3 vols. (Ottawa: The Queen's Printer, 1954).

Ouellet, Fernand. *Le Bas Canada 1791–1840: Changements, structuraux et crises* (Ottawa: Éditions de l'Université d'Ottawa, 1976).

Pangle, Thomas L. *The Spirit of Modern Republicanism* (Chicago: University of Chicago Press, 1988).

Plessis, Joseph-Octave. *Discours* (Montreal: John Neilson, 1799).

– "Sermon preché par l'évêque Catholique de Québec dans sa Cathédrale le quartrième Dimanche du Carême, 1 Avril 1810 (Quebec: À la Nouvelle-imprimerie, 1810)

Pocock, J.G.A. *The Machiavellian Moment* (Princeton: Princeton University Press, 1975).

Pope, Joseph, ed. *Confederation Documents* (Toronto: Carswell, 1895)

– ed. *Correspondence of Sir John A. Macdonald* (Toronto: Doubleday, Page and Co., 1921).

– *Memoirs of John A. Macdonald* (Toronto: Musson Co., 1930).

Pope, W.H. *The Confederation Question Considered from a Prince Edward Island Point of View* (Charlottetown: Hazard, 1866).

Pryke, Kenneth. *The Maritimes and Confederation* (Toronto: University of Toronto Press, 1979).

Reesor, Bayard. *The Canadian Constitution in Historical Perspective* (Scarborough: Prentice-Hall, Canada Inc., 1992).

Reichley, A. James. *Religion in American Public Life* (Washington: The Brookings Institution, 1985).

Reithmuller, Christopher. *Alexander Hamilton and the Rise of the American Constitution* (London: Bell and Daldy, 1864).

Robinson, Jonathan. "Lord Herschel and the British North America Act," *University of Toronto Law Journal* 20 (1970).

Russell, Lord John. *Memorials and Correspondence of Charles James Fox*, 4 vols. (London: R. Bentley, 1853).

Russell, Peter H. *Constitutional Odyssey* (Toronto: University of Toronto Press, 1992).

– "A Democratic Approach to Civil Liberties," *University of Toronto Law Journal* 12 (1969).

– *The Judiciary in Canada: The Third Branch of Government* (Toronto: McGraw-Hill Ryerson, 1987).

Ryan, William. *The Clergy and Economic Growth in Quebec* (Quebec: Presses de l'université de Laval, 1966).

Ryerson, Egerton. *The Story of My Life* (Toronto: William Briggs, 1883).

Scott, F.R. *Civil Liberties and Canadian Federalism* (Toronto: University of Toronto Press, 1959).

Schmeiser, D.A. *Civil Liberties in Canada* (Oxford: The University Press, 1964).

Schofield, Robert E. *Mechanism and Materialism in British Natural Philosophy* (Princeton: Princeton University Press, 1970).

Sharswood, George, ed. *Blackstone's Commentaries on the Laws of England* (Philadelphia: George W. Childs, 1866).

Shortt, Adam and Arthur G. Doughty. *Documents Relating to the Constitutional History of Canada, 1759–1791* (Ottawa: The King's Printer, 1918).

Silver, A.I., *The French-Canadian Idea of Confederation, 1864–1900* (Toronto: University of Toronto Press, 1982).

Simeon, Richard. *Federal-Provincial Diplomacy* (Toronto: University of Toronto Press, 1972).

Skelton, O.D. *The Life of Alexander Galt* (Toronto: Oxford University Press, 1920).

Slattery, T.P. *The Assassination of D'Arcy McGee* (Toronto: Doubleday Canada, 1968).

Smiley, Donald V. *The Canadian Political Nationality* (Toronto: Methuen, 1967).

– "The Case Against the Canadian Charter of Human Rights," *Canadian Journal of Political Science* 2 (1969): 277–91.

– "The Rowell-Sirois Report, Provincial Autonomy and Post-War Canadian Federalism," in J. Peter Meekison, ed. *Canadian Federalism: Myth and Reality.* (Toronto: Methuen, 1971).

Smith, David. *The Invisible Crown: The First Principle of Canadian Government* (Toronto: University of Toronto Press, 1995).

Smith, Goldwin. *The Proposed Constitution for British North America* (London: Macmillan, 1865).

Smith, Jennifer. "Canadian Confederation and the Influence of American Federalism," *Canadian Journal of Political Science* 21 (1988): 443–63.

– "The Origins of Judicial Review in Canada," *Canadian Journal of Political Science* 16, (March 1983): 1.

Smith, Peter J. "The Ideological Origins of Canadian Confederation," *Canadian Journal of Political Science* 20 (1987): 3–29.

Snell, James G. and Frederick Vaughan. *The Supreme Court of Canada: A History of the Institution* (Toronto: University of Toronto Press, 1985).

Solberg, Winton U. *The Federal Convention and the Formation of the Union of the American States* (New York: Bobbs-Merrill, 1958).

Stacey, C.P. *Canada and the British Army* (Toronto: University of Toronto Press, 1936).

Stevens, Richard G., ed. *The Declaration of Independence and The Constitution of the United States* (Washington: Free Congress Foundation, 1997).

Storing, Herbert J. *The Complete Anti-Federalists* (Chicago: University of Chicago Press, 1981).

Strachan, John. "A Sermon on the Death of the Honourable Richard Cartwright with a short account of his life," Preached at Kingston, 3 September 1815 (Montreal: W. Gray, 1815).

Strauss, Leo. *Natural Right and History* (Chicago: University of Chicago Press, 1953).

Strayer, Barry. *Judicial Review of Legislation in Canada* (Toronto: University of Toronto Press, 1968).

Sykes, Norman. *Church and State in England in the Eighteenth Century* (Hamden: Archon Books, 1962).

Tasse, Joseph, ed. *Discours de Sir Georges Cartier* (Montreal: Eusebe Senecal, 1893).

Taylor, Charles. "Alternative Futures: Legitimacy, Identity and Alienation in Late Twentieth Century Canada," in Alan Cairns and Cynthia Williams, eds, *Constitutionalism, Citizenship and Society in Canada* (Toronto: University of Toronto Press, 1985).

Tocqueville, Alexis de. *Ancien Regime et la Revolution*, J.-P. Mayer, ed. (Paris: Gallimard, 1967).

- *Democracy in America*, translated by George Lawrence, J.P. Mayer, ed. (New York: Harper and Row, 1966).
- *Recollections*, translated by George Lawrence, J.P. Mayer and A.P. Kerr, eds (New York: Doubleday and Co., 1970).

Trevor-Roper, H.R. *Religion, The Reformation and Social Change* (London: Macmillan, 1967).

Trotter, Reginald. *Canadian Federalism* (Toronto: J.M. Dent and Sons, 1923).

Trudeau, Pierre Elliott. *A Canadian Charter of Human Rights* (Ottawa: The Queen's Printer, 1968).
- *The Essential Trudeau*, Ron Graham, ed. (Toronto: McClelland and Stewart, 1998).
- *Federalism and French-Canadians* (Toronto: Macmillan, 1968).
- "The Values of a Just Society," in Thomas S. Axworthy and Pierre Elliott Trudeau, eds, *Towards a Just Society* (Markham: Viking, 1990).

Trudel, Marcel. *L'Église canadienne sous le Régime militaire* (Quebec: Les Études de l'Institut d'Historique de l'Amérique Française, (1956).

Tupper, Charles. *Recollections of Sixty Years in Canada* (London: Cassell, 1914).

Underhill, Frank. *The Image of Confederation* (Toronto: The Canadian Broadcasting Corporation, 1964).

Varcoe, F.P. *The Distribution of Legislative Power in Canada* (Toronto: Carswell, 1954).

Vaughan, Frederick. *The Tradition of Political Hedonism: From Hobbes to John Stuart Mill* (New York: Fordham University Press, 1982).

Vaughan, Geoffrey M. *Behemoth Teaches Leviathan* (Lanham: Lexington Books, 2002).

Vipond, Robert. *Liberty and Community: Canadian Federalism and the Failure of the Constitution* (Albany: State University of New York Press, 1991).

Voltaire, *Letters on England*, translated by Leonard Hancock (New York: Penguin, 1980).

Wade, Mason. "Quebec and the French Revolution of 1789: The Mission of Henri de Mezière," *Canadian Historical Review* 31 (1950).

Waite, Peter. *The Life and Times of Confederation* (Toronto: University of Toronto Press, 1962).

Wallot, Jean-Pierre. "La Révolution française, le Canada et les Droits de L'Homme, 1789–1840," *Etudes Canadiennes* 28 (1990).

Webster, Charles, ed. *The Intellectual Revolution of the Seventeenth Century* (London: Routledge and Kegan Paul, 1974).

Westfall, Richard S. *Science and Religion in Seventeenth-Century England* (New Haven: Yale University Press, 1958).

Wexler, Stephen. "The Urge to Idealize: Viscount Haldane and the Constitution of Canada," *McGill Law Journal* 29 (1984).

Whalen, Edward. *The Union of the British Provinces* (Charlottetown: Hazard, 1865).
- *Confederation* (Charlottetown: Hazard, 1866).

Wheare, K.C. *The Constitutional Structure of the Commonwealth* (Oxford: Clarendon Press, 1960).

– *Federal Government*, 4th ed. (London: Oxford University Press, 1967).

Whitelaw, William Menzies. *The Maritimes and Canada before Confederation* (Toronto: Oxford University Press, 1934).

Williams, David. *Letters on Political Liberty* (London: J. Ridgway 1792).

Wilson, Alan. *The Clergy Reserves of Upper Canada: A Canadian Mortmain* (Toronto: University of Toronto Press, 1968).

Wilton, Carol, ed. *Essays in the History of Canadian Law: Beyond the Law, Lawyers and Business in Canada, 1830–1930* (Toronto: University of Toronto Press, 1990).

Wolfe, Christopher. *The Rise of Modern Judicial Review* (New York: Basic Books, 1986).

Wood, Anthony. *Nineteenth Century Britain, 1815–1914* (London: Longmans, 1960).

Wood, Gordon S. *The Creation of the American Republic, 1776–1787* (Chapel Hill: University of North Carolina Press, 1969).

Young, Brian. *George-Etienne Cartier: Montreal Bourgeois* (Kingston-Montreal: McGill-Queen's University Press, 1981).

Index